ONE WEEK LOAN

D0514174

of related interest

Different Minds
Gifted Children with AD/HD, Asperger Syndrome,
and Other Learning Deficits
Deirdre V. Lovecky
ISBN 1 85302 964 5

Genius!
Nurturing the Spirit of the Wild, Odd,
and Oppositional Child – Revised Edition
George T. Lynn with Joanne Barrie Lynn
ISBN 1 84310 820 8

Gifted and Talented Children
A Planning Guide
Shirley Taylor
ISBN 1 84310 086 X

Bright Splinters of the Mind
A Personal Story of Research with Autistic Savants
Beate Hermelin
Foreword by Sir Michael Rutter
ISBN 1 85302 932 7 paperback
ISBN 1 85302 931 9 hardback

Caged in Chaos
A Dyspraxic Guide to Breaking Free
Victoria Biggs
ISBN 1 84310 347 8

Gifted Children

A Guide for Parents and Professionals

Edited by Kate Distin

Jessica Kingsley Publishers
London and Philadelphia

First published in 2006
by Jessica Kingsley Publishers
116 Pentonville Road
London N1 9JB, UK
and
400 Market Street, Suite 400
Philadelphia, PA 19106, USA

www.jkp.com

Library of Congress Cataloging in Publication Data
Gifted children : a guide for parents and professionals / edited by Kate Distin.-- 1st American pbk. ed.
p. cm.
Includes bibliographical references and index.
ISBN-13: 978-1-84310-439-1 (pbk.)
ISBN-10: 1-84310-439-3 (pbk.)
1. Gifted children. I. Distin, Kate, 1970-
BF723.G5G537 2006
155.45'5--dc22

British Library Cataloguing in Publication Data
A CIP catalogue record for this book is available from the British Library

ISBN-13: 978 1 84310 439 1
ISBN-10: 1 84310 439 3

Printed and Bound in the United States by Thomson-Shore, Inc.

To Michal Hambourg
and Barbara Sanders

Acknowledgements

Niki Adamson, Jacqui Foggitt and Sarah Talbot are members of the group who were prevented by other commitments from taking part in the actual writing of our book, but have all played an important part in shaping both our group and the book that has arisen from it.

Although she left the Counselling Service before our writing group was formed, Dorothy Reynolds has generously allowed us free use of the material in her research study, 'Giftedness in children between the ages of six and eleven years: a study of its relevance to the child, the family and the school', written as part of her master's degree from Birkbeck College, London, in collaboration with the Institute of Family Therapy.

We are grateful to Dr Keith Distin, to Professor Andor Gomme and to Dr Patricia Thompson of The Croft School for giving so generously of their time and expertise to provide constructive comments on previous drafts of the book.

'*Family first!*' To all those spouses without whose patience, understanding and shared commitment to the cause of gifted children the individual members of our group would have been able neither to make it to our writing group's meetings, nor to continue with the volunteer work that we did previously as NAGC counsellors, we offer out heartfelt thanks.

Our book is ultimately the fruit of the much-needed and valued Counselling Service which the National Association for Gifted Children created and financially supported from 1977 to 2005. Throughout these years it was a privilege for the members of our group to be trusted by so many families to support them on their journeys with gifted children. We are also grateful to all the trainers and supervisors who so ably and generously supported the volunteer counsellors throughout that time.

Contents

FOREWORD   9

THE WRITING GROUP   11

1. Introduction   13

Part 1: Gifted Children and their Families   21

2. What is Normal for a Gifted Child?   22

3. Giftedness in the Family   57

4. Beyond the Family   90

5. Giftedness and Schools   112

6. Gifted Children and Home Education   148

Part 2: Special Talents and Special Needs   157

7. Gifted Children with Special Needs   159

8. Gifted Children with Asperger Syndrome   163

9. Gifted Adolescents   178

10. What is it Like to be a Gifted Linguist?   190

11. Managing the Multi-talented Child   193

12. Giftedness and Creativity: Some Pointers   197

13. Musically Gifted Children   200

14. Effective Communication: The Way We Say It   211

Part 3: Conclusions   221

15. Living with Giftedness   222

APPENDIX: RELATED CONTACTS   234

INDEX   265

Foreword

I was extremely flattered to have been asked to write this foreword. I am not a professional educator or an academic. I'm a mother with a gifted child.

I can't tell you how much this book has meant to me. And how I wish someone at my daughter's first school had just mentioned the word 'gifted' to me.

Our daughter was nine years old when we were told she was gifted in language arts and maths. Why were we just learning this? Why hadn't anyone told us before? We had been told privately a couple of times by her teachers how she had scored highly on national exams for maths and English, but the words gifted, able or talented were never mentioned to us. We just thought, 'That's great. She's smart.' We loved going to parents' evenings!

It turns out that some schools believe it is best not to inform parents of their child's giftedness. Athletes receive repeated accolades at assemblies about their successes and artists' works are displayed around the school. But there is nothing comparable for children whose talents are academic. At our daughter's school, gifted children were praised at prize day on the last day of school – a ceremony to which only prize winners and their parents were invited.

Our daughter received an excellent education at her first school. Her teachers knew that she was gifted and she was challenged appropriately. This is crucial. If schools have to make special considerations for those with learning disabilities, then those who learn more quickly and want to delve into subjects more deeply should also be given the opportunity. But because our daughter's first school never suggested to us that she was gifted, we didn't realize when we moved back to the US that we should have been looking for a school with teachers who have had training in educating gifted children. Our very strong feeling is that parents should be told of their child's giftedness. If they are made aware of it, many questions and concerns they have about why their children do certain things would be answered.

Here is a book that discusses such areas as the signs of giftedness from a very young age; how to address the *thousands* of questions you will receive from your child both when you have the time to research the answers and when you really need to get dinner on the table; how gifted children learn differently; and how to talk to the school about your concerns without being seen as aggressive. I was in tears when I read some of the stories about other gifted children and their families. How often have I changed the subject (or accentuated the other child's skills) when another parent would ask me about whether one of my children was having difficulty in a subject their child was having great difficulty with and mine were excelling? How do you respond without sounding arrogant or offensive?

I truly believe that every parent whose child is gifted in whatever area should read this book. It will explain some of the trials, tribulations, and outright joys you will experience as a parent of a gifted child. It also provides many other references for further research into your and your child's specific needs.

Thank you to all of you who collaborated on this book. I'd recommend it to every teacher as a great way of gaining an insight into the world of gifted children.

Mary Rodewig, Ohio, USA

The Writing Group

This book has been written by a group of people who previously worked together for many years as volunteer counsellors for the National Association for Gifted Children in the UK.

Peter Carter was an NAGC counsellor from 1994 until the Service closed in 2005. Peter is a Registered General Nurse and Registered Mental Nurse, and the father of three children. He has acquired a specialist knowledge of Asperger Syndrome as it affects the gifted, through his efforts to understand his gifted son who was also (eventually) diagnosed as having Asperger Syndrome. Peter served as an NAGC Branch Chairman for five years.

Barbara Conchie was the Manager of NAGC's Counselling Service from 1994 to 2002; her background is in education. None of this book would have been written without Barbara, and indeed the NAGC's Counselling Service would not have developed into the close-knit, caring and professional group that it was if Barbara's firm but gentle guiding hand had not been on the tiller. Under her leadership, the Service in 1997 took part in the pilot study for the United Kingdom Register of Counsellors, the national system of self-regulation for the counselling profession. After a very stringent process, the NAGC's Counselling Service became only the twelfth organization to become a Registered Sponsoring Organization (i.e. listed in the UKRC).

Crystal Dickinson is the mother of three differently gifted children, all diagnosed as dyslexic although none is related to the others (one born, two adopted in infancy). She has been a local authority social worker, before training as a counsellor with the National Marriage Guidance Council (now Relate). She was an NAGC counsellor from 1997 to 2001 and now works with detained asylum seekers.

Kate Distin was an NAGC Counsellor from 1996 to 2002. She is the mother of gifted children and has a background in teaching. A Cambridge graduate with a PhD from Sheffield University, Kate's other publications include *The Selfish Meme* (Cambridge University Press 2005).

Susan Divecha was an NAGC Counsellor from 1984 to 2002 and an active member of NAGC Scotland for many years. Susan's background is in Information and Resources for Education, and she is also the mother of gifted children.

Susan Gomme was a founder member of the NAGC Counselling Service, serving from 1977 to 2002, during which time she was also active at Branch, Regional and National level in NAGC, including nine years' service as Chairman of the NAGC's Board of Trustees. A Cambridge graduate with a background in teaching, Susan has also seen her four gifted children through school, university and postgraduate qualifications. She has been an invited speaker at two world conferences on gifted children, as well as at universities and colleges, and was a keynote speaker at the joint NAGC/NASEN/NACE conference in 1997. Susan has contributed several articles on counselling to *Looking to their Future*, and is the author of 'The Role of the Family' in Michael J. Stopper (ed.) *Meeting the Social and Emotional Needs of Gifted and Talented Children* (David Fulton 2000).

The late **Michal Hambourg** was a distinguished pianist and Honorary Fellow of Trinity College of Music, who had for many years been the NAGC's Music Counsellor. She was the daughter of the pianist Mark Hambourg and, as an international concert artiste, Michal had appeared at the Proms and during the war at National Gallery recitals, as well as on the BBC as soloist and in radio dramas.

May Mackay was a founder member of the NAGC Counselling Service, serving as a counsellor from 1977 to 2002 and as Counselling Co-ordinator on the Board of Trustees for several years. She is the mother of gifted children, and from her experience of running a nursery she brings a knowledge of pre-school giftedness to our book.

The late **Barbara Sanders** was an NAGC Counsellor from 1995 to 2002. Barbara had a background in teaching, was the mother of a gifted child and was also a member of the Telephone Helpline Service for ovarian cancer sufferers.

Catherine Shaw was an NAGC Counsellor from 1997 to 2001 and is the mother of a gifted child. She is an Interpersonal Communication Skills Teacher, Assertiveness Trainer and Community Mediator.

CHAPTER 1

Introduction

This is the book that we needed when our children were younger. Our babies were not born with labels on their foreheads, 'Gifted – Handle with Care'. We were often not even sure that our children were gifted; afraid to admit they might be; struggling to believe that we really knew them better than anyone else. What we did know was that our children seemed different from most others, and that this made us feel different too. In our isolation we had no idea that our experiences were quite normal for the families of gifted children: that we were part of a scattered community of people-like-us. It is the companionship of this community which our book hopes to provide: the reassurance that the parents, grandparents and other carers of gifted children are not on their own; that they do know their own children best; that it is possible to find a comfortable place for giftedness in their family lives.

What is giftedness?

Intelligence is one of many human characteristics which, roughly speaking, follows a pattern called the normal curve of distribution, or the bell curve. What this means is that, like height and weight and longevity, intelligence is one of the areas in which most people are fairly average. Statistically speaking, there is not very much difference between the height, weight, life-expectancy or intelligence of about two-thirds of the population. Most people are pretty average in these areas: somewhat above or below, perhaps, but not very different from what we might think of as normal. The further away we get from the average, however, the more rarely do we see people of a particular height, weight or level of intelligence.

If we apply this information to school children and their performance, it means that we can expect approximately two-thirds of them to be reasonably clever, finding school work sometimes hard, sometimes easy, but generally appropriate for them. On either side of this block of children, though, there are others who will almost always struggle with the work set, and others still who almost always find it manageable. These are the people who fall into roughly the top or bottom sixth of the population, in terms of intelligence. Even amongst these children, there will be many who usually find that they can cope, both with school and with the other challenges that life throws at them. Some of them will need more help than others, but most of them will do all right in the end.

Within these groups, though, there are people at either end of the scale who need more support than anyone else – say the top and bottom 5 per cent, in terms of their ability. Self-evidently these children are in a minority. At the most, only 1 person in every 20 whom they meet will be very much like them. To put this in terms of an ordinary school, it means that few classes will contain more than one other person of similar intelligence to them. Some classes, and perhaps even some schools, will not have any at all. In this book, 'giftedness' refers to children who are of above average intelligence in this way.

It does not necessarily refer to people whom we might instinctively describe as geniuses. When we think of gifted people, names like Newton, Mozart and Bunyan spring immediately to mind, but in many ways these are unhelpful examples of giftedness. They are unhelpful firstly because there may be as big a gap between their abilities and those of most gifted children, as between children whose abilities are roughly average and children whom we might call gifted. They are unhelpful secondly because they are all people whose extraordinarily high abilities have been realized in correspondingly high achievements. As a result, thinking exclusively in terms of people like them can easily mask the important distinction between ability and achievement. This book is about the average gifted child, who has great potential but who, as a result of the complex mix of personality, opportunity and circumstance, may or may not go on to achieve great things as a result of her abilities.

Indeed the immediate response of many parents to the suggestion that their offspring may be gifted is frequently along the lines that, 'I wouldn't describe him as *gifted*, necessarily: he's bright, but he's not going to be the next Einstein.' For these parents the term gifted child is unhelpful in itself. In England, the Department for Education and Skills (DfES) uses the longer term 'gifted and talented'. It identifies gifted learners as those who have abilities in one or more academic subjects, and talented learners as those who have abilities in art and design, music, PE or performing arts such as dance and drama. In the US, most states also prefer the term 'gifted and talented', although a significant minority talk simply about 'gifted' students. Alternatively, some teachers prefer to talk about 'more able' children, and indeed this description may be less misleading and feel more comfortable to many parents. Nevertheless, 'gifted' is the word most commonly used in this area, and it is actually quite hard to replace with another so succinct. For these reasons we persist with its use.

In a sense the terminology is unimportant anyway: what does it matter whether John is gifted and Jane is highly intelligent rather than the other way around? The important thing is to gain a better understanding of each

> How does it feel to describe your child as gifted?

child. Good teachers try to find out each pupil's abilities, not with the aim of giving each a label (clever or average), but so that they know how best to help each child: by supporting one to grasp the most basic material and enabling another to tackle the most difficult, for instance. Similarly, if you can gain a good understanding of your own child's gifts then you are much better placed to support and guide him. Although each gifted child is an individual just as much as any other human being, it is possible to make some generalizations about this group of children. Nothing is cast in stone, but we can say things like *it is often the case that*, or *many gifted children have this characteristic*. When tempered by what you know of your own child, such generalizations can serve to shore up the foundations of your parental wisdom.

What is in this book?

Our subject matter is inevitably biased towards the problems that gifted children can face. Of course this should not be taken to imply that all gifted children will face all, or even any, of these problems. It is simply that their needs are brought most sharply into focus by the difficulties that some do encounter. There is also plenty here about the joys and advantages of being gifted or of having a gifted child, but the brutal fact is that there would be no book if that were the only side of the story. The positives are genuine and numerous, but the negatives are what provided the impetus for writing a book to support the families of gifted children.

Our aims in writing it are to help gifted children, their families and carers (including grown-up gifted children) to learn more about what is typical or

normal for gifted and talented children; to shatter some of the myths about
these children and their parents; to enhance their awareness of the emotional
impact of giftedness and thus to enable gifted children and their families to
live more comfortably with their giftedness, shifting their focus from its challenges to its rewards and possibilities.

Our book's content is somewhat idiosyncratic, being based on the
knowledge and experience of a somewhat idiosyncratic group of people. All
of us have in the recent past been counsellors for the National Association for
Gifted Children (NAGC) in Britain, for between 3 and 30 years.[1] As such, we
have a huge collective experience of being approached by the families of
gifted children who felt, at that moment, that they had no other source of
support. These parents were isolated by their experience of having a child
with this sort of special need and wanted desperately to talk to someone who
shared their concern for her social and emotional well-being. Of course we
believe that it is crucial for these children to be fulfilled creatively and intellectually – indeed, for many such children their emotional well-being will *depend*
on high levels of intellectual and creative stimulation – but we also recognize
that for each individual the needs and priorities will be different. Our concern
is to enable gifted and talented children to live fulfilled and happy lives.

As volunteers, the background that each of us brought to our counselling
work was extremely varied: all of us have different experiences of giftedness
within our own families or personal backgrounds. For each of us that experience has been enhanced and our understanding deepened by the many conversations that we have shared with the families of gifted children, as well as
by the ongoing training that the NAGC provided to support us in our work. It
is unavoidably the case, however, that the collective experience of such a relatively small group of people cannot cover the whole gamut of issues that
gifted children face. Although we have amongst us people with a deep understanding of the issues faced by musically gifted children and by gifted
children who also have Asperger Syndrome, for instance, we have less understanding of artistically gifted children or of those who also have cerebral
palsy.

In some ways, then, the topics covered here are incomplete. On the other
hand, no book can hope to contain the whole of a given subject. What this
one does offer is the product of many decades, between us, of work with
gifted children and their families. It offers those families a place within a
community of gifted children's families: a community which *to a certain extent*
has common experiences, shares common delights and faces common diffi-

culties. It is not an academic work, but one that hopes to offer support and understanding to a group of people who are all too often unsupported and misunderstood.

In particular, our aim is to explore the twofold theme which, more than any other, unites the families of gifted children with whom we have worked. First, there is the need to help gifted children and their families to find value in their difference: to be able to accept giftedness as an integral and valuable aspect of themselves, and to find a way to give voice to it in a culture where the response to giftedness is not always positive. Second, there is the need to find a place for themselves in that wider world: to be able to make contact with their age peers and to feel that they are a part of the context in which they find themselves. As for any minority community, then, their task is to find and preserve their own identity, whilst at the same time making mutually rewarding connexions with the predominant culture. Our hope is that this book will enable more gifted children and their families to avoid both the isolation that can grow from problems in interacting with other children and their parents, and the miserable frustration that can result from lack of provision for their gifts.

How does the book work?

There are three parts to this book. Part 1 is a truly collaborative work in which, as a group, we explore the world of gifted children and their families. We look at what it means to be a typical gifted child and at the impact that giftedness can have on a family. We examine the ways in which giftedness can affect the interactions of both children and their parents with others outside the family, and at the relationship with schools in particular.

Part 2 leaves behind the collective voice of our writing group in order to allow individual members to speak for themselves on their particular areas of expertise. This is a necessarily idiosyncratic collection of topics, covered in an inevitably heterogeneous range of styles, but its content draws on a wealth of personal experience and research on the part of each writer. Not all of these topics will be relevant to every reader, and for this reason each chapter within Part 2 is complete in itself, allowing readers to dip in and out of this section without losing any ongoing threads. If you have an interest in multi-talented children, for example, but no experience of Asperger Syndrome, then it would make sense to read the one chapter and skip the other, and Part 2 has been structured to allow you to do this.

Finally, in Part 3 we speak collectively once more, drawing together the twin threads that run through all of the topics that our book has raised: self-acceptance and communication with others.

Many chapters throughout the book end with a list of organizations and books that readers might find useful. Full details are given in the Appendix. All of the information is correct at the time of going to press, but it should not be taken as an exhaustive list of potential resources for gifted children and their families. Rather, it is a starting point for those who wish to explore particular issues in more depth or breadth than we have space for here.

Questions and case studies

In contrast to the self-contained nature of the chapters in Part 2, there is a more consistent style and structure to the writing within Parts 1 and 3, where we frame each chapter's discussion between an introduction and a bullet-point summary of its main points, and offer many illustrative personal stories in the course of our discussions. It is worth clarifying the nature of these personal stories. Although our knowledge springs to a great extent from our experience as NAGC counsellors, this book is not about the individual families with whom we have had contact. Those contacts were, and will always remain, confidential. When we write *many parents say* or *families often find*, that is exactly what we mean: we are not hiding real people behind our generalizations. Many of our case studies are amalgams: fictional in that there is no individual family which matches those exact details; factual in the truths that they illustrate. When we do use direct quotations or individual case studies to illustrate a point, it is with the full knowledge and consent of client families.

In addition to these case studies, the text is punctuated by opportunities for you to consider how our thoughts might be reflected in your own family's circumstances. These take the form of questions set aside from the text in shaded boxes, like the one earlier in this chapter. It should be noted that there is, amongst our group, a real divergence of views about the merits of such contemplative questions. Reading through the first draft of our book, some of us welcomed the space that these questions provided for reflecting on our experience of giftedness in the family. We thought that some readers would also value this opportunity to pause for thought. Others of us, it has to be said, were infuriated by the way that these questions-in-boxes interrupted the flow of text and thought! We wanted to read straight through without them. An animated discussion ensued … and the conclusion was that the questions should stay, with the proviso that readers who do not wish to reflect at that point on the issues they raise should not feel obliged to read them. The questions are not an essential part of the book's content and you will not miss any information if you do skip them. We hope that you will find them stimulating – helpfully so – if you choose to read them. We hope that you will not find them intrusive if you do not.

Note

1   There is also an NAGC in the United States. Unless otherwise specified, 'NAGC' refers throughout this book to the UK organization.

PART 1

*Gifted Children
and their Families*

CHAPTER 2

What is Normal for a Gifted Child?

We have already noted that gifted children are a minority: few of the people they encounter will be like them in this important respect. Of course being gifted does not define the whole person, and they may have plenty of other things in common with their friends and acquaintances. Giftedness tends, however, to pervade the personality in ways that set children and their families apart from those who have not shared this experience, and the rarity of encounters with others like them can make both children and their parents feel isolated and different.

This chapter explores some of the characteristics and emotions that gifted children often share with each other. Just as every person in the world is unique, so it is vital that individual gifted children are not buried under an avalanche of generalizations – but it is nonetheless true that some generalizations *can* be made. Used with care, they can be a source of understanding and support for gifted children and their families. For instance, if you feel different from the group of people with whom you spend most of your time then it can be a relief to hear that you are pretty normal by the standards of another group. Similarly, parents who may be struggling to comprehend or keep up with their children may be bolstered by an insight into what it is like to be a gifted child. It is this insight and sense of normality which this chapter seeks to provide.

Intellectual characteristics

The intellect is in a sense the most straightforward aspect of giftedness, and the easiest to understand: gifted children are simply more intelligent than the majority. Yet clearly there is more to it than this, and it is worth unpacking the meaning of the phrase 'more intelligent'. How does the gifted mind work? What are the emotional repercussions for children whose minds work in this way?

One key aspect of high intelligence is the ability to understand new ideas very easily. Where most children might need a second or third explanation before they grasp a novel concept, or rely on repetitious practice in order to master an unfamiliar skill, gifted children often will not. Instead they typically master new information very quickly, and find the answer to new problems either by means of mental processes that are too swift to be produced in words or text, or using no intermediate stages at all. Given this ability, they often find problem-solving highly enjoyable and gain great satisfaction from finding ever more efficient ways of reaching a solution.

Mental agility can, then, be the route to much intellectual pleasure, but also to a great deal of frustration and tedium. Inevitably teachers must go at the pace of the average or slower learners, and even in day-to-day life many people will direct only an oversimplified level of conversation towards children. What is this like for gifted children, who have already grasped what is being said and have constantly to mark time whilst the extended explanation or skill practice is completed? What is it like to be told again and again that it is essential to explicate every step from problem to solution, when your own mind has just 'seen' the answer because to you it is obvious? Such children are not only exposed to boredom and irritation but are also being marked out as different from all the others, for whom the teaching or conversational style may be quite appropriate.

They also risk losing their zest for learning anything new – and it is here time to dispel the myth of the Pushy Parent, who cannot see his child beyond the golden glow of her gifts and as a result is always thrusting her forward to the next level of achievement. Too often, in the experience of families with whom we have worked, their request for more appropriate or stimulating work for their child has been met with a dismissive reaction from the teacher or school, and the implication that they have a mistaken view of their child. Such a reaction is largely due, we believe, to a lack of understanding of this aspect of gifted children. Some gifted children have butterfly minds that flit from one new thing to another; others can concentrate for unusually long periods on their favourite topics and prefer to weave increasingly intricate webs of knowledge about them. What almost all have in common is the desire to *learn*, to *understand*, to *discover*. Far from being egged on by vicariously ambitious parents, such children can drive their families to exhausted distraction by their obsessive interests, their unceasing questions, their unflagging curiosity.

Indeed, gifted children are often distinguished by their unquenchable mental energy. Relative to their peers, they lack a sense of proportion and throw themselves heart and soul into every activity or topic. When Georgie's parents were worried about how tired she seemed to be as a result of having a lunchtime ballet lesson on top of her normal school day, they approached her class teacher to see whether she shared their concerns and to ask how the other children coped in the same situation. 'She does seem tired on a Wednesday afternoon', agreed the teacher, 'and more so than the others who do ballet with her. But then, you know, not many children put quite the same levels of *energy* into everything as Georgie does.' Such children also have a tendency to latch onto a subject and follow it relentlessly through to its natural conclusion (and, some parents would say, way beyond!), buoyed by a combination of this mental energy and their natural curiosity.

It can require some delicacy to avoid the risk of this zest for learning being extinguished. Joshua held the following conversation shortly after starting school: 'Mummy, I have a problem.' – 'Oh, what is it?' – 'Well, Mrs Thomlin says that when we are learning the words of a song, I must go on repeating it with the rest of the class even though I knew it first time through.' – 'I see. That is difficult. I wonder what we might be able to do about it?' A brief, thoughtful silence followed, then: 'I know. I'll do this.' Joshua took up his position, feet apart and hands behind his back, mouthing the words silently. The solution was practical, amusing and offended nobody, but it let him off what he saw as an unreasonable task. Who would have expected a five-year-old to come up with it? More, who would have expected a five-year-old to find himself in the position where such a solution was needed? What would have happened to his feelings about school if he had not felt able to talk things through openly at home?

Many gifted children are also perceptive and quick-witted. At much earlier ages than other children – often from the point when they first learn to talk – they are capable of abstract thought and of engaging in debate and logical argument. Mentally, they can skip not just several steps ahead of many adults but right into the next field and beyond. Frequently aided by quite astonishing powers of memory, their minds can leap between subjects that may appear to others completely unrelated, making original connexions and challenging orthodoxy. Their role seems to be that of the little boy in 'The Emperor's New Clothes': where the majority of people might accept and agree with what they are told, the gifted child is constantly popping up and shouting, 'But the Emperor has no clothes!'

Again, these skills can be a mixed blessing if they are misunderstood or even ignored. Not only can gifted children be misconstrued as showing off when they share their questions or thoughts, but it is not too strong to say that some adults refuse to believe that children can have such high levels of knowledge and intelligence. When Seetal first started nursery at the age of three, she was talking to her carer about what she could see in a picture: 'And what's this, Seetal?' the carer asked, pointing at one part of the picture. 'It's a daddy sparrow,' Seetal replied – to which the adult's response was, 'No, dear, it's a birdie.' Such stories are not uncommon amongst the parents of gifted toddlers.

Similarly, it can be hard for adults to keep up with a child whose mind has been taken via a complicated train of thought to a different topic from the one that was being discussed two minutes ago, with the result that his next comment appears to be a complete non sequitur and is brushed aside as irrelevant. By the age of four Barnaby had already become used to his knowledge and ideas being dismissed in this way. Not long after his birthday he took a toy into school which his teacher had not seen before, and reported to his father that Miss Lee had assumed that the toy must have been new for his birthday. 'Did you explain that you've had it a long time, since Grandpa sent it to you from New Zealand?' he asked. 'No, Daddy,' said Barnaby, 'I just agreed with her, because that way she believes me.' It is not hard to imagine the effect on the self-image of a child whose claims to knowledge about the world, questions or ideas are consistently undermined or ignored in ways that provoke such a response.

How can parents help their gifted children when they are faced with situations like these? As with all difficulties that our children encounter, the key is to find a balance in our response. It may be, for example, that a gifted child is perceived as arrogant because he really is behaving in an overconfident or dismissive way; then his parents' role will be to help him to understand a bit more about other people's feelings and how he might be coming across to them. Conversely, it may be that his abilities are being dismissed or resented as a result of others' insecurities; then his parents will need to focus more on reassuring him that he is not always responsible for other people's behaviour, and that despite *their* behaviour, *he* really is fine just as he is.

> Do any of these descriptions or stories ring true for your child?

Again, there will inevitably be times for all brighter-than-average children when they are forced to go at an average or less-than-average pace, and it may be helpful for parents in these circumstances to talk to their children about the need for compromise when you are one of 30 children in a class. On the other hand, if a gifted child finds herself constantly being held back, with no compromise being made for *her* benefit, and if her parents can see that her zest for learning is gradually ebbing away as a result, then they will need to approach the school about what is happening.

The same sort of balanced approach needs to be taken towards gifted children's tendency to challenge traditions or norms. On the one hand, there really are times when people's ways of doing things or the opinions they espouse are repeated rather mindlessly, and they may even benefit from the questioning approach of a gifted child. On the other hand, there may be times when his questions are not appropriate, either because the norm involved serves a genuine purpose (it's pretty crucial that we all accept our society's conventions about the side of the road on which we drive, for example), or because the people involved will not accept any criticism of their beliefs or actions.

Gifted children in these circumstances need guidance on two fronts. First, they need to know that there will be consequences if they do choose to reject commonly accepted traditions and values: you may choose to dress in that way, but other people *will* judge you accordingly; you may discard your school's convention that children don't tell tales about being bullied, but the other children *will* condemn you for it. This is not to say that the consequences should always put children off the challenge they wish to make or the question they want to ask, but they do need support in becoming aware of the fact that consequences there will be. Second, the discomfort of others, and the long-term effects on their reactions to a child who behaves in this way, may need to be gently explained to a gifted child in an attempt to increase his empathy with people whose reactions he may regard as irrational. It will help him to know that people do sometimes react with anger and fear when questioned or challenged.

The key, as emphasized, is balance. Of course it is important not to cast gifted children as the intellectual equivalent of the poor little rich girl – oh how hard it must be to be blessed with intellect and creativity! – but it nevertheless remains the case that their gifts *can* be a double-edged sword, and that an insight into how this arises can help in our care for these children.

Intellectual quirks

It is equally essential, however, not to paint gifted children as faultless innocents surrounded by obtuse adults and ogreish teachers. The intellectual quirks that often come with giftedness can erect barriers between such children and those around them, in ways that are both unintentional and in many cases unavoidable.

As well as being intellectually agile, gifted children are often very creative, showing original thought and imagination. The ways in which their minds work can be unusual, giving rise to unpredictable or divergent ideas and thought processes. Their sense of humour is often quirky and develops surprisingly early. All of these traits can bring great joy to gifted children and those around them, and ultimately of course they can be of immense value to society at large, but in the meantime it should be noted that they also carry with them an even greater potential for misunderstanding than their more conventional intellectual gifts. How, for example, were the Common Entrance[1] examiners supposed to respond to Amir when he handed in a blank piece of paper at the end of the mathematics examination? At the top of the question paper it had said, 'Answer as many questions as you like.' He answered none because he didn't like any of them.

On the whole adults are fairly confident about the sorts of answers or questions that they can expect from children in any given circumstance, and consequently they may ignore or reject any unexpected responses. They may also feel justified in their irritation with a child who keeps going off task because her mind has leapt to another topic; or with one who uses his creative and imaginative skills to enable him to avoid tasks that he dislikes or simply to get his own way; or with one who delights in putting shocking elements in his work; or with one who manipulates other children's behaviour to get them into trouble, whilst staying cleverly within the rules himself. Thus can the gifted child create, quite unknowingly, circumstances that do himself no favours; and thus can adults reinforce, quite unintentionally, the message that it would be better if he were more normal and produced more conventional responses.

In particular, the gifted child's sense of humour can mark him out from his peers. Usually we would not expect under-tens to have developed the sort of abstract conceptual ability that supports puns or intelligent associations. Although we often take for granted our sense of humour, in reality it requires the higher-level mental skill of being able to blend more than one type or classification of logical message. In some jokes we are led by the meaning of the words to expect one sort of outcome, and the humour depends on our ability to realize that the words also have an alternative meaning, so that the denouement is unexpected but also makes sense; some jokes are funny because we are able to see that the situation that they describe is ridiculous; others because they involve word-plays that depend on our knowledge of words which are unspoken but sound similar to those in the punch line. When you begin to unravel all that is involved in 'getting' even quite a simple joke, it is remarkable to think that many gifted children begin to develop a recognizable sense of humour and the ability to understand and repeat jokes long before they start school. Again this must influence the nature of the relationships that they form with both peers and adults, marking them out as different and opening them up to misunderstanding as well as appreciation.

'Why can't Daddy read my story?' asked four-year-old Milly as her mother tucked her into bed one evening and her father left for a local council meeting. 'Because Daddy has to go to a *very* interesting meeting,' smiled her mother, 'and talk to lots of *very* interesting people about lots of absolutely fascinating things.' Milly laughed. 'I think you're being a bit facetious, Mummy!' The same child had learned the words *transparent* and *opaque* when she first encountered the concept of opposites at the age of two, because within her family a delight in words was a natural part of life. Her mother quickly noticed, however, how ill-disposed other people could be towards Milly's wide vocabulary and accurate understanding of jokes and nuances. As she grew older, Milly too began to notice and be troubled by others' reactions to her abilities. In the first term of Year 7, at the age of 11,[2] she warned her mother before the first parents' evening of the year that she must not be disappointed about her mark in English. Was it bad, she wondered? 'Well, I didn't want to get very high marks, because people wouldn't play with me if I did,' Milly replied, 'so I didn't write the essay.' Her mark was still 70 per cent.

Gifted children can also shock adults by the force and conviction with which they express their emotions and opinions. Their minds are quick to challenge, question and criticize rather than just to accept the things that they read or hear. The problem is that if a child is surrounded by adults who persist in giving simplified answers and explanations – to the extent that some of their statements are actually untrue – then his respect for and trust in those adults is bound to wane. Very bright children are often capable of understanding quite complex information if it is presented clearly and within the limits of their vocabulary, and there is a host of negative implications in adult attempts to brush aside their questions with brief and inaccurate answers: that those questions are of no value; that adults are not trustworthy sources of knowledge; that the child's consequent frustration and confusion is of no importance.

'Don't ask Mrs Senior where her husband is when you see her,' said Mummy to six-year-old Earl. 'Why not, Mummy?' 'Because he has just died and she might be upset.' So Earl, urgently needing to know what being upset over a death might be like, approaches Mrs Senior at the first possible opportunity out of Mummy's hearing, and asks where Mr Senior is. It was not a naughty or malicious question, simply an exploration in depth. Fortunately, Mrs Senior was able to deal with it calmly and without distress. His mother's thoughtful advice was perfectly understandable, but so was Earl's urgent need to *know*.

It is vital, then, that assumptions are not made about the sorts of things that gifted children can understand, on the basis of the average child's achievements. Similarly, such children will work best when allowed to go at their own pace, unhampered by adult assumptions that someone of their age would not be able to succeed at a more advanced level. How can they learn from their mistakes if they are never allowed to have a go at tasks difficult enough to carry the risk of making them? It is not unusual for gifted children to be able to work several years ahead of their chronological age in subjects where they have a particular aptitude. It is essential for the gifted to be allowed to find their own limits, rather than to impose on them restrictions that are based on their contemporaries' abilities.

As Dominic, who benefited from such an attitude at Cambridge University, explains:

> My college supported me when I wanted to change degree subjects at the end of the first year, even though it would involve catching up on a year's course in a few weeks, and they allowed a friend of mine to take two degree courses concurrently. Later I received the same support when I wanted to change courses again at the end of the second year, even though it would mean catching up on two years' work over the Summer vacation. This time I discovered that it was just too much, but the fact that I was allowed to give it a go means that I am not left wondering 'What if?' and regretting a missed opportunity. I also value the fact that my tutors respected me enough to let me try, instead of just presupposing that I couldn't succeed.

If adults do persist in judging gifted children by the standards of their contemporaries then it can sometimes result in a child being praised for work that is of average or even above average standard, but which is well below her own abilities. If she is bright enough to realize this then it will not be surprising if she starts to lose respect for the adults around her, and eventually to lower her own standards. In these circumstances it will soon dawn on many bright children that there is little point in bothering to try very hard, as nobody seems to mind much if they achieve good rather than excellent results.

Again there are questions of balance and perspective to be addressed here, and in Chapters 4 and 5 we look at some of the ways in which other people respond to the idiosyncrasies of gifted children. It may sometimes be the case, though, that a child is genuinely behaving in ways that make life harder not only for other people but also for himself. The important thing for parents to remember in this situation is the distinction between their child's behaviour and him as a person. So the essence of the message from parent to child will be: 'I love you. Your behaviour is unacceptable.' This may be realized in words like, 'You are a lovely little boy, and I know that you don't usually behave like this. There is no point in being naughty in the hope that I'll send you to your room and you won't have to tidy your toys, because I'm afraid that it just has to be done. Come on, let's see how quickly we can do it.' In addition to the crucial fact that the parent here has separated the child from his behaviour, a gifted child will respect the fact that she has also understood what lay behind his behaviour, acknowledged that this task is something he dislikes and presented herself as an ally in tackling it.

> In what ways does your child's mind appear to work differently from other children's?
>
> In what ways does he sometimes make life harder for himself?
>
> How do you respond when your child behaves in these ways?

Language development

One particular intellectual gift deserves special attention at this point. Early language development has been identified within our group as a key influence on the relationships that gifted children form, both within their families and with their peers. From the moment of birth, babies are surrounded by sound and more specifically by speech. Their own initial response is by cries, gurgles or smiles, but the interpretation of these can be limited or approximate or simply wrong. If Nicola is bored and wanting to have a go in her baby-bouncer, then she will find it frustrating when daddy thinks that she is yelling because her nappy needs changing. So a degree of alertness to the huge variation of sound which is presented to her in speech, especially if certain combinations of sound constantly recur, is likely to produce the incentive to make her communication more precise. Of course the same is true for any child, but a gifted child may develop this understanding exceptionally early.

Parents often look eagerly for the first words from their children, so a baby who develops early speech is generally rewarded by a very positive reaction. If you produce your first sentence (' 'nk a' go' ') by the age of ten months, and are met with delight and a reward ('Is your drink all gone? Would you like some more?'), then the result of your effort makes it well worth continuing. Further, if the expressions and ideas that you produce are idiosyncratic and charming, then you will have gained the goodwill of the people with whom you are communicating. Wanting a lot more of the Christmas fudge than he has been given, William will probably pick up the fact that his mother's instruction to his brother, 'Go and fetch the F.U.D.G.E.', is a prelude to its arrival at the table. So William's claim, 'My want F.G.G.' is received with benevolent laughter…and a piece of fudge.

From charmingly idiosyncratic toddler-speak the bright child soon progresses, again by copying and extending a process demonstrated by the older people around him, to an understanding of cause and consequence, and then to a precocious capacity for logical argument.

When Helga, at the age of three, was sitting at a table in the living room and called through to her mother in the kitchen, 'Mummy, just get me that red crayon from the box, will you?' Mummy, equally busy, answered, 'Why don't you get it? You're nearer.' 'Yes,' came the immediate response, 'but your legs are longer.' What parent is likely to resist such delightful logic? Mummy laughed, put down what she was doing and took the crayon across to Helga. In so doing, she was reinforcing Helga's belief that provided she gets the argument right she can control her surroundings.

From such small beginnings grows a wonderful confidence, often noted in bright toddlers and infant school children,[3] that to master the system is the recipe for ruling the world. Anthony, in the Reception class at school,[4] believed that he was superior to his brother James, the elder by 18 months. When Anthony announced that he was king, James after some consideration asserted that he was emperor. Anthony promoted himself to being head of a neighbouring empire, so James threatened war and conquest. During that week the Reception class was introduced to the Creation story. Anthony, recognizing his brother's greater size and strength, decided on a private satisfaction of his ambition: late at night his mother overheard him saying quietly, in the privacy of his bedroom, 'In the beginning, Anthony…'

Later on, when other necessities come into force or adults have a more pressing agenda whose causes are not apparent to the child, a battle of wills may ensue which is technically won by the child's argument but where the result is not changed by it. 'Why do I have to go to school?' is a question faced by many parents. Often their answers seem to the child logically inadequate. 'Because you'll learn a lot of things there,' may seem to the adult to be a reasonable response, but 'I know all the work,' complained five-year-old Helen, 'and I don't like the custard.' The claim that it's because 'you'll make lots of friends there' may turn out to be equally untrue: Darren, who spent his playground time walking around with the adult in charge, was only silenced by the answer, 'Because I'll be sent to jail if you don't.'

A conviction that logic and justice should rule the world may well turn out to be a double-edged sword for a gifted child. On the whole, you don't become popular by always being right or winning the argument, and teachers as much as your age-peers may react badly to your skill. If you are regularly branded as a boff or geek, or if you are never asked for the answer even though you put up your hand for every question, then you will soon lose enthusiasm and may even begin to wonder what is wrong with you. At the same time, families and teachers may put undue pressure on you by equating logical skills with being sensible, which is a quite different and more emotionally rounded characteristic. The assumption that because you are articulate you are equipped for dealing with difficult situations is sometimes a cruel one, which ignores your need for emotional support. There is indeed no guarantee that the intellectually advanced child is equally emotionally mature. More than this, it is crucial for adults to apply normal discipline and boundaries to the gifted children in their charge, as it can be very unsettling for one so young to realize that he is able to manipulate the grown-ups around him.

So the confidence that learning can set you at the controlling centre of the universe changes gradually into disillusionment and even, in some cases, to a potentially self-destructive position. Isolated and unpopular, because too different, the child who only receives affirmation through and for his skills of logical thinking faces personal annihilation if these break down. 'Of course I realize,' said Mary despairingly when she dropped out of university, 'that I am only personally acceptable insofar as I succeed academically.'

The agony of such misinterpretation, echoed poignantly by Stevie Smith ('I was too far out all my life, and not waving but drowning'), can nevertheless be transformed by other personal characteristics: an innate human understanding or a strong sense of social justice may turn a young person's desire for total control outwards into an attempt to make life better for other people. Given contact with adults who are nurturing, understanding and supportive, highly developed skills in language and logic can form a channel for offering great gifts to society, not only literary but interpretive, critical or statesmanlike.

> In what ways have you noticed that your own child's language development has influenced the sorts of relationships that she has formed?
>
> How has this affected you as a parent, the ways you respond to your child, or the assumptions that you make about her?

Intellectual inconsistencies and surprises

As well as expressing itself as advanced skill in language, giftedness may crop up in one or more of a number of diverse areas. Some children have excellent spatial awareness, some excel at design or invention, and some at listening to and understanding other people's problems and needs. Sometimes these gifts may be ignored because they fall outside the traditional school timetable. Such children experience the double whammy of spending most of their time doing things at which they do not necessarily excel, and never having the opportunity to do the things at which they do, with predictable results for their self-esteem.

One of the problems faced by such children is in fact quite common amongst those we call gifted: very often, their gifts are specific rather than general. Whilst some gifts will influence a person's abilities in almost any subject area – such as the capacity to grasp new ideas with ease, to make links between topics or commit things effortlessly to memory – others will be limited to given fields of knowledge. The same child who romps through problems in mathematics, plays county level hockey or enthrals a concert hall with her violin recital may well have quite average ability in other areas, and struggle with some subjects as well. Nor is it unusual for gifted children to have learning difficulties like dyslexia or conditions such as Asperger Syndrome.

What effect will these inconsistencies have? Gifted children are on the whole quite bright enough to see that their achievements in some areas are not very good when compared with what their peers can do. Moreover, even if a child's abilities are quite reasonable in some areas, the extent to which he excels in other fields can make his average achievements seem disproportionately poor by comparison. Again, if he is used to scoring top marks in most school subjects without even trying then it is bound to come as a shock to find that he has to practise just as hard as everyone else before he can master a new practical skill like playing the piano. In these circumstances children often feel that they *should* be able to learn as quickly in one arena as any other, and are unduly harsh in judging their own abilities and achievements.

The key to their predicament lies, quite frequently, in a mismatch between their intellectual skills and emotional maturity. Mentally, they are alert enough to have noticed that their abilities in a given area do not live up to their own usual standards, or perhaps to the standards of those around them. Where most children might not even notice that some other people's work is much better than their own, or think much about the fact that they find French harder than maths, the highly intelligent child often will. More than this, she will *expect* to be able to produce results as good as her neighbour's, or to learn as easily in one subject as in any other, and will often come to the conclusion that because she cannot, she has failed. Although gifted, she is still a child and there are many things that she cannot yet grasp: that she may still be reasonably good at French, rather than completely useless, for example, even though she is better at maths; that her neighbour's work is beautifully neat and tidy because presentation is important to that girl, whereas her own rather scruffy efforts are the result of rushing through work that is far too easy for her.

Gifted children's *perception* of failure is, then, often quite different from the norm, and it is enhanced by their characteristic lack of proportion. They tend to compare themselves unfavourably, not only with other people, but also against their own unrealistically high standards. Being bright enough to ruminate on the standards that *can* be achieved in a subject (100%, A*, etc.), they curse themselves when their achievements fall short of this ideal. Such frustration and self-blame can all too easily lead to a loss of confidence in their own talents and a consequent lack of self-esteem: perfectionists who set themselves unrealistic standards will inevitably fail to meet their own targets, and after a while they come to see themselves as failures.

Thus many gifted children surprise the adults who care for them by lacking confidence in their own abilities and being almost crippled by self-doubt, even though they succeed by anyone else's standards in almost everything. As Oliver's headteacher exclaimed in frustration to his parents, 'I can't believe that Oliver's opinion of himself isn't higher, when he's achieved so much!' The problem, of course, was that by Oliver's own standards his achievements were neither here nor there: *of course* he would get top marks in maths and the sciences; they were easy. But what about the B in Spanish?

It would be fruitful to pause for a moment here and reflect on Oliver's assertion that maths and science are easy; clearly he gains little self-respect from the fact that he scores high grades in these subjects. This is another experience typical of a gifted child: that the expectations of adults, or of educational systems like exams or assessments, are so low in relation to his actual abilities that they are not, in the child's view, worthy of respect. If this is the case then it may be that the only other target he can see is perfection. Having gifts that lie somewhere on the scale between an irrelevant target and an unattainable one, he is left without any clues as to his true level of ability and develops an unrealistic picture of himself.

Nor are past achievements, for many gifted children, a guide to future possibilities. Every time there is a new challenge they are convinced that this time it will end in failure. Hoda's parents had always tried to restrain her own tendencies to push herself too hard, rather than exerting any pressure themselves. Regardless of this, Hoda, who had never had a grade below A in her life, 'phoned them from university after taking her finals to explain that, 'I know you're used to me getting top marks, but I really don't want you to be disappointed if I don't do well.' Past evidence is dismissed as irrelevant by young people like this, because 'this time it's *different*' in some pertinent way. This is not false modesty, but a genuine ignorance of their abilities as compared to other people's, stemming perhaps from their focus on their own unattainable goals.

A not uncommon response to these feelings among gifted children is to spend a lot of time sitting and watching what is involved in a particular activity before they are prepared to give it a go themselves – although it should be noted that after extended observation and planning, they then reach decisions more quickly or produce more accurate results than the others can manage. In older children who are learning a foreign language, for instance, this tendency may be manifest in a refusal to say anything at all unless they can guarantee that it will be correct: thus they can gain a reputation for saying very little in language lessons, but whatever they do say tends to be right in every particular.

Younger gifted children also frequently display a tendency to hold back in new situations, as if checking out all of its implications. They may refuse to help or to answer questions before they know all the details involved, and may be initially shy in social situations. Some aspects of their development, like walking and talking, may actually appear to be delayed but then emerge fully formed: Paul hardly said a word until he was 20 months old, but then started speaking in paragraphs. By the time he was four his conversations were so fully punctuated and hedged with qualifications and corollaries that, in his quest for linguistic precision, it took an inordinate amount of time for him to say anything: 'Mummy, Khalid says that you can buy Star Wars Lego at the supermarket (not the supermarket we usually go to, but the one near to his house – well, quite close anyway – that he goes to with his mummy, or whoever he goes shopping with). So next time you go shopping – or if Daddy goes, or you both do – could you go to that supermarket, and buy me some Star Wars Lego?'

Even more extreme than this sort of caution, it is not uncommon for gifted children to become so convinced that they are poor at something that they actually refuse to attempt tasks in that area. Indeed one of the skills that many highly intelligent people hone, almost unconsciously, is the ability to spot an opportunity for failure at a hundred paces and take avoiding action. As a result they have few opportunities to learn from their mistakes. It is not unusual for a driving test to be the first thing that a young gifted person has ever failed. If, in addition, they have never had to struggle to keep up in a subject then they may lack skills of perseverance and concentration, just giving up if something seems too hard. They may have difficulties, too, in areas where being clever can't cut corners, like subjects where you need to learn some things by rote, or skills like playing a musical instrument which demand patience and regular practice. When Bella first started to play the violin she used to screw up her face in frustration and exclaim, 'I *know* what my fingers are meant to be doing! Why won't they do it?'

Whilst it is obvious, in theory, that one can learn valuable lessons from making mistakes, from the gifted child's point of view the avoidance of failure makes perfect sense. Since he finds learning easy, there are genuinely few instances where the risk might arise, and this adds the fear of the unknown to his dread of getting it wrong. Moreover, his intelligence enables him to see, in a way that his peers just do not notice, the vast amount of knowledge and skill that he lacks in certain areas. A small child who sees adults producing, with an apparent lack of effort, a sheet of evenly formed and swiftly executed hand-writing, can easily be intimidated by the distance between his own level of skill and the grown-ups'. Rather than make mistakes and risk looking silly, it may seem preferable to him to distract the adults by misbehaving and in that way avoid doing any writing of his own. The same can apply to reading or indeed to anything else. Despite his intelligence, he is not yet mature enough to understand the reason for the gap between himself and the adults. Putting it simplistically, the child comes to believe that 'I can't and you can' because 'I'm stupid and you're clever,' rather than for the true reason: that 'I haven't learnt yet, and you have.'

It is easy for parents to feel helpless in the face of a child who persists with an unrealistically low assessment of her own abilities and worth (and for many gifted children the two are intimately linked). Part of the problem for these children is that the area in which many of them are used to excelling – academia – is one in which they are constantly measured and given grades. What happens to them, then, when they grow up and go into life situations in which they are ungraded? Often these children are blessed with extreme sensitivity as well as intelligence, and rather like canaries down a mine they can sense what matters to their parents, even when they try to hide it, and long before anyone else does. Rather than risk anything less than perfection, they will simply refuse to carry out any task in which failure is a possibility. Many carry this approach into their adult life.

How does your child perceive himself and his achievements?

In what ways is he affected by perfectionism?

How does he respond to failure or its prospect?

What can be done to heal these children of what can be an almost crippling level of self-doubt? In a nutshell, what they need is *evidence* of a sort that they can *respect*. In order to understand what is meant by this, we need to look in a bit more detail at what targets and achievements involve for gifted children.

As we have described, a gifted child will not necessarily welcome praise for having achieved at the highest level that is conventionally measured, for he may not deem that particular target worthy of respect: if the exam system is such that he can achieve the top grade with little effort, then that top grade will not be worth much to him. Reuben, for example, is far from the only teenager whose seven A grades at O level[5] were utterly eclipsed, in his own perception, by the two B grades that he was also awarded. To many people his response may be laughable or even offensive, but to Reuben the only meaningful O level target was a clean sweep of top grades. On the day that results were published, having set his face into a fake smile all morning in response to other people's congratulations, he finally burst into tears when his best friend's mother's reaction was, 'Oh Reuben, I'm sorry.'

Similarly, Alex's own perception of her achievements was masked by her clean sweep of A grades at A level. General studies she regarded as a matter of chance, since it required no exam preparation; she found maths so easy that the top grade meant very little; Latin she found time-consuming but not intellectually challenging, so that again its A grade gave her satisfaction but no real sense of achievement. Physics A level, on the other hand, was a real challenge for Alex: it was perhaps the first subject in which she had ever truly struggled, by her own standards, at least, but she had devoted so much time and effort to it that in the end it too became easy. *That*, for Alex, was a real achievement.

Thus the first step towards helping a child like this must be an attempt to understand what her targets and achievements mean *to her*. Not until this step has been taken can adults begin to respond in ways that accord with her perception of the situation.

The next step is, however, equally important, and that is to begin to explore with the child to what extent her perception of the situation accords with *reality*. When Bella began to express such frustration with what she perceived as her pitiful attempts to play the violin, her teacher's response was to talk to her about the reality of learning to play any musical instrument: that the pupil is not 'useless' because she cannot yet achieve the standards of people who have been playing the instrument for many years; that with practice she will make progress towards those standards; that progress has actually already been made, despite what she sees as her current low levels of achievement. In other words, the teacher was exploring with Bella the unrealistic nature of both the targets that she had set herself and the assessment that she had made of her achievements.

In order to convince Bella of the reality of what he was explaining to her, her teacher gave her some evidence that even she could not dismiss. In addition to her standard preparation, he gave her the same short but challenging exercise to practise, week after week. After a while, he presented her with a new and, by her standards, extremely difficult composition. When she threw up her hands in despair at the thought that a violinist so poor as she could attempt such a piece, he quite casually asked her to run through the now familiar exercise that she had been practising for so long. 'Do you hear how well and easily you play that exercise, Bella?' he asked her, 'And do you remember how very hard it was when you first tried it? Well, you can play it so well now because of how you have practised it. The same thing will happen again with this new piece.'

Thus her teacher gave Bella incontrovertible evidence that she had made progress from her previous standard of playing; he invited her to make the undeniable inference that she could therefore do the same again from her current standard; and at the same time he gave her the unspoken message that therefore her own highest goals in music may well be achievable, with work, *at some point*, even though she had not yet reached them. Her previous assessment of her ability and achievements was just unrealistic: the fact that she was not yet as good a violinist as him, for example, ought to be irrelevant to her assessment of her own potential. On the other hand this teacher was not completely dismissing the relevance of that comparison. Bella was right in her assessment of their relative *skill* levels; she was mistaken only in her assessment of what the current gap between them implied about her own *potential* as a violinist.

This sort of technique can obviously be applied to a child who is engaged in learning any type of skill, be it something practical like sport or music, or something more academic like reading or writing. Its essence lies in the presentation of evidence of a sort that the child can believe and respect. This evidence cannot be a simple restatement of the level of his past or present achievements. To say, 'But you read very well, darling, much better than most children your age,' or 'You're bound to do well in your A levels; just look at how high your GCSE grades were,' may, as emphasized, be of very little help to this particular child. The most useful sort of evidence in these situations will, rather, be information that is both relevant to the particular situation and related to the child's own experience.

Thus it may well be relevant to point out that his reading level is higher than average, but at the same time it would be useful to remind him of his progress (what sorts of books did he struggle with last month?), and of how long Mummy and Daddy have had to practise their reading. Similarly, it is not ill-judged to remind a child of her success in previous exam situations, but she needs also to be reminded of how equally unconfident she felt before *that* success, and of the similarities between the work that she is putting in now and how she managed to achieve that past success. In this way such children have a chance to air what they see as any relevant differences between the past and present situations – perhaps they can honestly say that never before has the subject matter or skill level been so challenging *for them* – and to begin to think their way around any obstacles that do genuinely exist.

Having taken the time to understand a gifted child's perception of his targets and achievements, and made the attempt to anchor that perception in reality, the next important step is to ensure that the child understands the difference between ability and achievement. It is this which can provide the key to how he handles situations in which he perceives himself as having failed. Even the most well-balanced child, who is able to work realistically towards the next target without being dazzled by his end-goal of perfection, will every now and then come up against a situation in which that target is not met. Talented footballers have off-days when they are not picked for a team; brilliant musicians do not always give brilliant performances; gifted mathematicians can make silly mistakes in an exam situation. More than this, in a competitive setting there may well be another child whose gifts exceed their own, so that the fair outcome *is* that they are out-performed by the other child. How can parents help their gifted children to cope with circumstances like these?

The answer is to highlight for the child the difference between a particular measure taken on a particular day, and the facts about her abilities. Liana, now at university studying English, well remembers the day that her English teacher at school succeeded in making this distinction real to her. She had been increasingly panic-stricken about her A level results, and was not at all reassured by the universal assertion that 'Liana is an outstanding student and bound to achieve the top grades.' Eventually her English teacher took her to one side: 'Liana,' she said, 'You are indeed an outstanding student. You write fluently and poetically, and you're a perceptive critic. You're blessed with a reliable memory and you have a remarkable capacity for organising information. *None of this will stop being true if you don't get an A.*' Liana eventually went on to get the grade that she wanted, but her friend Alan was not so lucky in his chosen subject. It was the same teacher who said to him, 'Alan, I'm really sorry that you didn't get an A. I think that you underachieved, and I think that you're worth more than that.'

Indeed there may be longer-term practical implications of the failure to meet your own targets, and these may not be trivial: Alan was not able to go to his first choice of university. There is a crucial distinction, however, between the practical implications of failure and its emotional impact. Gifted children can avoid many of the long-term *emotional* implications of failure if they have learnt that no given measure of your achievements can fully reflect your abilities or worth. Of course this is an important message for us all, not just for gifted children, but in their case it is particularly significant because high achievement can become so tightly bound up with a gifted child's estimate of his own worth; and because gifted people are often cast as an infallible persona by those around them, making failure so much more difficult and shocking when it does occur. If we can help them to see beyond the confines of targets and achievements then, whether or not they have realized those dreams, they may be able to avoid the feeling that *therefore* they are worth more or less than would otherwise be the case.

We must foster in them a sense that failure is not a dreaded disease but a natural part of life, from which growth and progression is always an option. When 16-year-old Charlene was awaiting her GCSE results, all her hopes and fears were focused on her favourite subject, history, in which she needed at least a B in order to study it at A level. Despite her teacher's prediction of an A* she had nightmares on a regular basis throughout the summer as her anxiety grew. Her parents suffered with her, but their attempted reassurances were to no avail. Then, one Tuesday morning just before her results were due, Charlene strolled down from her bedroom in an evidently relaxed frame of mind. She laughed as she explained over breakfast, 'I can't believe that I've been so silly. If I don't get my B in history then I'll just do a different A level. It's not the end of the world!'

Such maturity is rare in a 16-year-old, but Charlene's is the message that we need to convey to other young gifted people. We cannot pretend that everything in the garden is rosy and that a positive outcome is inevitable in every anxious situation, but the point is that other options are always available. Missing an educational step now does not mean that the chance has been lost for ever, and indeed educational achievement is not the only measure of success; we need to emphasize to our children the reality of the value of alternative paths.

Moreover, not only gifts but also multiple other factors have to be acknowledged when assessing a person's success. Crucial amongst these factors is personality, which does have to be taken into consideration. In some gifted people, their personal approach marks the converse of what we have been discussing. Having the ability to make a realistic assessment of them-selves, they may not feel the need for external validation in the form of formal qualifications – especially if, as mentioned, they cannot respect the assessment process or standards. Frustration that someone's potential has not been realized may be unrealistic given the complexities of his situation, the ways in which he is beginning to fit into the world, the compromises that he is prepared to make and the realities of what feels safe to him.

In conclusion, then, what a gifted child needs is for her parents to try to understand how *she* feels about her targets, achievements and abilities; for them to help her to make a comparison between these feelings and the situation in reality; to present her with relevant and respectable evidence of this; and for them to put into perspective the significance of those achieve-ments and goals – their practical implications, and what in reality they can tell us about her abilities.

Finally, on the topic of self-esteem and achievement, it is especially important for the parents of gifted children to dissociate the *person* from his *deeds*, and to do so from the earliest age. At the most basic level, this means for example that 'good boy' does not mean the same thing as 'well done' and that neither is equivalent to 'clever boy'. If parents use such phrases interchangeably then the child at some level receives the message that *in order* to be a good boy, he must do well.

> In what ways does your child's perception of herself and her achievements surprise you?
>
> What sort of evidence could you present to your child to help her gain confidence in her abilities?

So, for instance, when a child first learns to tie his shoelaces or does some particularly neat colouring, an appropriate response would be something like, 'Well done', or 'What a lovely picture', *not* 'Good boy.' If, on the other hand, he has let another child share his toys, then it might be appropriate to praise the way that he has behaved with words like, 'Good boy', or 'Thank you for sharing so nicely.'

This highlights another key element of useful praise, which is to make the praise specific rather than general. On the whole, neither 'well done' nor 'good boy' actually gives the child much helpful information, whereas 'What neat handwriting', or 'I'm really pleased that you were honest and owned up to having broken the ornament,' tells them exactly why they are being praised and carries much more meaning and force as a result.

Other useful techniques for raising a child's self-esteem when commenting on his achievements are described by Joan Freeman (1998). The child needs information about consistency: for example, 'You did that well again.' He is helped by what is called consensus information: either 'You got that all right, and most people find it really hard,' or conversely 'I know you struggled with that. Most other people find it hard, too.' He needs information about his particular talents: 'This topic suits you,' or conversely 'The other subject suits you better, doesn't it?' He needs his parents to emphasize the role of effort as well as ability: 'If you try that again then it will soon become easier.'

Of course all of this is good advice for all parents, but for the parents of gifted children it is of particular significance, for as we have emphasized it is all too easy for gifted children's self-esteem to become bound up with their perception of their own achievements. If they become used to their parents separating the two from an early age, then they are far less likely to have that dangerous confusion in their own minds.

> In what ways do you help your child to know that he is valued for more than his gifts?

Emotional skills

In the previous section we considered a small child who despairs because his literacy skills are not comparable with those of the adults around him. It may seem blindingly obvious to most adults that they can read and write simply because they have benefited from decades of teaching and practice, but this does not mean that even a gifted child can see the same thing. No matter how bright the child, *he is still a child*. This is a mantra that is worth repeating, for gifted children are vulnerable to all manner of misconceptions. It is very easy to assume, when faced with an articulate child who is able to grasp the meaning of just about any combination of words that you might use in a sentence, that she is also able to comprehend the significance and ramifications of the topic of conversation. It is easy to forget, when recommending books for an able reader, that the emotional content of the more difficult books may be completely inappropriate for such a young child.

Corresponding problems can stem from the fact that the gifted often have an unusually heightened awareness of the world around them and the issues that it raises. From a very early age they can be troubled or puzzled by current events, by the snippets of history that they pick up and by the environmental, theological or ethical questions that occur to them. They can also become fascinated by the difference between reality and fantasy, with an urgent need to analyse the different levels of pretence involved in books or films. Where most children might be ready to accept an adult's evasive answer about difficult issues, or a very limited and sanitized version of events, the more able are hardly ever satisfied by this approach. Their minds are swift to ferret out the gaps or inconsistencies in an explanation, and their intellectual abilities may lead them into areas for which they are emotionally unready. Thus neither the three-year-old who is curious about why everyone seems to be wearing poppies nor the seven-year-old who saw the news on 11 September 2001 is likely to be ready for the answers to his questions. The world can feel much more frightening to an observant, perceptive and thoughtful child than to one whose gaze rarely lifts above the parapet of her crayons and toys.

Indeed, not only may such children have an intellect that far outstrips their chronological and emotional age, but their emotional age may actually be *less* than their chronological age. Some bright children are, despite their intelligence, emotionally immature. Ironically, this is exacerbated if they are also unusually sensitive and perceptive, for they can be exposed to an awareness and intellectual understanding of difficult situations long before they are able to cope with them emotionally. Gifted children are sometimes characterized as having one skin less than others: their feelings seem to develop very early, and to be heightened and extreme when they do emerge. One mother described her son as 'a child who could look right through to your soul'. As she put it so powerfully, 'People couldn't take it, and their vengeance on him was very great.' This was also an intensely moral boy, who could not tolerate untruth in people's behaviour, or how they treated each other. Not only can it be genuinely difficult for other people to understand and absorb this intensity of feeling and perception, but the gifted child himself will at times find his own feelings unfathomable and overwhelming.

Neil's mother became pregnant with his sister when he was two-and-a-half, and he seemed to be much more affected by this than were any other children his parents knew, perhaps because the majority of children are not really aware of what it means for their mother to have a baby in her tummy. In Neil's case, however, he appeared to be fully aware of what it meant: the knowledge that his family life was going to change so enormously, in ways that he could not comprehend and at a time that seemed at once immediate and indeterminate, was the cause of the greatest anxiety that his parents have ever observed in him. Throughout his mother's pregnancy he displayed many of the textbook reactions to the *arrival* of a new baby: refusing to settle at night, going back into nappies, behaving badly, and so on.

Two important points emerge from Neil's anxiety. The first is that he is far from being alone in his response to an impending younger sibling. A gifted child will often find this situation much more taxing than his peers. Being sensitive enough to pick up on his parents' excitement and anxieties, he may be deeply unsettled by the changes that he senses in them. Being bright enough to understand that a pregnancy means that a new baby will arrive, he may develop a terror of losing his special place in the family. When adults make cheery comments about how he will be able to help Mummy to look after the new baby, he may be overwhelmed by a sense of unmanageable responsibility. All of these responses are unusual in their extremity – but not for a gifted child.

Neil's response to his mother's pregnancy is also fairly typical of a gifted child in a second way: the key to it seemed to lie in his inability *fully* to com-prehend what was happening. He obviously understood it well enough to react as many children do to the baby's actual arrival, but equally obviously he could not have had a proper understanding of the situation. His parents had by this time often noticed that the unknown was a great source of anxiety for him: once something actually happened, no matter how difficult it might be, Neil almost always rose to the occasion and coped beautifully. If problems were going to arise then it would be in the waiting time before a significant or challenging occasion. Indeed, following an awestricken first encounter in hospital, Neil has seemed to be a genuinely happy, adoring and protective big brother. He is not a jealous child and indeed his intense sense of justice will at times lead him to defend his sister's rights at his own cost. So the baby herself was not the problem.

The problem, rather, was that Neil, in common with many other gifted children, has an urgent need to *understand* a situation – to get an intellectual grip on it – before he feels able to cope with it. This problem is compounded by the fact that, being still children, they are often unable to express and indeed may be unaware of exactly what is the vital missing element in their comprehension. Thus their parents become used to having to guess what question it is that their child is asking internally but cannot find the words to express, and this can at times present an enormous challenge. When Selina, aged three, developed a sudden anxiety about her parents' death, it was several distressing days before they lighted on the issue that lay at the heart of her fear: she wanted to know what would happen to *her* and to her beloved house and toys, in the event of her being abandoned, as she saw it, by them. Once they had hit on the relevant gap in her knowledge, they were able to fill it with a brief and matter-of-fact description of the arrangements that they had made: who her guardians would be, the fact that she would still have her toys, and so on. At that point her obsession abated as suddenly as it had appeared.

Conversely, Neil's parents regret the fact that they never did get to the bottom of what aspect of the new baby was causing him such worry, and thus they were not able to relieve that worry until things were resolved naturally by the baby's arrival. Sometimes even the most gifted child's mind remains impenetrable.

It is very hard for parents to protect a child who is so attuned to emotional undercurrents, and who has just enough insight into complex situations to allow him to feel scared by or inappropriately responsible for them. He cannot be kept out of an adult world for which he is just not ready, and indeed his exposure to it will often be twofold. First, his unusual perception enables him to pick up on unspoken issues and conversational meanings long before his peers could. Second, adults tend to take him into their confidence long before it is appropriate because they assume that such a bright child will be able to understand; indeed, that such a bright child deserves a full explanation of things.

The pressures on young children in these circumstances will be exacerbated, once more, by the unrealistically high expectations that they have of themselves. They may not even recognize the fact that they are not able to cope with the situation, believing rather that their adult level of information gives them also an adult level of involvement and responsibility. Lacking the maturity to understand that the situation is one beyond their control, bright children often believe that they should be able to make things better. After all, past experience tells them that problem-solving is not so hard: here is a problem that is making the people they love unhappy; surely the thing to do is to solve it. Children who are inevitably unable to resolve adult problems can not only feel guilty about their perceived failure, but also internalize the implication that adult problems, whether with partners, at work, in health or in friendship, are therefore insoluble.

Part of the difficulty faced by gifted children is that theirs is a world in which high academic achievement comes relatively easily and intellectual pursuits afford great enjoyment. Their absorption in the processes of thought and cognition, logic and deduction is thus reinforced by the double reward of high marks at school and great personal fulfilment. Why should this be described as a difficulty? Because the world of *thought* can exclude the world of *feeling*, depriving the gifted person of a whole realm of discourse, understanding and coping mechanisms. It is not unusual for very bright people to be able to analyse complex human situations with perception and clarity, whilst completely missing out their own feelings about it all. Like the avoidance of failure, this can appear to be an excellent strategy for self-protection: 'I'm in control because I understand what's going on here.' Yet just as when failure is unavoidable it must therefore loom disproportionately large, so emotions can overwhelm the gifted when eventually they do have to be faced. The world of thought is a pretty safe place, and a sheltered existence within it can leave children vulnerable when at last they emerge.

Fortunately, this is another area in which the parents of the gifted child need not feel helpless. There are practical techniques that can be used to begin to foster in children an emotional awareness and ability to speak about their feelings, and these are explained in Chapter 4. Beyond this, parents should be reassured by the truth that their child will be aware of and appreciate the very fact that they are trying to understand her feelings and fears. That in itself is an acknowledgement that the feelings are real, even if the cause of the anxiety is a misunderstanding or simple lack of knowledge. Although parents like Neil's can feel as if they have let their child down when they fail to identify the source of his worry, it is almost equally useful to say something like, 'I don't want to guess what you're feeling because I could get it wrong, but I'm here whenever you want to tell me about it,' or 'It's really scary when we don't understand what's going to happen next, isn't it?' or even simply, 'Whatever it is that's bothering you, I want you to know that the grown-ups are in charge of it and you don't have to worry.' The message here is clear: I care about what's worrying you; it's okay to ask for help; I'm here whenever you need me; the responsibility is not yours.

> What sorts of situations cause your child most anxiety?
>
> Does your child have a need to understand a situation before she feels that she can cope with it?
>
> How easy is it for your child to speak about her feelings?

Social skills

Gifted children can struggle not only with their own feelings but also in encounters with other people. Intellectual advancement is no guarantee of social ease, and the gifted are just as much at risk of being painfully shy or socially gauche as any other children. Furthermore, they may simply have nothing in common with most other children of their own age. They may have all-absorbing hobbies or interests that exclude others, so that they're seen as loners. They may be too parental in their dealings with their peers, which other children quite understandably do not like.

They may also lack the social skills to deal with others' insecurities, so that they seem arrogant and intolerant. This is a more complex situation than it first appears, because it is too simplistic to condemn their peers for jealousy or hostility. Blessed with a good memory, delighting in the abstract and relishing debate, it is easy for able children to make others feel insecure, and then self-confident intelligence may not seem so very different from arrogance. The gifted rise to the challenge of any task described as difficult, and their easy comprehension of new ideas may make them unwilling to slog in order to understand anything that they do *not* immediately grasp. Their difficulties in coping with the unfamiliar experience of failure can compound the situation, and all of this can be perceived as conceit.

Of course both pupils and teachers can be hostile to difference of any kind. How much worse if the exceptionally able child is also exceptionally socially inept! For many gifted people, their childhood is characterized by bullying and miserable isolation. Their confidence and self-esteem suffer a consequent decline. From a very early age, when they reach milestones abnormally quickly, they might sense apprehension within their parents' pleasure. It can be hard for parents to hide their nervousness about their gifted children's futures: as Angharad explains, her choice of a highly academic prep school[6] for her son was influenced by the thought that 'I don't want Huw to be always the one on his own in the classroom.' In such children, a latent niggle may begin that they are not like other children, and this can be further stimulated when they try to make friends with those others. The more able are often so advanced in their understanding and language development that they find it almost impossible to enjoy talking to their own age group. If they have an unusual depth of knowledge about their favourite subjects then it is unlikely that other children will know what they are talking about. If they are used to adults answering their questions sensibly then they may find it hard to adapt to monosyllabic or irrelevant conversations with their fellow toddlers.

As noted already, early language development can exert a powerful influence on the relationships that gifted children form. With their peers the problem is twofold. On the one hand the other children resent and react against the language skills of the brighter child, or at a more basic level are simply not able to understand his communications, especially when they are intellectually playful or display sophisticated humour. On the other hand it can be hard for gifted children to guess what ideas and phrases are peer-appropriate, against the background of their own precocious intellectual and linguistic development. Furthermore, if social problems do arise as a result of the gulf between their own linguistic development and that of their peers, then the gifted may further flounder when they find that language use cannot rescue the situation. Dorothy Reynolds (1998) quotes two little boys who, being bullied, each independently lamented that 'It doesn't matter what *I say* [her emphasis], I can't stop them.' If their social problems arose in the first place as a partial result of their unusual language skills, then a reasoned and articulate response to their peers is hardly going to remedy matters.

Quite understandably, therefore, children who are blessed with a sophisticated language and sense of humour often prefer the company of adults or older children to mixing with their peers. On the one hand this is clearly not a long-term solution for gifted children who are struggling to find a place in the lives of their peers. On the other it affords both adult and child great pleasure and stimulation, and why shouldn't we choose interesting people over same-age people as our friends? It may simply be the case that the gifted child, emotionally immature though intellectually advanced, is just not ready to mix with others as early as the majority of children are.

All children take a few years to be ready to play together: toddlers will usually play happily in the same room as each other, but this is not the same thing as being able to play *with* each other. Most are of primary school age[7] before they begin to develop friendships and really interact with each other. The gifted child whose nursery teacher is concerned that he doesn't mix with the others, or whose mother worries that he doesn't seem to want to join in with the games at parties, may just not yet be ready for it. He may feel quite happy and at home on the fringes of the crowd, and be totally unembarrassed about playing his own games while the others play together, just as a toddler does, because that is the stage of development that he has reached. The older gifted child may well be at the same stage of *social* development as the toddler, despite his intellectual abilities (or perhaps because of them? No child can rush ahead in every area of development at once). This is just another area in which the gifted do not conform with expectations.

> Is there a gap between your child's intellectual abilities and his social or emotional development?
>
> What sorts of social situations does your child find difficult?
>
> Which people does your child like and feel at ease with?

Chapter 4 looks in more detail at the ways in which parents can support their children in their interactions with people outside the family.

Being different

Of course it is important not to dismiss the social problems that gifted children can face, brushing them aside as something that comes right with time. Often this is indeed the case: as the children get older their social skills have time to catch up with their peers', and things become correspondingly easier for them. One significant difficulty can persist, however: the feeling of being *different*.

Probably all of us have experienced the feeling of being different from those around us. Perhaps you moved house as a child and your accent stood out at your new school; perhaps your parents wouldn't buy you the latest craze toy or outfit; perhaps nobody else wanted to listen to the music that you secretly preferred; perhaps you started a new job and everyone else seemed to know exactly what he was meant to be doing; perhaps you weren't a bit interested in the World Cup...

Everyone experiences some level of difference, both at school and in later life, but it will be less acute for those whose abilities are closer to the average, because they will be surrounded by more people whose abilities are similar to their own. Gifted children feel different from other people almost all of the time. By definition they are in a minority, and they are often ridiculed rather than respected by their peers; think of all the terms of abuse that are available to the tormentors of bright children: boff, swot, nerd, geek, clever clogs, and so on. They find that they don't have very much in common with people their own age: the others don't share their interests and seem to have very different priorities. Gifted children may also be much more aware of differences than others, and much less willing to make compromises or settle for second-best, in friendship as in any other area. Gifted children and their peers are in many ways mysterious to each other, and from the other children's point of view, the gifted child can seem different in a way that is enviable and even threatening. As a result, she can begin to feel isolated and may even be ostracized or bullied by her peers.

When they feel that they don't fit in somewhere, not surprisingly many people become lonely, unhappy and frustrated. Sometimes they find themselves behaving in ways that they know are out of character but which they just don't seem to be able to help. Naturally quiet people may become loud and aggressive; confident people may become quiet and withdrawn; normally well-mannered pupils become disruptive in lessons. It is not uncommon for people to try to hide their intelligence, knowledge and achievements in order to fit in better.

Such loneliness may be intensified if it is coupled with unreasonable expectations from teachers or family. Jacek's timetable was too full for him to include an A level in music as well as maths, physics, chemistry and general studies, so he decided to take the exam out of school with his piano teacher. After just one year of only an hour's lesson per fortnight, he achieved a B grade. 'Oh,' said his headmaster thoughtlessly, 'we expected you to get an A.' Jacek still feels a failure in this respect.

The difficult thing for intelligent young people is that they are often very perceptive: they can see what's happening and know that they don't want to behave like that. What they lack, quite often, is the maturity to see that it is quite normal for *everyone* to feel miserable and out of control sometimes, and that being clever doesn't mean that you have to blame yourself for not being able to cope, or for not being able to solve a situation, or for needing support. What is more difficult for them is that they will probably experience these feelings of being very different from the surrounding context much more often than most other children. Again this can lead them, quite understandably, to seek out contexts in which they are less different: the company of adults, of older children, or if at all possible of their intellectual peers.

It may be, too, that it is less of a problem at home, where they have some crucial characteristics in common with at least some members of their family. As for many other children who find the external world challenging, the home can be a real haven for the gifted, providing a safe space in which they can relax and let off steam. This letting off steam can be horrible and worrying for their parents, but at the same time can ultimately be very positive. Home may, for instance, be a place where children can practise the sorts of social interactions that they observe as successful between their peers, but which they don't have the confidence to try out for themselves in the playground. If their parents perceive these behaviour patterns as rude or inappropriate then there will be conflict at home, but this in itself can provide a useful learning experience for the child: he might begin to see that different ways of interacting are appropriate in different contexts, or that popularity with that particular peer group might not be such a desirable goal as he'd first imagined. What matters is that he had the confidence to try it out at home, where he knew that the consequences of failure would not be catastrophic: his parents might be cross or disappointed, but they would still love and accept him.

> In what ways is your child different from most others?
>
> Which aspects of your child bring you the most joy? When do you feel most proud of her?
>
> Which aspects of your child are the most difficult, or cause you the most worry?

One of the most important gifts that parents can give to a minority child is an arena in which she feels normal: the reassurance that her family is, for her, the basis against which she can judge normality. One of the more puzzling aspects of being different from your peers is the feeling that, to you, what you're like *is* perfectly normal. If you spend a big chunk of most days feeling like an alien from another planet then the sense of coming home, metaphorically as well as literally, can be incredibly healing. It can help you to cope better with situations where conformity is non-negotiable, if there are also circumstances where you are allowed to be yourself.

This means, for instance, that parents need to guard against the temptation to pin early labels on their offspring. Many of the characteristics of giftedness overlap to a certain extent with conditions like Asperger Syndrome: gifted infants may experience unusually intense levels of distress about separation from their parents, about changes in their routine or about not getting a task done with absolute precision; they may find it hard to socialize with their peers and be perfectly content in their own company. From none of this does it follow inevitably that they have Asperger Syndrome or indeed any other special need in addition to their giftedness. Worrying though such overlapping behaviours can be, from the gifted child's point of view they may merely reflect what the world seems like *to him*.

This insight is, for our group, the key to provision for the gifted. In this chapter we have focused on the problems that gifted children can face as a result of the many complex ways in which giftedness can impact upon their personalities and preferences. We have tried to draw together something of what it feels like to be a gifted child. It is our firm belief that help for gifted children must start here, with an exploration of their feelings. Gifted children live with an atypical set of perceptions and priorities, and it is crucial to make the attempt to see the world from their point of view. Not until they have been enabled to see that none of what they feel is weird or unusual *for a gifted child* can children begin to find a context in which they feel normal.

What to tell the child

It is relevant here to mention the controversy about whether it is a good or a bad thing to tell your child that she is gifted. Some writers claim that it is harmful to label children in this way. Others believe that because in reality she already knows that she is different, unless you give her some explanation then the danger is that she will 'manufacture her own explanations, such as that she is unlikeable, or that other children have little value' (Webb, Meckstroth and Tolan 1994, p.58).

Our feeling is that whilst it is important not to focus only on a child's gifts – you can also draw her attention to the things that she does have in common with at least some other people, and to other people's gifts as well – nonetheless two significant benefits can arise from being open about this aspect of your child. First, if she sees that you are not embarrassed to use words like clever, very bright or even gifted on occasion, then her difference may begin to feel more acceptable to herself. We wonder whether some people's embarrassment about the *term* 'gifted' might stem largely from their embarrassment about the *concept* of a person's being gifted? Second, it gives her the chance to see that there *is* a group of people out there with whom she does share this unusual aspect of herself: she is not alone.

Realistically, however, it will not often be necessary to use a convenient shorthand like gifted to describe a child. It will more often be appropriate to *describe* the specific ways in which she behaves, the particular aspects of her personality or the direction of her enthusiasms, than to give her a more general *label* like gifted.

Summary

- Gifted children are part of a minority.

- Their minds are more agile and energetic, more able to make leaps and links, more urgently in need of knowledge and understanding than most children's.

- Their sense of humour and irony may develop earlier than other children's, as may their language skills and their capacity for logical debate.

- Gifted children often have strong feelings and opinions, and are not afraid to challenge the adult point of view.

- All of these traits will have an impact on the way that gifted children form relationships with their parents, teachers and peers.

- Gifted children are often perfectionists who fear failure and confuse their *worth* with their *achievements*. It is important for parents to separate these concepts from the earliest days: 'good boy' does not mean the same thing as 'well done'. Parents need also to help their gifted children to be realistic about their personal targets and achievements.

- Their gifts are rarely universal. They may even lag behind their peers in some areas of the curriculum, or have additional special needs like dyslexia or Asperger Syndrome. They may be emotionally and/or socially immature, compared with their peers.

- Gifted children often have an urgent need to grasp a situation intellectually before they feel able to cope with it emotionally.

- Gifted children feel different from their age peers and may find it hard to relate socially to them. This may simply be what is normal for them: to prefer their own company or that of their intellectual peers, including adults.

- Help for gifted children starts with an attempt to see the world from their point of view. They need reassurance that they and their families are normal *for them*.

Notes

1   An examination for pupils transferring from junior to senior independent schools in the UK.

2   As a rough rule of thumb, children in England and Wales are four to five years older than their year group's name, so Year 7 children are aged 11–12.

3   In England and Wales, infants are aged 4–7, juniors aged 7–11 and senior school children aged 11–16.

4   Reception children are aged four to five.

5   In the UK compulsory education ends at the age of 16. Most children now sit examinations called GCSEs (these used to be called O levels) aged 16. If they do choose to stay on at school then they will take A levels aged 18.

6   A prep school is a fee-paying school for children aged 4 to 11 (or, traditionally, 13).

7   Primary schools take infant and junior pupils up to the age of 11. Secondary or senior schools take pupils aged 11–16.

References

Freeman, J. (1998) *Educating the very able – current international research*. London: Office for Standards in Education, The Stationery Office. Available from: http://www.official-documents.co.uk/document/ofsted/veryable/able.htm

Reynolds, D. (1998) *Giftedness in children between the ages of six and eleven years: a study of its relevance to the child, the family and the school*. Unpublished Masters Dissertation, Birbeck College, London in collaboration with the Institute of Family Therapy.

Webb, J.T., Meckstroth, E.A. and Tolan, S.S. (1994) *Guiding the gifted child: a practical source for parents and teachers*. Scottsdale, AZ: Gifted Psychology Press.

Related contacts (see Appendix for full details)

United Kingdom
CHI (The Support Society for Children of High Intelligence)
National Association for Gifted Children
National Association for Gifted Children in Scotland

International
World Council for Gifted and Talented Children
European Council for High Ability (ECHA)
Hoagies: the all-things-gifted resource

United States

American Association for Gifted Children
Belin-Blank International Center for Gifted Education
Center for Gifted Education
Council for Exceptional Children (CEC)
Gifted Development Center
GT World
John Templeton Foundation
National Association for Gifted Children
Ohio Association for Gifted Children
Supporting Emotional Needs of the Gifted (SENG)
Dr Sylvia Rimm

Canada

Association for Bright Children of Ontario
Calgary Action for Bright Children (CABC)
Gifted Canada
Mensa Canada Society
Ontario Gifted

Australia

www.austega.com/gifted
Australian Association for the Education of Gifted and Talented
Australian Mensa Inc.
GERRIC
Gifted and Talented Children's Association South Australia
Gifted and Talented Children's Association of Western Australia Inc. (GATCH WA)
www.gifted-children.com.au
NSW Association for Gifted and Talented Children Inc.
Queensland Association for Gifted and Talented Children Inc.
Tasmanian Association for the Gifted Inc. (TAG)
Victorian Association for Gifted and Talented Children Inc. (VAGTC)

New Zealand

The New Zealand Association for Gifted Children

Books

Adderholdt, Miriam and Goldberg, Jan (1999) *What's bad about being too good?*
    Minneapolis, MN: Free Spirit Publishing.
Explains the differences between healthy ambition and unhealthy perfectionism and
gives strategies for getting out of the perfectionism trap. Gives adults insight into how
their behaviour and expectations can contribute to perfectionism in teens they parent and
teach.

Axline, Virginia (1990) *Dibs in search of self.* London: Penguin.
Through psychotherapy and love, the brilliant trapped lonely child was released by himself.

Galbraith, Judy (1999) *The gifted kids' survival guide: for ages 10 and under.* Minneapolis, MN: Free Spirit Publishing.
An introduction to growing up gifted. Based on surveys of hundreds of gifted kids, it includes first-person advice from boys and girls.

Galbraith, Judy (2000) *You know your child is gifted when... A beginner's guide to life on the bright side.* Minneapolis, MN: Free Spirit Publishing.
Light-hearted, illustrated introduction to life with a gifted child.

Goleman, Daniel (2005) *Emotional intelligence.* Tenth anniversary edition: New York: Bantam Books.
Explains how the rational and emotional work together to shape intelligence and why empathy, self-awareness and self-discipline are essential to success and positive human interaction.

Greenspon, Thomas S. (2001) *Freeing our families from perfectionism.* Minneapolis, MN: Free Spirit Publishing.
Perfectionism is about believing that if we can just do something perfectly, other people will love and accept us – and if we can't, we'll never be good enough. This book explains perfectionism, where it comes from (including influences outside the family), and what to do about it.

Leyden, Susan (2002) *Supporting the child of exceptional ability at home and school.* Third edition: London: David Fulton.
Overview of issues that arise at different ages, with practical guidance and specific examples.

Lowe, Gordon (1972) *The growth of personality: from infancy to old age.* London: Penguin.
Outlines how personality may be expected to develop from infancy through to old age.

Miller, Alice (1996) *The drama of the gifted child: the search for the true self.* New York: Basic Books.
Reclaiming life by discovering own crucial needs and own truth.

Pomerantz, Michael and Pomerantz, Kathryn Anne (2002) *Listening to able underachievers: creating opportunities for change.* London: NACE/Fulton.
The authors, a university lecturer in educational psychology and an educational psychologist, based this book on interviews with secondary school pupils. Contents include developing relationships with peers, parents and siblings and responding to personal and emotional needs.

CHAPTER 3

Giftedness in the Family

If there is a group in society whose needs have been more neglected than those of gifted children, it is their parents and carers. Becoming a parent is amongst the hardest things that most people ever do, and becoming the parent of a minority child can be doubly challenging. In addition to meeting their child's needs and (often somewhere at the bottom of a long list of priorities) meeting their own needs, these parents have to manage the impact of the child's special needs on the rest of the family. For special needs like giftedness, which can run in families, the repercussions can be felt throughout the generations: parents are reminded of the time when they were gifted children; grandparents relive their experiences as the parents of those gifted children; old patterns of rivalry and tensions are resurrected in the extended family; new patterns are shaped by the latest gifted child and her siblings. Here again it can be a relief to realize that these experiences are shared by many families of gifted children.

Family dynamics

Gifted children bring to their families an intensity of interaction which resonates throughout all of the usual patterns of family relationships. All parents struggle to achieve a balance between the needs of their various children, but the parents of minority children have this problem magnified. In the case of gifted children's parents the need is to protect and provide for the gifted child at the same time as protecting and providing for the rest of the family – and whilst avoiding the tendency to make the gifted child the centre of the family's universe, to the detriment of all.

Similarly, all children put some sort of pressure on their parents' relation-ship with each other, even if only through being a drain on the time and attention that the adults have for each other. The parents of gifted children can additionally find their relationship strained by differing views on how best to meet their minority child's needs, or by unhelpful advice and interventions from the extended family or in-laws, or simply as a result of the exhaustion and confusion that they are experiencing as individuals. In the rest of the family, any of the usual problems that can occur between siblings will often be heightened by the giftedness of one or more of the children involved. If less gifted siblings feel jealous or left out by their parents then they may develop strategies for drawing attention to themselves. From a child's point of view, even negative attention counts. Indeed, negative attention may actually carry more force than positive: there is often real power and emphasis involved, whereas in our positive interactions we are gentler and less emphatic.

Of course the greatest gifts that parents can give any child are love and acceptance, right from the beginning, but it is important to acknowledge that gifted infants can even cause difficulties in this respect. More than most babies, they present from birth a clearly defined character. A few hours after the birth of her son, it felt to Samantha as though, 'I looked into the cot to see what I'd got, and he looked back to see what he'd got.' He was, of course, dis-playing the precocious motor control often observed in gifted infants, who are regularly reported as focusing early, talking early, walking early and above all as being very aware of the external world. It is precisely this unexpected quality of reaction from the child which may encourage, undermine or distort the social interaction, depending on the way in which the family responds or the flexibility of their social norms. The challenge of such a personality may develop into a constant, unproductive struggle or, conversely, an exciting and rewarding exploration.

This is especially true if the child's development is met by the experts with disapproval. Fatima, still in hospital after the birth of her first baby, was scolded by the midwives for putting her down on her side rather than her back. They refused to believe that Yasmin had turned over by herself. By the age of ten months she was in perpetual motion and Fatima met more disap-proval from the health visitor:[1] 'You really should make her lie down to have her nappy changed.' By this time Fatima's confidence in herself as a mother had reached rock bottom, and she needed considerable affirmation from a counsellor before she could allow herself to follow her instinctive responses to Yasmin's behaviour.

Even though the vast majority of their interactions are not with professionals, the parents of gifted children can find the simplest sorts of social situation a challenge. It is not at all uncommon for parents of gifted toddlers to avoid social interactions altogether because their children's behaviour seems so odd or unacceptable. 'Would you like a bikky, dear?' asked a family friend whom they were visiting at tea-time. 'That's not a bikky, it's a biscuit,' replied two-and-a-half-year-old Sunil scornfully. It was a long time before his mother was prepared to take him out to tea again.

With a repetition of such exchanges, it is easy to see how the parents of young gifted children can become socially isolated and mistrustful of their capacity to bring up their family according to accepted norms. This uncertainty, in turn, undermines the idea of the family as a safe haven for the children, making it feel more like a camp armed against a critical world.

Under such pressure, inconsistencies and misunderstandings may also appear within the family. If disputes are not to move from irritation to fractures in the relationship, it is important for parents to check that their often unspoken assumptions about family life do coincide with one another. Fran's mother was a lone parent, obliged to go out to work all day, and consequently Fran had an idealized view of what 'real' family life was like. So did her husband, Steve, who had been discriminated against by his stepmother in favour of her own, younger children. As a result of her early experiences, Fran was very indulgent to her sons' moods and as a result of his, Steve wanted to take the whole family out on exciting expeditions every weekend. The boys argued, sulked and never wanted to do the same things, so Fran and Steve became upset and confused that their efforts seemed to go so badly astray. They greatly benefited from the opportunity to work out a consistent, joint approach to their two very different sons, rather than simply reacting out of their respective, very different backgrounds.

In addition to a conflict between their unspoken assumptions, parents can disagree openly with each other about how to bring up their children. The possibility of confronting authority could be unthinkable for one parent, whilst the other is keen to address every concern that arises in their child's schooling. One parent might regard an academically selective private school[2] as the only solution to their child's educational difficulties, whereas the other may be ideologically opposed to moving her out of state education. Discipline, extra-curricular opportunities, religion and the amount of time that a child should spend on homework or practice can all be fertile ground for parental conflict. None of this is unique to the families of gifted children, but any potential for disagreement is more likely to be fulfilled when parents are under the additional stress of having a minority child. Again it can be helpful for parents to take the time to talk about why a particular issue is so important to them both that they find themselves arguing about it; and again this may be easier with the support of a third party such as a relationship counsellor.

Against the background of this evolving adult relationship, it can be a difficult balancing act for parents to accommodate the differences between their children while still holding them within a safe set of rules and boundaries. Yet the management of this tension between individual needs and the demands of the basic social group will provide one of the essential building blocks of adult life. Many factors may contribute to the complexity of the situation, and each family needs to work out its own approach to what is acceptable or unacceptable. Consistency and communication are very important so that everyone knows where he stands, but many families find that they do better if they think carefully and limit the absolute rules to as few as possible, in order to avoid constant argument. Basic safety must be the prime factor, and this is not always easy with an independent-minded, physically competent toddler. Am I actually making it more dangerous for my two-year-old by insisting that she hold my hand while scrambling around these ruined castle walls? It obviously compromises her phenomenal sense of balance. Perhaps I can let go here, but when we are crossing the road on the brow of the hill I will insist that she does keep hold of my hand. If she objects that she can see the road is clear, I shall have to lift her up to get a view of the dip which hides an approaching car.

Such actions and decisions may sound easy in the quiet reading of a book. As parents know, the reality is much more stressful. Acutely demanding situations can arise out of the blue, often when parents are already overtired, and need immediate, off-the-cuff action.

Aiko, about to carry her baby daughter up a steep cliff path, instructed her toddler, Mai, to put her shoes on for the climb up from the beach so that she didn't hurt her feet. Mai, relishing the feeling of sand between her toes, refused, so Aiko sat down, with the baby on her lap, and firmly put on Mai's shoes. Taking her by the hand, she got Mai, crying, half-way up the cliff. There the tears culminated in a temper tantrum. Mai threw herself down on the path, screaming and blocking the way for the other home-going holidaymakers, who stared critically at Aiko as they waited. With unexpected strength, Aiko shifted the baby to one hip, lifted Mai to the other and carried her, still screaming, to the top. The encounter left Mai rebellious, as there was no proof that she would have hurt her feet. It left Aiko humiliated by the stares of the other people, angry that her pre-emptive concern had gone so badly wrong, and above all exhausted.

Obviously this was not the best time to work out how to have managed the situation better. It is often hard for parents to allow themselves time out to unpick the dynamics in such situations, but the opportunity to talk about it later, with an impartial but understanding person, can be invaluable in finding alternative reactions or tactics for the next time. If the encounter is a one-off incident then it is soon forgotten. Mai recognizes that Mummy means what she says and Aiko realizes that Mai may need to experience sharp rock underfoot to know that it hurts, or tries diversionary tactics another time: 'Let's watch everybody else. Can you see anyone going up the path without shoes on? Look how soft the sand is: you can make foot shapes in it. Can you do that on the rock?' But if constant repetition of instruction and defiance develops into an entrenched battle of wills, reinforced by the expectation of further encounters, then there is a danger that what started as a nurturing relationship will turn into an emotional drain for both mother and child.

Indeed it is not at all easy for parents to maintain an appropriate balance between independence, confidence and experimentation by their children on the one hand, and dependence, the need for advice and support, assurance of love, acceptance and provision on the other. Add more children of varying ages and the question becomes even more complex. One of your family may be perfectly capable of cycling home from school, but his elder sister is such a dreamer that you would not think of letting her do it.

Again, there may be situations where the whole family works on a level, in sharp contrast to others where the difference in their ages separates them off from each other. 'The trouble with her', remarked a teacher friend to the parents of seven-year-old Mercedes, 'is that she doesn't know what age she is.' Mercedes was in the throes of a temper-tantrum because her older brother and sister refused to let her play tennis with them. Small wonder: she was not big enough or well enough coordinated to make an acceptable contribution to their game, but they had all just been involved on level terms in a hand of cards, and she generally took an equal part in any family discussion. So her age, within a brief time-span, had ranged from, say, emotionally four-and-a-half (screaming and kicking in inarticulate fury), through seven in terms of chronological and physical development, to fourteen or fifteen in her intellectual competence.

It is not always the youngest who comes off worst in such encounters. Indeed the eldest may end up with a misconstrued estimation of where she stands and suffer inappropriately low self-esteem, expecting those following her to outpace her. As so many long-distance athletes know, running at the shoulder of the leader gives you both physical and psychological advantages, so you are well placed to move to the front in the finishing straight. In terms of family life and sibling rivalry, this may turn out to be a real blow to the eldest (front runner) unless their parents have been positive in affirming all the good qualities in each of the children, whatever their place in the race.

It can be oddly reassuring for parents to reflect that stumbling blocks on the path of family life are inevitable, especially when one or more of the children in that family has special needs. Tensions are bound to arise as children make the journey from a baby's omnipotent beginning to a child or adolescent's sense of himself as an individual person. Much depends on the gradual way in which his recognition of self and other develops after birth. At first, although physically separate, the newborn infant will make little distinction between himself and the person who cares for him. As his needs are met, his carer simply seems an extension of himself and he remains the centre of his universe. As the baby develops a true sense of separateness, inevitable conflicts arise. What a child wants or needs may not dovetail neatly with Mummy's agenda. How is the compromise going to be made? There is no one-size-fits-all answer here. Different parents have different priorities: if Mum goes to work in the morning then the timetable for dressing and eating breakfast cannot be negotiated; other parents, whose work schedule is different or whose metabolism is late-evening orientated, may be quite relaxed about getting-up and dressing times.

Furthermore, parents of more than one child often remark on how early they observe differences between them. Why does this particular baby, Pippa, cry so constantly? Why is she so intolerant of any sort of disturbance or discomfort when her brother Nick, whom they believe they treated in almost exactly the same way, was generally placid and good-humoured? Each child is born with a unique genetic makeup which is bound to modify the interactions with those who care for her. The child's reaction will, in turn, draw out different responses from her parents, depending on their expectations of children's behaviour and their own overt or hidden emotional makeup. It is helpful, though, as so often, very difficult amid the pressing demands of small children, to recognize Pippa's awkwardness as part of the definition of her personality. She is not going to sit down under adverse circumstances but will do what she can – in this case screaming is her only option – to bring about some improvement. Her nature is to take action in a situation, where her more thoughtful brother might be aware of other issues, needs or signals from outside. Where Pippa screams about her mother's failure to meet her need, Nick by contrast is aware that there is also a satisfaction in waiting until his mother is able to give the attention willingly.

Inherited characteristics, which the parents either like or react badly to in older members of the family, may spark off predetermined attitudes to their children. Family members who claim to see likenesses to older generations, although often partial in their observations, may be offering a useful pointer here. When two-year-old Didier's stubborn determination became apparent, his two grandmothers competed to attribute it to each other: it was in fact probably inherited equally from both, but what the argument did was to offer his parents the reassurance that this somewhat intractable behaviour was within the family norms. It also indicated, to some extent, how such a characteristic might develop into adulthood. Presumably the way they dealt with it will have been guided, at least in part, by their relationship with the relatives concerned. Did they value and therefore reinforce it, or did they find it unacceptable and try to persuade or discipline the child into modifying or suppressing it?

> Which of your child's characteristics remind you of other family members?
>
> How are your responses to these aspects of your child influenced by your feelings about the relatives they bring to mind?

It is worth remembering that even quite small babies can absorb and react to unexpressed feelings in those around them. The more the feelings are concealed, the more possible it becomes for the child, who after all has no in-built encyclopaedia of the ramifications of human psychology, to misinterpret the discomfort they produce. And the younger the child, the more egocentric the interpretation is likely to be. Children can believe, for example, that it is their bad behaviour which has caused their father's long absences or separation from the family. Others can experience a sharp downward spiral in their own self-esteem as a result of their parents' concern about their lack of social skills. This, ironically, can in turn increase their friendlessness. Even if it was not true in the beginning, the perception that they are socially inept becomes a self-fulfilling prophecy.

Most discussions of good parenting agree on the basic principle that the related negative emotions of anxiety and guilt are the most undermining of constructive family input. A sensitive child may well interpret these feelings as being his fault, even if it is the parents who actually believe that they are failing in some way. This is particularly true if there is no discussion about where or why the anxiety or guilt arises.

In this respect the parents, as much as the children, need to be freed from unrealistic expectations. The comforting concept of being a 'good enough' parent is probably not good enough for their image of how they should be. Add to this the common anxiety about knowing how to cater for the exceptional needs of a gifted child, and the unexpressed worry in the household may well be at a high level. There is a great burden of responsibility in making decisions about providing for the specialist education which may be required, especially if the idea of having a gifted child is completely unexpected or the gifts fall outside the family experience. The cost to the family in time, energy and commitment as much as in finance may be extreme.

It is not always easy to avoid resentment by a gifted child's siblings of the apparent cuckoo in the nest, or to be successful in demonstrating that the care for all of them is equal even though the distribution of resources is apparently unfair. The way in which these tensions are handled may make a considerable difference to the child's perception of himself and so to the degree of pressure to succeed at all costs. Learning to share is as important as learning to succeed or be best, and the family ethos is the safest situation in which to learn it. It depends, in essence, on a respect for the contribution that every member of the household brings to the family, on affirmation of what each does well and constructive criticism of the things that are out of line or distressing to other family members. In this, as in most things, openness is generally the most productive approach, especially in allowing an airing of difficulties or resentments before they become inflamed.

Gifted children and their siblings

It is not easy to generalize about growing up with siblings: there is so much possible variation, including where the gifted child comes in the family, what the capacity, gender or difficulties of the other children may be, and indeed what experiences the parents have had in their families of origin.

If it is sensitively managed then the presence of siblings is rather like the proving ground of a litter of young animals: learning through play; sham or real fighting; competition for attention; argument; and reactions to one another that are played back honestly and promote adaptive behaviour, all make a safe place for the beginnings of wider socialization.

Of course, a litter of kittens is born together. There is no sense for them, as there is for the oldest child in a family, of a special place usurped by a new arrival, or of resentment at having interesting activities curtailed by a sibling who is not old enough to join in. A sensitive first child may well interpret the arrival of the second one as an indication that she was inadequate. If the second child is very alert or advanced then the defensiveness in the first can be exacerbated by the experience of being challenged or overtaken – even to the extent of the younger growing taller than the older.

Geoff and Angela, aware that their elder son, Edward, was being overtaken and outshone by his younger brother, Nicholas, decided that Edward should have his own special thing, and took him for swimming lessons. Unfortunately, because they had no one to baby-sit, Nicholas had to come too, but they firmly told him that this was Edward's time and he was to amuse himself and keep out of the way. Part-way through Edward's first lesson, a small form appeared on a diving board at the other end of the pool and executed a neat dive into the water. 'Who is that?' asked the swimming coach excitedly. 'I must have him. He's an absolute natural!' It was, of course, Nicholas.

Sometimes there may be considerable aggression towards the younger child, as an unwanted intruder on the scene. Murray, fed up with his newborn brother's insistent and demanding crying, asked sharply whether Jamie could now be put back into Mummy's tummy. And the arrival of a third child often produces in the second a sense of being squeezed: the first special because the oldest; the third attracting huge attention because she is the baby. Such tension needs careful and delicate handling by the parents to reinforce the specialness of each child and to celebrate their different qualities equally. This is often easier if the gender or interests of the children are different.

A family in which the differences between children are affirmed, even when they are experienced in the short term as tiresome and frustrating, can offer invaluable resources of support and understanding. Jenny never liked playing anything competitive with her younger brother because he always won, and at the time this made a considerable extra burden on the family, playing cards or board games with Rob while helping Jenny with making dolls' clothes, drawing or gardening. But they also all did a great deal together, making expeditions, going to concerts and theatres, and camping abroad in the summer holidays. By the time she grew up, Jenny had shared so much experience with her brother that she said quite freely when he followed her to the same university, 'I think Rob is my best friend.'

> If you have more than one child, how did the older one(s) react to the arrival of the younger one(s)?

Diversion from explosive situations and affirmation of good experiences are valuable strategies in family life. Nevertheless, there are times when bad feelings need to have room for expression and acknowledgement if they are to be dealt with productively, particularly if the parents themselves have had similar, uncomfortable experiences. Alison had always felt inadequate in relation to her much younger but highly competent and self-confident sister. When she saw the same situation repeated in her own two daughters, she became very defensive of Megan, the elder. This constantly repeated protectiveness left Megan, too, feeling she was not good enough if she needed to be so often reinforced and supported.

In some ways Lucy, the younger, came well out of the situation, a competent high-achiever like her aunt. But in later life she realized that when she faced a difficult confrontation, she found it almost impossible to make free use of all her knowledge and skill. She was always inhibited by the guilt of having an advantage over her antagonists and concerned at the hurt she might inflict. 'It's as though I always had to fight', she said, 'with one hand tied behind my back.' It was an adjustment she felt both temperamentally obliged and conditioned to make. Her father had always responded to her petulant or aggressive demands to have what she wanted with the phrase, 'You're not the only pebble on the beach.' Her own innate need to belong and be loved caused her to internalize this uncomfortable aphorism. Her response to aggressive jealousy, spoken or unspoken, was to be protective of the aggressor and do her best to live with her own anger at the unfairness of the attack. Her success is likely to be dependent on her ability to channel the energy of that repressed anger into productive activity.

What Alison had in common with almost any other parent was the lingering effects on her own parenting style of the place that she had within her own family of origin. This is so powerful because siblings almost always seek out a particular role within a family, and of course this will be carried through to their own children if they have them. Siblings keep a close eye on each other, and 'If one child adopts a role' then 'another sibling is unlikely to lay claim to that role, even if the role is one she is capable of playing' (Webb, Meckstroth and Tolan 1994, p.162). Ranjit had wanted to become a doctor since he was a very small boy, and his younger sister Jaswinder clearly decided that Ranjit was the bright one. She became the funny one instead; if asked about her own plans, then she would say that she wanted to be a nurse, *if she could*. Only when Ranjit took a gap year abroad did Jaswinder feel free to take on the role of the bright one as well, and came to admit that really she too would like to take the more academic route of training as a doctor. Both have now been successful in their careers, and obviously both were 'the bright ones', but their case shows how unconscious family roles can be inhibiting as well as reassuring.

The reassurance comes from the safe feeling that each member of the family has his own role, and can count on the others to play theirs. What matters is that no member should be trapped in just *one* role, but that parents in particular should find several different roles for each child. Thus Asher will sometimes be the helper and sometimes the funny one; Ruth is sometimes the reminder and sometimes the comforter, and both are sometimes the naughty one, too. This last point is more important than it might at first seem, for positive roles can at times be as limiting as negative ones. It seems obvious that it will be hard for Asher if he is always the naughty one and Ruth the helper, but what about when Ruth feels angry or put-upon: how can she refuse to do her bit, if she is the helper? How can Cathie stand back from her friends' relationship problems, if she is the peacemaker?

Of course it is well nigh impossible for parents to avoid making comparisons between their children, just as siblings will constantly compare themselves with each other. As Ranjit and Jaswinder show, it can be particularly tempting for families to ignore the gifts of younger siblings when their personalities are very different from that of a gifted firstborn. Quite apart from making mistakes in their assumptions about the varied children in a family, however, it can be difficult enough for parents to know how to handle it when it really *is* the case that one is more gifted than another. How are parents supposed to react when one child achieves straight As and the other struggles to collect a handful of pass marks?

> Do you think that each person in your family plays a particular role?
>
> Which of these roles is positive, and which negative?
>
> When do your children surprise you by acting outside their roles?

It is a statement of the obvious to say that what children need is for their parents to value each of them as an individual, but how can parents show this in practice? Especially valuable will be the praise and distinction that they give to each child's very different achievements and gifts, for it is true to say that every child is special and will be better at *something* than his siblings. On the other hand children are not stupid, and 'every child has his own special gifts' is clearly not synonymous with 'every child is gifted': the first statement is true and the second is false, in the sense in which we are using the term gifted. So a parent's emphasis on the different contributions that each child brings to the family, and the varied strengths of each, cannot mask the fact that one sibling always achieves higher grades than the other. If Eric passes and Dan fails an English exam, then it may not be possible for that to be swept·under a carpet of praise for Dan's maths result.

It may be, of course, that maths is Dan's thing and he isn't much bothered about English, in which case a parental emphasis on the boys' different strengths will be important. It may be, though, that both care a lot about English, and that no matter how hard Dan works he just cannot match his brother's performance. Here again it is vital for parents to give their children the space to express negative feelings. Tracey and Craig, 14 months apart in age, ended up taking their final university exams at the same time because Tracey's course was a year longer than Craig's. Craig had breezed through every previous exam with little preparation, gaining a First in his first two years' exams.[3] This time it seemed as if he were doing less work than ever, but there was no reason to suspect that the same thing wouldn't happen again. Tracey always struggled for a respectable grade and was desperate for a 2:1. She revised for hour after hour, requested extra tutorials and read widely around her subject. 'Well, if anyone deserves a 2:1, it's you, Tracey,' said her mother at last. 'Yes,' replied Tracey wryly, 'I can think of someone else who does, as well.'

At times like these, it is just not relevant that Tracey plays hockey for the university and is widely valued for her loyalty and discretion as a friend. At that moment, Tracey cared deeply about a goal that she shared with Craig, and cared equally deeply that he was likely to hit it and she was not. Her parents needed to acknowledge *both* that she was not so academic as Craig *and* that this mattered to her. If she were merely underestimating her own abilities then their role would have been to bolster her self-esteem. As she was actually being rather realistic about herself, the most pertinent question for them to ask was how much this mattered to her. It could have been the case that it didn't matter very much at all. A different personality might not be very keen on her brother beating her, but may ultimately care more about other things than scoring the highest mark possible in a set of exams, such as maintaining her social life, or going on to work in a field where academic scores aren't very significant. Here the parental role would be to remind her of where her own strengths lie, and to emphasize how much more those areas matter to her than the one where she is currently struggling.

But for Tracey's personality the failure lay in an area that *did* matter to her, and not only because it was galling to be beaten by her younger brother. For her, the simple facts were that the path into her chosen career would have been so much smoother with a 2:1 than a 2:2, and that she was unlikely to achieve a 2:1 whilst her younger brother was likely to exceed it. She knew that her parents valued them both as people, and was as realistic about her own strengths as about her weaknesses. She did not need reminding of her sporting prowess or of Craig's lack of physical coordination.

What she needed was the space to express her feelings of resentment that Craig could achieve a higher grade than her with a fraction of the work; her distress at the impending failure; her consequent fears for the future. After this, she needed someone to help her to do a bit of a reality check: a 2:2 is not actually the end of the world, and even if she went so far as to fail her finals there would still be options open to her. Granted, they would be different options from the ones that would have been open if she had passed, but options there still would be. We all have choices about how we respond to failure, and Tracey also needed to be reminded that the current situation was a result of earlier choices that she had made. Academic work was always quite a struggle for her, but she had chosen to work hard enough to be accepted by the same university as her much brighter brother. She had chosen to pursue a path that was much steeper for her than the one that led to a less academic institution or to a non-graduate job. These choices were to be applauded, showing her determination and stamina. The chances were that the same qualities would take her a long way, regardless of the class of her degree. Equally, Craig's lackadaisical approach was bound to have an effect on his life choices, regardless of the class of his degree.

The key point, then, of this rather extended case study is that parents need *both* to show how much they value their children as individuals, regardless of their relative gifts and special needs, and to be honest in meeting their children where they are. When a child compares himself unfavourably with his siblings, it is not always enough to remind him about the areas where he does better than them. If this is something that he cares about then he may also need his parents to help him to deal with the areas where *they* do better than *him*.

Sometimes, of course, the only thing that he cares about is that his sibling is beating him. Mothers of boys in particular can find their children literally fighting over them: when two-year-old David took to shoving his older brother off their mother's lap when he came home from school, Wyn responded by shouting, '*Stop* it, David! She was my mummy before she was yours,

If you have more than one child, do issues like this arise for them?

you know!' No parent enjoys witnessing his children squabbling, but it is important to remember at times like these that sibling rivalry, and the unpleasant ways that it is manifest, can be an acting out of underlying feelings in the same way as any other behaviour can: feelings that one child feels left out, less valued or whatever. Parents need to listen carefully when their children squabble, to try to hear the source of their rivalry; often this is as simple as the desire for parental attention.

Helpful responses include the parent overtly stating that she will not get involved in the squabble, overtly stating the cause of the squabble and overtly stating that she trusts the siblings to be able to sort it out themselves: 'I can see that you both want to sit on my lap at the moment. Wyn, you haven't seen me all day, and David is feeling a bit left out now that I'm giving you some attention. I know that you two can sort this out for yourselves.' It can also help to remind the siblings of the positive aspects of their relationship: 'I feel sad when you push Wyn like that, David, because I know how much you miss him when he's at school, and how much you love it when we all cuddle up together.' Finally, it is also worth reflecting on how the adults in the family settle their own disagreements in front of the children, and in particular, how often disagreements are in fact *not* settled in front of the children. It is not unusual for adult rows to blow up in public but their resolution to be put off until after the children have gone to bed, with the unfortunate result that the children actually never see adults making up after an argument. The ways in which adults resolve (or fail to resolve) tensions with their loved ones can provide, like anything else, an important model for the children who observe them in action.

What is it like to be the parent of a gifted child?

The family dynamics and sibling issues that arise within the families of gifted children can be seen, then, as mirroring those of many other families, but often the situations that arise may feel more intense or greatly magnified than they do in other families. What lies behind this magnification or intensification of feelings and interactions? What additional factors do children's gifts bring to their families?

The parents of gifted children are blessed on a daily basis by the presence of a small person whose company is so interesting and rewarding. From the earliest days with such babies the joy at being constantly surprised by their interests and achievements is immense. The age at which interaction with such infants becomes a genuinely two-way process, with parent as well as child being stimulated by the encounter, can be quite astonishingly early, as can the ages at which the child reaches the standard developmental milestones. Quite apart from the pride that parents may feel in their children's swift progress, in lots of ways it makes life much easier for them all, too. An early grasp of language, for instance, not only makes it much simpler for adults to communicate with a child, but also helps him to avoid many of the frustrations that toddlers usually face when trying to express their thoughts and feelings.

As they grow, children who are quick-witted and articulate make interesting companions, and conversations with them can be a source of great delight. It is easier to explain things to a bright child; easier to teach her the skills or information that she needs at any given time. The intense curiosity of gifted children is often manifest in projects and hobbies that can involve and excite the whole family. These children will often prefer the company of older people to that of other children, and from a very early age they can develop hugely rewarding relationships with other adults in the family circle of friends and relatives. Not only is it heart-warming to watch a friendship grow between our offspring and those whom we love, but these relationships can also support and enhance our own relationships with both our children and the other adults involved: everyone benefits from the shared affection, and from the affirmation of being liked by someone outside the immediate family.

Against the background of the blessings that gifted children undoubtedly bring to their families, how can it be that they also cause their parents such concern? There are two main areas in which problems can arise for most parents: the challenges that gifted children present to them *as parents*; and the challenges that can arise, as a result, for the parents *as people*. In this section we explore the parenting problems that can arise in the families of gifted children, and in the next we focus on some of the potential personal difficulties. We postpone until the following chapter the additional struggle faced by parents as they strive to find ways to help their children to survive in the world outside the family.

> When do you most enjoy your child's company?
>
> Which aspects of your child do you most like?
>
> Which people in your family's circle does your child get on with best?

Intellectual demands

Within the family, one of the main challenges for parents is that gifted children are almost ineffably demanding of one's time and energy. From a very early age their interactions are unremittingly intense. Although it is true that many can become absorbed in their own interests for long stretches of time, negating any need for parental interaction, it is also the case that many gifted children have a constant need for stimulation. This is perhaps particularly the case when they are very young, and do not yet have the skills (reading, organization and planning, etc.) to stimulate themselves adequately. Thus, as three-year-old Brigitte's mother so typically put it, 'I'm exhausted. No matter what I do, she always seems to need more.'

It is hard to describe the sort of strain that gifted children put on their parents, because it sounds much too negative to describe them simply as being demanding. What they demand is not merely attention, but *full* attention, *alert* attention, *thoughtful* attention, *one-step-ahead* attention…and this from the moment that their eyes pop open in the morning – or indeed in the middle of the night, should the occasion arise – to the moment that they shut in the evening. On car journeys, it is amazing that their parents can make it safely from A to B against the background of a stream of intellectually stimulating word games or questions about life, the universe and everything. These questions are not often one-offs, either: there is a logical progression from one to the next, until the topic has at last been exhausted to the satisfaction of the small interrogator, which might not be for several weeks or indeed months. The parents of gifted children become used to sitting vivas in theology or astronomy whilst bathing their pre-school offspring, and to the corresponding examinations in biology or psychology on the morning journey to nursery.

Gifted children, from early infanthood, can become deeply absorbed in activities or topics, engaging with ostensibly trivial tasks with an almost disturbing intensity. Their questions are endless and their thirst for learning so great that parents may be genuinely stretched by the intellectual probings of a child who still lisps and wets the bed. How do you explain the workings of the solar system in terms that will satisfy the curiosity of a pre-school child (whilst warming up his Bob the Builder pasta)? What do you say to the four-year-old whose reply to your final 'Good night, sweetheart', is 'Night night. Mummy, how did God make the very *first* baby? Because if there were no grown-ups first, then where did the baby come from?'

On the one hand it must be stressed, again, that there is a hugely positive side to this aspect of gifted children. The sorts of conversations that one can have with a gifted four-year-old are often much more interesting from the adult's point of view than the standard pre-school fare; and the sorts of topics that capture the gifted child's imagination will often hold a fascination for all ages. The difficulties arise when either the questions, or at a more basic level the demands for attention and interaction, carry on beyond the point of a reasonable adult's ability to cope.

Part of the problem here is that parents are often uncertain about what *is* reasonable. If your child is content with helping you to post the letters then that is fun for both of you. If your child would like to write her own letters, and make envelopes for them, and stick stamps on and then post those, then that can be fun too. But what about when this isn't enough, and she wants also to know what happens to the letters once they've been dropped into the post-box: how they are sorted, how distributed, how delivered, and so on? And what if, when you have explained all this to the best of your ability, and perhaps found her a book about it or let her have a chat with the local postman; when you have helped her to play-act the process in the comfort of her own bedroom, making a post-box and post lady's uniform, setting out a sorting office; when you have even arranged a trip to the local sorting office – this is still not enough? Or what if it is enough, but no sooner is that topic exhausted then the next obsession crops up, like another of Hydra's heads? What is reasonable then?

At the heart of this dilemma is the universal, and laudable, parental concern to *meet their children's needs*. For a gifted child, the needs that are traditionally perceived as rather esoteric – intellectual stimulation, pursuit of knowledge, logical debate, freedom to be creative – are known by his parents to be his bread and butter. How, then, can they deprive him of these things? How can they say no when he asks for more of them? Wouldn't they be letting him down if they failed to give him what he needs?

In one sense the answer is obviously yes – but only when we realize that what he needs is for his parents to provide for him not only as a *gifted* child but also simply as a *child*. It is quite reasonable for any parent to say to her child, 'You have had enough of that now,' or even, 'I can't give you any more of that at the moment.' This statement is obviously true when applied to a favourite food, and remains true even if that food is something healthy: it may be that the parent in her adult wisdom knows that the child needs a change from that food now, or perhaps she simply has to say that she cannot afford to buy him any more of it until next week. It is equally true, however, of the more abstract demands that our children put on us. It is perfectly reasonable for a parent to say, 'I know that you're interested in this, but I think we should give it a break

> How do these images ring true with your own child?
>
> When have you felt challenged by your child's questions?

for now,' or perhaps, 'I need to do something else now [or even just: I need a break from this now], so if you want to carry on then that's fine, but I'm not able to help you for the time being.'

It is reasonable, too, for a parent to say something like, 'I love being with you, but just now there are some jobs that I need to do. Here is a video/a book/a puzzle/some colouring, and I'd like you to get on quietly by yourself until I've finished. I'll just be in the next room, so I'm here if you need me, but I do need to do this for the moment.' It is reasonable for a parent to take the same approach if she has reached the end of her tether, and what she needs to do is sit quietly with the newspaper for half an hour. Of course we are not talking here about parents who routinely neglect or ignore their children, but about the sorts of conscientious parents who so frequently feel unable to say, 'Enough is enough', in the face of their offspring's unremitting demands.

Sometimes what a good parent has had enough of is the need to explain his reasons to a young and insatiably demanding child. There are occasions when the phrase 'because I say so' may well be appropriate, because there isn't the time to explain fully now, or just because the parent is too exhausted to say anything more. Bernhard's father still recalls with a slight shudder the time when, drained of all his inner resources by the interminable yes-buts and what-ifs, he shouted at his son, 'What on *earth* possesses you to think that at three-and-a-half years old you know more than I do at thirty-three-and-a-half?'

Of course the important thing for a parent in this sort of situation is the ability to reflect later on what it was that reduced him to bellowing in this way, and to repair things with the child; but at this point we want to emphasize the fact that there is actually something in *what* he shouted. The reality is that, gifted and quick-witted though Bernhard undoubtedly is, he has nonetheless accumulated three decades' less experience than his father. It is reasonable for gifted children to be reminded from time to time that age and experience do count for something, and that certain things are as they are because that is what experienced adults have decided on behalf of the whole family.

Indeed, more than just reasonable, it is actually necessary for parents to put these sorts of boundaries down for their children. From the parents' point of view, it is important for them to take care of themselves so that they don't burn out. This is true of all parents, but gifted children have such intense needs that their parents in particular can end up feeling that they have nothing left to give, if they are not careful to meet their own needs as well as their children's. It is not unusual for the parents of young gifted children, especially those whose partner is absent either permanently or through the demands of work, to have to battle even for the chance to take a shower in peace; or to make a sandwich and then have time to eat it; or to speak briefly on the telephone to their own friends.

At around four months old, Peter went through the first of what was to be a regular experience in his early life: an intense period of frustration due to not *quite* having reached a particular developmental stage, which was in this case becoming mobile enough to reach toys on the other side of the room. His mother now laughs when she recalls how frequently she missed her own lunch when he was tiny, because she just didn't have a minute to make it. 'Why didn't I let him cry for five minutes whilst I grabbed a sandwich?' she asks. 'It was so silly. How much harm would that have done him, when for the rest of the day he had my undivided attention?' She is able to reflect on this now with the wisdom of hindsight, but at the time it felt genuinely impossible for her to refuse his demands, when her prime aim in life was to meet his needs.

Boundaries are also important from the gifted child's point of view. Again, all children need boundaries, but it has been our experience that gifted children seem to have a greater need for them than many others. It may be that the often forceful personalities and wide-ranging minds of these children makes the world seem very big and potentially frightening. They may be aware at some level that if they argue strongly and logically enough, or mimic others' manipulative behaviour closely enough, then they can on the whole guarantee getting their own way, and that this too is rather frightening. Whatever the reason, gifted children frequently seem to need and welcome the safety that comes from adults who say, 'I'm in charge here. This is the boundary. If you go over it then X will happen.' So long as a rule has first been explained to them so that they can understand it, they seem to appreciate a strong and simple link between cause and effect: if you behave like this, then that will happen.

When Latasha was five, she went away to a hotel with her parents one weekend and shared their bedroom. Her behaviour had been challenging during most of Saturday, and when she woke at five in the morning on Sunday she refused either to go back to sleep or to lie quietly, ending by disturbing her older sister as well as her already exhausted parents. During the awful dark hours of hissed instructions between five and seven a.m., Latasha lost various privileges for that day, until eventually the ultimate sanction of the time was imposed: 'If you can't be quiet now, then we shan't video your favourite programmes while you're at school this week.' Latasha's joy when she came in from school was to relax in front of the one or two favourite short children's programmes that she'd missed during the day, yet even this threat did not quell her that Sunday morning.

So what happened? Well, her parents followed through with all of the promised sanctions, except that her father actually taped two or three programmes towards the end of the week when he saw how much Latasha's behaviour had improved, and how she did not once complain or even ask about what had been taped, normally her first question on arriving home from school. On Saturday morning he gave Latasha a big hug and explained how pleased he was with her, and how lovely it was to see what a big effort she had made to make up for her behaviour last weekend. As a special treat, he said, she could watch a few programmes that he had videoed for her after all. Latasha's response? This child of five looked at her father in shock and evident disappointment, and said accusingly, 'You *lied* to me, Daddy! You said I couldn't watch *anything* this week.' It has, he says, taught him an important lesson: 'Latasha needs boundaries, and she needs them to be firm. As far as she's concerned a promise is a promise, and it doesn't make a bit of difference whether the promise is that something good will happen or something bad. She needs to know that what we say will happen, *will* happen. Only then does she know where she stands, and feel safe.'

Gifted children, then, are like any others in that they need their parents to be in charge, to be reliable and to tell them where the boundaries are. Parents on the brink of exhaustion need to reassure themselves that when they feel obliged to say no they are doing their job as parents, just as much as when they feel able to say yes.

Emotional demands

Exhaustion, for the parents of gifted children, is brought on not only by the intellectual and physical energy that is needed to keep up with them, but also by the emotional energy that is expended on their protection. At the same time as answering their questions, parents need to stay one step ahead in order to keep them safe from knowledge and issues for which they are not yet ready. Very bright children are fascinated by complex subjects like how our bodies work, what happens after death, how people behave towards each other and the environment, and items that they pick up when their parents are listening to the news. At one level they need a proper answer that honours their intellectual capacities. At another, the answer has to be suitable for their age and for each individual child's maturity, and it would often be wholly inappropriate to give them the full gory details. As we have already mentioned, gifted children are more aware of the big issues than other children, and as a result they are confronted at an earlier age by subjects that can be unsettling or saddening even for adults. Thus, at the same time as seeking an adequate child-language paraphrase of the facts and uncertainties involved, their parents must struggle to present the information in a way that is emotionally manageable for their individual child, given her particular tendencies and vulnerabilities.

> **What sorts of subjects unsettle or obsess your child?**

One of the most important things for parents to remember when faced with a child who is fearful or anxious about something, or who conversely is blithely pushing forward into subjects which hold unknown horrors ('But Mummy, *how* was Hitler such a bad man?'), is that they as parents know their child better than anyone else in the world does.

If your instinct is that this particular topic will deeply unsettle your child then you are probably right – and even if you're not, you may well feel that it is better to be safe than sorry. You know your child's needs best, and it is important to trust your feelings about when he is ready for something, be that a life skill like dressing himself, a particular activity like attending parties on his own, or a perplexing subject like war or God. Richard, the father of two gifted children, offers this warning to other parents:

> The times when we have most regretted our actions, and felt that we have really let the girls down, have been when we have accepted 'professional' advice against our own best instincts. In retrospect, we *knew* that Amy wouldn't be able to cope with acceleration out of her year group at primary school, and we were right to think that Suzy's unhappiness at her new middle school[4] was more serious than the average teething troubles. We've since learned to be a lot more confident about the fact that we do know the girls better than anyone else does.

The other thing to remember, when it comes to the sorts of issues that unsettle gifted children, is that it is actually impossible for us as parents to protect our children from everything. Some subjects really are puzzling or upsetting, and at some stage our children will be exposed to them. It is hard for a gifted child who comes upon them at a much earlier age than would normally be the case, but the essence of the parental response is much the same whatever the age. A combination of approaches can help, including some or all of the following ones.

Parents can to a certain extent contain the issue, particularly with younger children, via a censored discussion that does not unnecessarily highlight its most unsettling aspects. Often the child will be upset by one particular aspect of a problem and, once that has been resolved, the whole topic can be laid to rest without the need for every other element of it to be fully explored. As we have seen, this can lead parents into the difficult situation of trying to second-guess what that particular aspect is; but this can often be elicited with a gentle admission that the parent does not know what it is, and the offer of an ear whenever the child feels ready to raise it.

Another approach is to admit that the parent herself finds this subject difficult, as do many other people, and to reassure the child that it is quite all right not to be able to understand everything. Parents can also share their own coping mechanisms, talking about the value of sharing worries with other people, and reassuring the child that they are always there with a hug whenever it is needed. This approach contains the issue with a practical demonstration of the fact that adults too find things difficult or upsetting, but that there are ways of coping with these feelings without being overwhelmed by them.

Finally, parents might want to think about whether there is anything underlying their child's anxiety, which has ostensibly been caused by an abstract issue like death or kidnap. It is often the case that children's, and indeed adults', fear becomes focused on something entirely removed from its actual cause. They may be genuinely unaware of what is really troubling them, but a convenient way for a troubled mind to avoid an issue is to divert its anxiety onto a different topic, or to subvert the anxiety into fantasies or dreams. Winston, normally a relaxed and contented seven-year-old, went through a distressing period of nightmares from which he awoke shouting and crying. His parents could not think of any traumatic event which might have caused such a change, and especially could not trace the source of any of the disturbing images that were recurring in his dreams. Winston became afraid of going to sleep, and very anxious around bedtimes as a result. It was only when he successfully took the entrance exam to the school at which his elder sister had already gained a place that the bad dreams stopped, and his parents understood that he was afraid of not being good enough, and even that this might split up the family.

Challenges to authority

A further drain on parents' emotional energy is caused by the constant tendency of many gifted children to challenge the information they are given, or what they are asked to do. When children can speak fluently and argue logically at the age of two it is bound to affect their relationship with their parents. Such children frequently challenge parental instructions and make very early challenges to parental authority: their arguments carry the full force of a toddler's emotions and are bolstered by the infant's inability to accept other people's points of view. As Prem's mother put it, 'His behaviour at the age of four was a lot like my 14-year-old nephew's behaviour at the same time.'

What makes this situation even harder for gifted children's parents is that they may be faced with adolescent challenges to their authority, an almost adult level of reasoning and articulacy, and a toddler's tantrums and physical limitations, all at the same time. It is not surprising that these parents find it hard to know how to accommodate the out-of-stage behaviour, when their child might at any moment revert to more chronologically appropriate behaviour. This can also make it difficult for parents to accept their clever, articulate child's need to revert to behaviour that is more appropriate to younger children – wanting babyish books, toys or videos; playing or speaking in a babyish way – even though she really does need this time to relax and feel safe.

It is hard for parents when children behave in these contradictory ways: hard because the individual behaviours are themselves challenging; hard because the combination of behaviours is so rare, relative to the average child, that there is little guidance to be found about how to deal with it; hard because the child can switch between the adult/adolescent/toddler behaviour far too quickly for the parental reaction to keep pace; hard because the sheer force of emotion behind these behaviours can provoke equally strong feelings in the parents; hard because it is unavoidable that parents will sometimes feel that their consequent reactions have been misguided or regrettable.

> In what ways does your child's behaviour jump between age groups?
>
> How do you respond to his inconsistency?

It is really important to spell out how difficult this can be, because parents can feel that they are failing their gifted child when they have no idea how best to respond to the extreme behaviour and emotions that he displays. In reality: who *would* know, instinctively, how to deal with a situation like this?

For many of us parenting is one of the most challenging journeys that we ever make in life, and it is vital to acknowledge the additional complications that are thrown into our path by our children's giftedness. Parents should not blame themselves for feeling confused or lost when faced with circumstances that are genuinely trying: they find the situation hard because it *is* hard, not because they are not good enough parents.

As is often the case with gifted children, some of the most helpful pointers towards solutions are actually applicable to almost any child. It's just that in the gifted child's case things are intensified and expanded to an extreme degree. So, for example, it is useful for parents to bear in mind that in difficult encounters with their child their own feelings are often a reflection of the child's unspoken emotions. In other words, if you are feeling confused and anxious because you don't know how to deal with the situation then the chances are that you are mirroring your toddler's unspoken emotions. The child acts out his feelings and you pick up on them without even realizing what you are doing. This is helpful information for two reasons. First, it gives you an insight into your child's world at that time. Second, it can free you from emotions which, odd though it might sound, weren't really yours in the first place.

Another universal toddler-rearing tip that seems particularly useful with gifted children is the idea of giving children choices, in order to restore in them a feeling of being in control. The world can feel quite frightening to a small child, particularly to a very bright one, and even the small decisions of which they are capable can help them to feel a bit more at ease. The key here is that the decisions should be *real*: don't say 'Shall we go for your bath now?' if what you mean is, 'It's bath time now.' And they should be *manageable*: it can be fun for a toddler to reach into the drawer to choose which pair of socks he is to wear that day; it would be unreasonable to ask him to choose the whole outfit. It is up to the parent to provide safety by offering *limited* options within a *fixed* outcome: you *are* going to get dressed for nursery; would you like to do it now, or after breakfast?

Finally, it is also worth repeating the mantra that gifted children *are still children*. It is therefore inappropriate either to engage in the sort of verbal spat that can be so tempting for adolescents and their parents; or to involve them in the sorts of decisions or discussions in which such a young child would not normally take part. The best guide here will again be the parents' knowledge of their own child. Even if they have sometimes got things quite spectacularly wrong, parents do still know their own children better than anyone, and learning to have confidence in this knowledge can be the key to more fruitful provision for them.

Feelings of helplessness

The problem for many parents is that, unsure how to respond to the complexities of their gifted child, they can begin to feel completely overwhelmed and lost in the experience. It is frightening for any parent to feel that he cannot meet his children's needs or resolve their problems, and this can be compounded for some by a feeling of inarticulacy when talking to their gifted children, even at a very young age. As Sean asked in despair, after an encounter with his son, 'What is it like for him to see his dad as less than him: not able to keep up?' Such feelings of inadequacy are often compounded in gifted children's parents because they are gifted people themselves, with the same tendencies towards self-critical perfectionism as their children. As individuals they are used to being able to find efficient solutions to problems, and to being amongst the best at whatever they tackle, but parenting is one of those jobs that is ungraded. Nobody can tell you whether you are doing well, much less whether you are doing better than average; yet this is something whose outcome feels more important than anything you have ever done before.

Often, the only feedback for parents will come from health or educational professionals. Unfortunately, these professionals' reactions to the interaction between gifted children and their parents can sometimes increase the parental sense of helplessness. Parental responses to a minority child are inevitably going to be unusual when compared with the norm, but it can be hugely undermining for a health visitor or teacher to pass an adverse comment on the unusualness of the parental response, without taking into account the unusualness of the child who provoked it.

Even without any outside interference, however, a gifted child can quickly reach the point at which his parents feel lost and unable to cope. There may be genuine constraints on their ability to meet his needs, be these financial, physical or intellectual. Ironically, a different cause of anxiety for some parents is the feeling that what their child receives at home is so much richer than what he gets elsewhere, for this can lead to a feeling of helplessness and pessimism about what life holds in store for him and about their own abilities to make things better for him. These feelings can then be compounded either by the knowledge that their child feels desperate to fit in with his peers, or by the secret knowledge that they themselves often share this wish: why can't he just be more normal?

Once more it is crucial to say to parents who feel over-whelmed and helpless in the face of their gifted child: this is normal, natural and completely understandable. You are not a bad parent but a parent who faces a rare and *genuine* challenge. If you have sometimes let your child down, then you are still the best parent for him because you love him more than anyone else does. Nobody else will ever have the feeling for him that you had when he was brand new, or that grew for him as he grew. The most perfect parent in the world would have children who made bad choices – but in fact there *is* no perfect parent in this world. We all fail sometimes, and that too is natural and normal: the important thing is to face the failure and move on from it. We are all limited in some way when it comes to provision for our children: for some of us the limitations are intellectual, for some financial, for some emotional and for some physical. This too is okay: one important task for parents is to help their children to cope with frustration, to help them to look for alternatives and to free them from unattainable goals. Children actually need parents to fail from time to time.

> Does your child ever crave normality and try to blend into the crowd?
>
> Do you ever wish that your child were less different from the others?

Furthermore, the relationship between a parent and his child is like any other: the product of the individuals involved, and therefore unique. You do not have the same relationship with your partner as with your children; neither of you has the same relationship with your child; and if you have more than one child then your relationships with each will be different. All of this may sound obvious, but the result is that parenting is really not something that can be judged objectively. Of course there are general principles that can be applied and helpful tips that can be shared, but what is right or successful within one family may be totally inappropriate for another. Whether the choices involved are educational, disciplinary, material or moral, it is up to each parent to filter other people's suggestions – including all the suggestions here, in our book – through his unique knowledge of his unique family.

None of this is meant to trivialize the genuine feeling which gifted chil-dren's parents frequently express, that they have made mistakes and do not know how to cope with their child; that they sometimes feel overwhelmed by her special needs and have wished her to be less different. Our intention is rather to acknowledge that there are genuine reasons behind these genuine feelings: gifted children can be hard to raise. More than this, though, we want to emphasize that the job of their parents is essentially no different from the job of any other parent: to love their children. This is no mere platitude. Imagine four children, each of whom has unlimited access to only three out of the four following blessings: intellectual stimulation; the financial backing to pursue any chosen activity to any level; guidance in developing social skills; parental love and support. Which child would lack the most?

Parents as people

The parents of gifted children are, then, like many others daily enmeshed in the joys and tensions of family life, facing the ongoing challenge of managing relationships both within and beyond the family. But every parent knows that there is more to having children than their day-to-day care. Underneath mummies and daddies there are real, grown-up people with a range of social, emotional and intellectual needs of their own. In addition to the parenting challenges that they face, their experiences as parents can present them with challenges to themselves as individuals. All parents are reminded of their own childhoods as they observe their offspring: memories are revived and resonances felt as their children grow. Children's difficulties can sometimes stir up painful memories and emotions, and this is of course as true of those with gifted children as of any others. In particular, their children's giftedness can itself provoke a whole range of thoughts and feelings.

The classic misconception of a gifted child's parents goes something like this: overbearingly proud of their child's talents, they thrust her relentlessly towards the realization of their own unfulfilled dreams and ambitions, basking in the reflected glory and taking an unhealthy, vicarious pleasure in her achievements. Families like this may well exist: certainly there are some who can be perceived in this way, for the media have a tendency to hunt them down and hold them up for all to mock. They are so few and far between, though, that the collective experience of our group has yet to encompass one.

In reality, most parents of gifted children fall into one of two camps: those who are themselves grown-up gifted children, and those who feel less gifted than their offspring. For both groups a whole range of issues can be thrown up by the arrival of a gifted child in the family. We have already spoken about the feelings of inadequacy that can be prompted by a child's giftedness, and here we want to concentrate on a group of parents who have been much neglected in the literature: those who were gifted children themselves.

For these parents it can be particularly hard to disentangle their child's current experience from their own past experiences. If the parent is a high achiever, for example, then it might be difficult to accept that his child, who is just as able as himself, might yet lack the personality traits like application and stamina which enabled his own abilities to be realized so effectively. Conversely, if the parent was for some reason prevented from reaching her full potential, or had to fight against circumstance in order to do so, then she might be left with all sorts of unresolved issues from her own past. The sorts of challenges that face gifted children today are not unique to our time but were also faced by many who are now adults, and they must have repercussions in these adult's current lives, especially when they are forced to let their children out into the wider world of school and society, to confront the very situations that caused them such pain when they were small. The combination of fear for her child and the unexpected resurrection of her own childhood hurts can cause a sometimes shocking level of upheaval in a parent's emotions and ability to cope.

Many adults may not realize quite how badly bruised they were by the difficult times that they had at school. Not until they have children themselves are they forced to confront the memories that they had previously been able to put to the back of their minds. A parent who has formed a secure and supportive circle of adult friends may nonetheless have been bullied or ostracized as a child; another who is now settled and happy in his chosen career may nevertheless have had his abilities doubted and undermined by his teachers at school. If they have never come to terms with those childhood experiences, and if she sees her own child begin to struggle socially or he begins to suspect that his children's teachers have not recognized their gifts, then this may well be the trigger for an explosion of long-buried feelings of rejection, inadequacy and confusion. This can also be true of grandparents, of course, who struggled with their own gifted children and then find their feelings resurrected when they observe those children wrestling with their own offspring's gifts.

There is often a two-fold effect of such unresolved issues from a parent's own past: they can make it difficult for him to *see* his child's situation clearly and objectively; and they can make it equally hard for him to know how to *handle* it effectively.

From the beginning, the pain that these parents have experienced will inevitably make them wary on behalf of their child. Many grown-up gifted children carry a fear and a determination that their children should not suffer as they did at school, and this is bound to colour their dealings with teachers and children at their children's schools. On the one hand it may make them more pessimistic than they need to be about what school will be like for their child, feeling over-defensive and concerned about any negative incidents that do arise. On the other hand it can also help to raise their awareness of any problems that genuinely do crop up for their child, the challenges that he might face as a result of his gifts and the need to tackle any difficulties as early as possible, before they have a chance to develop into the sorts of situations that caused his parents such pain. The difficulty for the parents in these cases is knowing whether they are being slightly paranoid about circumstances that are not easy for their child, but which cannot be avoided and need to be overcome; or whether the alarm bells are ringing for a good reason, with their own experiences acting as a very good guide to what is best for their child.

The question that these parents need to address – and this is often much easier said than done – is what their feelings are *about*. Am I feeling hurt and fearful because my child's teacher is genuinely refusing to acknowledge her gifts? Or have my feelings been triggered by the memory of what it was like for me when my teacher discounted *my* abilities? Of course the answer will rarely be entirely straightforward: the intensity of my feelings may well be the result of what happened to me, but at the same time there may be real justification for my worries about my child.

Similarly, unresolved childhood issues can make it hard for a parent to see how best to handle a difficult situation. If she was bullied, for instance, and the problem was never curtailed, then it may be impossible for her to see how to support her child in the same circumstances. Indeed, she may not believe that it *is* possible for bullying to be stopped, because she has no model of how that can be done. Another parent, who at school was constantly in trouble and formed poor relationships with his teachers, may feel fearful and impotent in dealings with his child's school. Many parents of all sorts of children find themselves resurrecting their own childhood reactions to school. It is not uncommon for gifted adults to find themselves somehow trapped in the role of troublesome school child when they are talking to their own children's teachers.

Again there is a question to be addressed here about the source of the parent's feelings. Do I feel helpless about my child's situation because there really is no way out of it? Or do I feel helpless because when it happened to me I had no help? When I find my dealings with my child's teachers so frustrating, is it because they are actually being unhelpful and dismissive, or am I reacting out of my uncomfortable memories of being a pupil at odds with the teacher's authority instead of acting as a responsible adult? Once more, the answers to these questions are almost bound to be rather complex: I may well be responding poorly to my encounters with my child's teachers, but they may also be behaving unhelpfully.

For any parent caught in this sort of no-man's-land between his own past and his child's present, it could be helpful to take the opportunity to look again at the things that happened to him and the effects that they have had. Whether this is something that an individual can do alone, or whether the support of a friend, partner or counsellor is needed, is inevitably a personal decision. We have found that parents often feel much more able to understand and support their children once they have come to terms with the things that caused themselves such pain. In particular, parents who are able to address their own emotions about schools and teachers can be freed to deal more objectively with any obstacles that their children might face at school.

It is important to acknowledge, however, that some parents will just not feel able to face their own issues at a time when so much of their personal energy is devoted to raising a family and keeping their heads above the daily tides of tasks and pressures. Some people will know instinctively that the time is not right for them to open the floodgates of past emotions and experiences. Their personal decision will be to focus on their child's present rather than their own past – and this decision is as valid for them as the alternative is to a different individual who is at a different stage, personally, in her life. It is helpful to be aware of the separation between the challenges facing our children and the resonance that those challenges might have for us as individuals, but this does not mean that every parent is obliged to look further into the reasons behind that resonance.

For some people, becoming a parent will be a good opportunity to work out some things from their own childhood. For others it will not, and it will be enough for them to bear in mind the possibility that sometimes their perception of their children's difficulties will be less clear than they would ideally like, and that consequently they may from time to time need to check their perception against that of a trusted third party. Just like the parents who do decide to look more closely at their own past – and indeed like those who are content that their own childhood is not relevant to this bit of their children's experience – these parents are acting in the way that they judge to be best for their family, which is made up of individuals whom nobody else knows better, living in circumstances that nobody else fully understands. This is all that any of us can do.

Summary

- Gifted children bring much joy to their parents, but also demand from them an almost unbelievable amount of intellectual, emotional and physical energy.

- Gifted children, with their often forceful personalities, need their parents to keep firm boundaries in place within the family: disciplinary boundaries, but also boundaries around the amount that their parents are able to give to them.

- Gifted children can behave in ways that are consistent with many different ages, within a few short minutes. Although gifted, they are still children.

- Parents often find it enormously difficult to know how best to respond to all the challenges that a gifted child throws at them. This is because it *is* difficult.

- Your child does not need you to get things right all the time. She will learn many valuable lessons from how you respond when you get things wrong.

- The precocious and intense interactions of gifted infants will inevitably shape the relationships that they form with the rest of the family. Parents' own feelings about relatives whose traits their children share, and about how families should operate, will also shape those relationships.

- Differences between siblings can cause tensions. Parents need to show that they value those differences, but also to be realistic about the ways in which some children outshine the others: children know when their siblings are better at something than they are and may need support to come to terms with this.

- Parents are also people, and ignoring their own needs does their children no favours. Parents who were themselves gifted children may find it unexpectedly painful when they see their children having experiences that resonate with their own childhood. Some people will find it helpful to reflect on their past at this point; others will not.

- What children need most is the unconditional love of a parent. This is not just a platitude.

Notes

1   A health visitor is a trained nurse who works within the community to promote health and prevent illness in all age groups. A key part of this role is her work with the mothers of young children.

2   Independent school and private school mean schools which are self-governing and funded independently of the state, normally by the parents whose children attend them and sometimes (more often in the US than in the UK) by religious or other endowments.

3   In the UK, university degrees are awarded by 'class' rather than grade: 1st class; 2nd class – which is divided into an Upper Second, or 2:1, and a Lower Second, or 2:2 – and 3rd class.

4   In some areas of the UK there is a middle school system: pupils attend a primary school up to the age of 10, a middle school up to the age of 13 and a secondary school from 13 to 16.

Reference

Webb, J.T., Meckstroth, E.A. and Tolan, S.S. (1994) *Guiding the gifted child: a practical source for parents and teachers.* Scottsdale, AZ: Gifted Psychology Press.

Related contacts (see Appendix for full details)

United Kingdom
Childline
Childline Cymru/Wales
ChildLine Northern Ireland
Childline Scotland
Institute of Family Therapy
Parentline Plus
ParentLine Scotland
Parents' Advice Centre
Samaritans
Stepfamily Scotland
Young Minds
Young Minds Parents' Information Service

United States
Childhelp USA
Family Support America
Gifted Child Today Magazine
Gifted Development Center
www.kidsource.com/kidsource/pages/ed.gifted.html

Books

Apter, Terri (1998) *The confident child: raising children to believe in themselves.* New York: Bantam Books.

How to raise a child to solve problems, to be socially active, manage emotion and express feelings appropriately.

Bowlby, John (1983) *Attachment.* New York: Basic Books.

First volume of Attachment and Loss series with two new chapters and revisions to incorporate major developments in theory and empirical research.

Bowlby, John (1990) *Secure base: parent–child attachment and healthy human development.* New York: Basic Books.

Explores the nature of early parental bonds and offers evidence of how strong emotional ties promote mental health.

Faber, Adele and Mazlish, Elaine (1998) *Siblings without rivalry.* Tenth edition: London: HarperCollins.

Positive approach with suggestions that parents can use.

Greene, Ross W. (2005) *The explosive child: a new approach for understanding and parenting easily frustrated, chronically inflexible children.* London: HarperCollins.

Therapist offers parents skills to defuse explosive situations to lower tension and hostility levels.

Skynner, Robin and Cleese, John (2001) *Families and how to survive them.* London: Ebury Press.

Using family therapy model the authors show how understanding can be developed in family relationships.

Teare, Barrie (2004) *Parent and carers guide for able and talented children.* Stafford: Network Educational Press.

Comprises three sections: effective communication with school, developing skills and recommended fiction.

Walker, Sally Yahnke (2002) *The survival guide for parents of gifted kids: how to understand, live with, and stick up for your gifted child.* Minneapolis, MN: Free Spirit Publishing.

Explores what giftedness is (and isn't), what makes gifted kids so special, how kids are identified as gifted, and why some kids fall through the cracks during the identification process. Includes practical tips for living with a gifted child.

Webb, James T., Meckstroth, Elizabeth A. and Tolan, Stephanie S. (1994) *Guiding the gifted child: a practical source for parents and teachers.* Scottsdale, AZ: Gifted Psychology Press.

Topics include motivation, stress management, depression and relationships.

CHAPTER 4

Beyond the Family

Despite all the challenges and the gradient of the learning curve, for many parents the impact of their child's giftedness is much easier to contain within the family than it is when they begin to interact with other people and institutions. It is at this point that both gifted children and their parents begin to feel the pressure to conform, and are obliged to cope with other people's reactions to their difference.

Gifted children in the wider world

Within the home, and the rather limited circle of family and friends with whom she normally has contact, a child's world is (unless the home situation is abusive) relatively sheltered. She receives a fairly consistent set of messages about social norms like what is right and wrong, what is ordinary and unusual, what standard of behaviour is expected, and so on. She probably shares at least some of her interests with some other people; she probably shares at least some of her intellectual foibles and personality traits with some other people, too. Unless the home situation is disturbed or dysfunctional, she is surrounded by people who love and accept her despite the times of conflict that are inescapable in any family. Within her usual context, then, she feels pretty normal.

Once a gifted child steps out of this sheltered environment, however, on the whole she will find fewer situations in which she, her gifts and attitudes are typical. At nursery or school she will be surrounded largely by children who are much less intelligent than she is, whose interests and level of conversation are consequently different, and whose reactions to her are very unlike her own family's responses. Her carers and teachers will often be people who expect children to conform to a particular pattern of abilities, enthusiasms and characteristics. In short, she will find herself in another world. Her task is to find her place in this world, and its completion may be the work of a lifetime.

Reactions to giftedness: mixed messages

In practice this means that gifted children have to come to terms with both other people's reactions to their gifts and their own feelings about them. Some very able children may be genuinely unaware of how much more advanced they are than their peers, especially when they are very young or if their school consciously tries not to allow children to be compared with each other. Others may be much more aware of the situation and feel a whole range of emotions about their gifts, from pride to embarrassment, from anxiety to guilt, from denial to resentment.

The more negative feelings can often spring from the jaundiced or confusing ways in which other people have behaved towards them. It is hard, for instance, to know how to respond to a person who is dismissive or derisive about your abilities in your presence, but vicariously boastful of them in your absence – and these sorts of mixed messages are not uncommon. The uncle who chaffs a teenager for being a swot, perhaps as a defence against comparisons with his own less academic child, may nonetheless be overheard in the pub later telling all who will listen about his niece who has won a place at university. The teacher who encourages her pupils by giving lots of praise or merit awards for good work might also have a tendency, when she asks the class a question, to ignore the gifted child's raised hand in order to let someone else have a chance. Such contradictory attitudes towards her gifts can in many ways be as damaging to a child as the more straightforwardly negative reactions that people can have, for they imply that it is acceptable to be gifted only so long as you keep quiet about it.

> Have other people's reactions to your child at times been contradictory or confusing?

Reactions to giftedness: pressure to conform

It can be difficult, in these circumstances, for gifted children to discover how to relate to other people and how to fit in with accepted ways of communicating. As discussed, their unusual articulacy and intellectual capacity will set them apart from most others, who will often resent and even mock these attributes. The gifted therefore need to find a way of communicating with people of more average intelligence, and this may involve a huge personal sacrifice. There will be an important part of themselves that cannot be shared, even with people whom they like a lot and with whom they do have other things in common. With some children they may share interests like football or a certain type of toy; they may enjoy the company of others who have similar sporting or musical abilities. With very few will they be able to have the sorts of conversations that really interest them, or share one of their intense enthusiasms.

The positive side of this situation is that giftedness clearly does not define the whole person and there may well be plenty of other things that the very bright can use as bridges to friendship with other children. The negative side is that their gifts are, equally clearly, a significant factor in shaping their personalities. The need to sideline that aspect of themselves can not only place a huge strain on the gifted, but also be something that takes a long time to learn. In the meantime, they may suffer socially and absorb all sorts of unpleasant messages: that bit of you isn't very interesting; you're strange; you care about things that don't really matter.

It can also be very confusing for a gifted child when she first comes to realize that others are not interested in the same things as her. For many children the priority is to be liked by others and fit in with the current trend, be that toys for the younger ones or fashions in music or clothes as they get older. For many gifted children, these things just do not cross their minds. As 13-year-old Claire put it so succinctly: 'Why should I want to wear makeup just because all my friends do? "Oooh, I look so much more attractive because my eye-lids are blue"!' Being so absorbed in the world of their own interests and hobbies, they may just assume that this is what it's like for everyone else, too. So Fabio is interested in Action Man, which happens to be what all the other boys in Tom's class are into as well, but Tom doesn't see the point of Action Man; he really likes building things. A child like Tom may be less attuned than the majority of his peers to the social consequences of his attitude about the latest crazes. From his point of view, we all have different interests and that's fine. He may also have learned early that he does not completely belong, so he cannot understand the urgency of the group all to be the same. What he fails to see is that, from the other children's point of view, this makes him strange, and that most people cope poorly when confronted by difference.

It is not only their peers but also the adults around a gifted child who can react badly when she fails to conform to expectations. Many adults, including teachers and the parents of other children, tend to make assumptions about what all children enjoy or dislike, find difficult or easy. If they refuse to shift from those assumptions, or simply fail to notice that this child does not match up to them, then the gifted child can be left feeling misunderstood, frustrated and ignored.

Imagine living in a world in which almost every activity or situation – from the pace of lessons to the content of storybooks, from playtime games to your friends' parties – feels irrelevant, difficult or dull to you.

> In what ways does your child not conform, and what effect does this have on her?

Because these things are designed with the more mainstream child in mind, you can see that almost all of your peers seem to accept and enjoy them, and you may begin to feel that your own abilities are merely a nuisance. What are the implications for a bright child, who is gradually becoming aware of the ways in which she is different from most other children? Since her interests strike her peers as silly and boring, she might begin to feel that she had better hide them and not try to share them with anybody. Since lessons are so irrelevant, she might begin to feel that school is an irrelevance to her. Since all of her peers seem to enjoy the sorts of parties and games that she hates, she may begin to feel that there is something wrong with her.

Reactions to giftedness: pressure to socialize

In particular, she can receive some very negative messages about her preference for her own company or that of older people. A gifted child is often criticized for her limited ability to socialize with her age peers, and labelled rather pejoratively as a bit of a loner. Yet if a child is constantly being thrust into crowd situations in which the activities involved appear difficult or boring to her; if in addition the other children in the crowd seem to be enjoying these activities together, making her feel excluded and different; if she is overpowered by the number of messages she is picking up from the busy activity all around her; and if conversely her experience of being with adults in a one-to-one situation is that the activities and conversations that they share are generally interesting and rewarding, then it is really not very surprising that she should prefer to be alone or with just a few others with whom she has something in common.

The emphasis on developing social skills comes early in a child's educational career. Pre-school teachers often see the development of social cooperation as one of the prime aims of their work, equal to acquiring skills in reading, writing and physical coordination. In terms of managing a class of 20 to 30 disparate individuals it is essential that small children readily learn the basic rules of social cohesion: listen to what the person in charge says; do what is asked of you; don't disrupt the group but learn acceptable ways of claiming attention. Nonetheless, some of the ways in which these expectations are laid on children can be particularly difficult for the gifted. Teachers have been known to burden parents with concerned comments about how their child 'finds it hard to mix with the others; he plays happily on his own or on the edges of the group', with the teacher's concern presumably stemming from the fact that the child is on his own or on the fringes.

Yet isn't the key element of such statements, in fact, that the child is playing *happily* in those circumstances? Some people, adults as well as children, are not really comfortable in big groups and will always prefer to be with just one or two others. If this is what is normal for those people, then it is to be expected that such a preference will begin to manifest itself in childhood. The difficult thing for a child like this is that he has much less control over his surroundings than a similar adult does. The vast majority of children attend school, for example, so that the bulk of their time is spent with a crowd of other children, the constituent members of which they cannot choose. Why should we find it surprising that for some children this situation is stressful and challenging?

Of course there are individuals for whom socializing is really a problem. They may be being bullied or ostracized by the group rather than choosing to be on its fringes, and then adult concern and intervention will be justified. In general, however, there are two things to bear in mind about a child who is often to be found alone or in a one-to-one situation. First, it is perfectly possible that the child has chosen this way of being. It is a perfectly appropriate and normal choice to make. Second, when his social skills are being questioned it is important to look at the ways in which he interacts with the people whose company he does enjoy: if a child is able to form warm, mutually rewarding and stimulating relationships with some adults then, even if he does not currently have this ability with any of the children he knows, the chances are high that he has no real problem with socializing, just with the circumstances in which he finds himself.

What can be particularly hard for children with any kind of special need is that in new situations like starting at school or joining a club, the understanding and allowances made at home are not necessarily available. So the developmental dislocations often apparent in gifted children may well become stumbling blocks in the social group, where they find that their age peers are less advanced in their intellectual development; yet older children may also be unsuitable companions as a result of their more advanced social and physical development. Such disparity between different aspects of a child's growth is difficult for everyone to manage, and most of all for the child. To say of a gifted six-year-old that 'you can talk to her like an adult' may be to put expectations on her which make it even harder for her to reconcile those conflicting elements. If the approval she gets is for being like an adult then how can she come to terms with the violent and childish frustrations which are also part of her makeup? Such children need the safety of being contained within the known structure of a loving family and an understanding school, which will acknowledge the predicament without condoning unacceptable behaviour.

Nevertheless, for many gifted young people the socializing quandary remains acute. It is a question of balancing the pros and cons, of learning that other people have as much right to their priorities as you have to yours. This can lead to hard choices between companionship and the pursuit of a compelling interest. 'I like physics', said 13-year-old Frances, 'because I can lose myself in a problem for days.' For her this was an escape from the social pressures of her urban comprehensive school,[1] where she felt quite out of place. But it is no fun being so lonely. Later, after long and agonizing thought about her choice of university place (she was especially taken by the lively, well-thought-out course offered by a young and energetic department at Sheffield), she finally concluded, 'I think I'll go to Oxford, because there I have a chance of being me, and not just "the clever one".'

Wherever or however the socializing forces kick in, they have to be seen by the child to be worth the effort. Emma, aged five, was referred to an educational psychologist because she lacked social skills. There she complained that the children in her class were boring. Why was that? 'Well, they don't read *The Spectator*, so I can't talk to them about what I find interesting in it.' Is it not acceptable for her to seek out adults for a conversation? She needs intellectual as well as social companionship. Where the gap is hard to span she needs an understanding person, be it parent, grandparent, teacher or friend, to recognize how stretched she feels and to reassure her that it will ultimately come right. Meanwhile she needs affirmation that it is all right to be where she is now.

The gifted: a minority

The challenge that faces a child like this, perhaps earlier and more acutely than it does other children, is to find a way of living with her circumstances.

One element of this task is to discover what sorts of people she likes or finds difficult and what sorts of situations make her feel uncomfortable or at ease. Another aspect of it is to find ways of coping when she cannot avoid the situations that make her uncomfortable, or is forced to spend time with the people she finds difficult. Gifted children are not alone in facing such challenges, but these tasks are perhaps more pressing for a child who is a member of a minority group.

Like all minorities, the gifted face a twofold challenge: to find value in their differences and simultaneously to find a voice in the world of the majority. There is an irony here: the minority cannot begin to fit into the world of the majority until the differences between them have been defined and acknowledged. As in a jigsaw, the things that make each piece different from all the others are the very *same* things that define how it fits into place amongst those others. If you began by turning all the pieces over, so that all had the same blank grey surface, then success would be almost impossible. In order to slot any one piece into a secure place within the bigger picture, you must first take the time to see what is special and different about it.

When the pieces involved are people rather than cardboard shapes, of course the process is much more complex and fluid; but the principle is the same. We have described some of the challenges that can face gifted children in their search for a place within the bigger picture of society. Our belief is that they will hardly ever be able to succeed in this task unless they are first able to acknowledge what is special about themselves and find value in that difference. This is a process which must start with their *feelings*.

The unheard gifted child

When children feel isolated and different it can be easy for them to conclude that the majority is somehow better than they are. When they are in a group and they suspect that what they are thinking and feeling is not the same as what the others are thinking and feeling, it can be easy for them to conclude that the others must be right and they must be wrong. What effect can this have? If a gifted child spends most of his time feeling different and cut off from the majority, and if at the same time he desperately wants to be able to fit in, then it is likely that he will begin to try to hide his differences. In group situations, for example, he may withhold his contribution because he does not want to draw attention to that difference; alternatively the contributions that he does make might be disruptive and designed to draw attention away from it. In either case the effect of his actions is that he is getting into the habit of hiding his true self from the world.

The irony is that, in his reluctance to draw attention to his difference, he does not give anyone else the opportunity to accept and value it. Thus can a vicious circle be established in which, since nobody ever has the chance to accept his true self, he begins to feel that this part of him is

> Do any of these descriptions ring true for your child?

actually unacceptable. Since he feels unable to contribute, he starts to believe that his contribution is not worth making. In this way his feeling of being different and separate from his peers is reinforced and his desire to hide it is heightened. These feelings are validated every time someone reacts badly to him. When people respond positively, on the other hand, it can feel as if they are acting out of kindness or sympathy: being nice despite what he is like, rather than because of it.

A safe place to be heard

The good news for gifted children and their parents is that it is possible to break this vicious circle. What gifted children need is a safe place to be heard. Many of them spend so much of their lives hiding or downplaying their giftedness that this crucial aspect of themselves goes through life unrecognized. Once they have been heard and valued, however, a foundation of confidence is established which enables them to present their true selves to the world. Once a child finds a person whom he can trust, with whom he feels able to share his thoughts and feelings, then the mere fact that someone wants to hear his contribution can help him to feel that it is worth making. Some have described this process as a sort of emotional inoculation, where positive experiences enable a child to withstand negative ones and 'The positive self-regard acquired from one person allows him to mentally discount the stresses of destructive criticism, blame or even ridicule that he may encounter elsewhere' (Webb, Meckstroth and Tolan 1994, p.37). Putting this another way, just being heard can be enough to help children to find value in themselves, for when there is a context in which they are accepted, the implication is that they are acceptable.

Once this foundation has been laid, a child can begin to feel able to make her contribution in other, more daunting or risky circumstances. Instead of feeling compelled to keep quiet, she is empowered to speak out and be heard: whether the group accepts or rejects her contribution, the value that she herself has put on it will enable her to feel that it is worth making. Even when someone reacts negatively to her contributions, she is able to see that this does not mean that there is no value in them. Because there is a forum in which she *is* valued and accepted, she can see that she is still valuable and acceptable, even at those times when she is not being valued or accepted by those around her. Just as the child who has not learned to see value in his difference is unable to put his trust in the occasions when others accord him value, yet is reinforced in his feelings on every occasion when they do not; so the child who is confident in herself will have that confidence reinforced by the times when she is accepted by others, and will be more able to cope with the times when she is not. Her contribution is offered as a gift, and even if the others are not ready in their own development to include her by accepting it, at least she has made the contribution and *been heard*.

Of course the fact that a child is no longer unheard, and that she believes in the value of her difference, cannot change the ways in which the world responds to her. She is never going to stop being different from most other children and British society will not, overnight, begin to celebrate her talents. If she finds herself in a group of children with whom she has little in common and who are ostracizing or even bullying her, then she will find the situation as miserable as any other child would. If she has a personality clash with her teacher or if a relative is resentful of her gifts, then she may need help in learning to handle a difficult situation. She will need to develop the sensitivity to know when it might be best to withhold her contribution, not because it is worthless but conversely because the situation is so hostile that it would be a mistake to offer something of such worth, only for it to be crushed and rejected. She will need, in short, to develop the same sorts of social skills and personal coping mechanisms as any other person. Simply being heard will not take away these challenges, but it can take away their potentially deadly cumulative effects on her self-esteem. It can give her the ability to see them as challenging situations rather than as confirmation of her own unworthiness. Just being heard may not change other people's reactions to her, but it can change the way in which she is able to respond to them.

Not only she but also the others will benefit because she is able to say, 'You may see it like that but this is how it feels for me.' Without her contribution, wider society is denied the gifted view and is left like the crowd when the Emperor had no clothes, unable either to see that the majority view is mistaken or to speak out if they can see it.

Space to be heard: the home
What sorts of circumstance can offer gifted children this much-needed safe space to be heard? They might find the support of a particular adult: a significant person in their lives who values them for themselves; who understands their individual needs and abilities; who accepts them as they are. This person

may well be the child's parent. We should never underestimate the value of emotional support at home and an obviously unshaken belief in a child's qualities. The awareness that his parents will always love him, no matter what he does or does not achieve as a result of his gifts, can provide that safe space in itself. To put it in the most obvious terms, a child who has daily evidence that his parents enjoy his company, delight in his humour, find his questions worthwhile and interesting, believe in his abilities and love him unconditionally is much more likely to be able to cope with life's vicissitudes than one whose parents wear his gifts like a trophy, are unaware of them or see them as a burden.

Needless to say, no one could manage to maintain a supreme level of parental virtue on a permanent basis. There will be times for all parents when they are too tired to answer yet another fascinating question; when the things that their child finds difficult appear to be dominating their family's life far more than his gifts ever do; when there are just not enough hours in the day to allow for every minutia to be ordered in the way that is so urgently vital to him. There is not a parent in this world who has not snapped something regrettable at her child, unfairly denied him attention or failed to notice something that is upsetting him. None of this matters as much as the ability to apologize, to reassure him that he is still loved and to help him to learn from what happened. From his parents' normal human reactions he can learn that sometimes even a very tolerant adult will behave unreasonably, if he pushes too hard when they are feeling tired or unwell; that adults also behave in ways that are unconnected to anything that he has done; that we all make mistakes; that it is possible to say sorry for your mistakes, to put things right and to move on from them.

Parents who sometimes feel helpless in the face of their gifted child's problems can be reassured to know that their very existence, as parents who are aware of her gifts, is actually helping her to overcome those problems. Other parents can feel under pressure to ensure that their child is constantly being stretched, stimulated and enabled to achieve to her full potential. Without wishing to belittle how important it can indeed be for a gifted person to have the opportunity to exercise her talents, it must also be emphasized that these parents are doing an equally essential job at the times when they give their child the space and freedom to relax and be heard. The gifted, like other children, need time to dream, to absorb moods, to reflect and to process information. Creativity is fostered as much by the provision of this space as it is by more concrete forms of discipline and tuition. When children have a place where they feel safe and confident in the knowledge that they are accepted as themselves, this provides not only a haven at times when the wider world is frightening or painful, but also a springboard to self-acceptance, creativity and, ultimately, achievement.

Space to be heard: outside the home

Children for whom such support is not available in the home environment may nonetheless find it elsewhere. So long as there is some one person in the life of an able child who will in effect act as a mentor in identifying and nurturing her gifts, and supporting her in her vulnerabilities, then it is possible for her to be heard. Within the ordinary limits of child safety concerns this person could be a teacher, neighbour, relative or family friend rather than a parent.

Support can also come from contact with other gifted children. In support of our belief in the need to start with these children's feelings, studies have shown that when children can interact with others like themselves their confidence and self-esteem rises (Mason and Essen 1987; Moore 1996). When they can exchange ideas with children whose minds are like their own they no longer feel forced to pretend to be less intelligent than they really are, and no longer feel so very different.

The leader of a local club for gifted children was bemused by the regular appearance of Lui at their meetings. He brought his own electronic circuitry to build and sat in a corner all by himself all session. Why did he keep coming? Because he was welcomed and nobody looked askance at what he was doing. For him, for now, that was affirmation enough.

The quick, demanding minds of the gifted need constant stimulation: able children can provide this for each other, and so can help each other towards more realistic expectations of themselves. For all of us it is reassuring to enjoy the company of people who have shared some of our most painful, enriching or formative experiences. For the gifted this can be the only time in which they feel like their age peers, and thus it can provide an invaluable bridge to society.

> Does your child have access to this sort of safe space?
>
> What part do you yourself play in providing it?

Whatever the location and nature of the safe place where the gifted child can be heard, the effect will be the same. Having experienced what it is like to be valued and accepted, he becomes more capable of valuing and accepting himself, and of ensuring that he is heard by others outside that safe place.

Finding the words

Having given a child the confidence to engage in society, there is another key skill that she needs: just as important as being able to *make* her contribution is the ability to *express* it clearly. Here we are not talking about articulacy, vocabulary or comprehension, all of which most gifted children have in abundance, but about the global language of feelings. Once they have the courage to present their contribution, few gifted children have a problem in expressing opinions, points of view or reasoned arguments. They may need support in learning what conversations they can have with different sorts of people, and in gaining the ability to talk at different levels when necessary, but on the whole the expression of *facts* is not hard for gifted children. The difficulty arises, as it does for many other people, when it comes to putting *emotions* into words. For the gifted as much as for anyone else, being able to say how they feel is paramount in their growth. If we focus too much on their intellectual gifts, showing them that we are only interested in the head, then gifted children will feel emotionally deprived and fail to engage. Their ability to fulfil their intellectual potential may well be curtailed too: how much point can we expect a child to see in attaining top grades, if she is unable to make a friend?

This part of a child's education is all too often missing. Children are taught all kinds of languages but rarely the language of feelings and emotions, yet this is the foundation of where any child, including the gifted, can feel secure. How, in practice, can it be achieved?

To begin with, the child needs to know that feelings are common to us all, including grown-ups. If we deny our own feelings then how can a child make sense of difficult emotions like rage or sadness, fear or jealousy, shame or blame? Gifted children are often highly perceptive and can sense a feeling even when the adults around them are not owning it. They can feel frightened or burdened by the disowned emotion, and end up owning it themselves. Consider how a toddler's parents can feel helpless and frustrated in the face of his tantrum because they are picking up on *his* feelings of impotence and frustration. In just this way, a perceptive child can feel overwhelmed by the sorrow of a grieving adult who believes that she is putting on a brave face; the child of parents who try to hide their anger can be found acting out feelings of rage in the playground; a teacher's failure to understand a gifted child can result in the child herself feeling a failure.

Conversely, children feel reassured if adults admit when they are frightened, sad or angry. If they can say, 'Sorry. I was cross with Daddy and you got the brunt of it,' or 'I've been really sad since Grandma died. I'll feel better in time, but I'm just not myself at the moment,' then the child receives all sorts of unspoken messages. She learns that these emotions are normal because other people have them too; she learns that the adults who feel like this are not ashamed to admit it; that some emotions are difficult and painful but that the adults who have them are not overwhelmed by them. Or, if she can see that they *are* overwhelmed at the moment, then she learns that a good way of dealing with this is to express the feelings and accept support from loved ones.

Having seen that adults have and are able to express the same sorts of feelings that he experiences, a child needs then to be given the ability to express them for himself. Right from the earliest days with a toddler it is possible to help him towards this goal, and parents of gifted children are actually at an advantage here, as their offspring tend to pick up new concepts so easily. A very simple first step is to say out loud the feelings that you observe in your child: 'I can see that you're sad about Grandad going away'; 'I know that you're cross because I won't let you have that toy'; 'Poor Mahmud, you're feeling so tired and fed up today.' It is remarkable how effective this technique is, both as a step towards giving your child an emotional vocabulary and as a means of bringing their behaviour back under control. It seems that the act of putting a feeling into words is empowering for the child in all kinds of ways: it tells him what his feeling is called; giving it a label brings it under some measure of control; it implies that other people have this feeling too, otherwise why would it have a name?; it shows him that we can talk out loud about things that we feel inside; it tells him that the adult is aware of his feelings and finds them important enough to acknowledge; it shows him the distinction between behaviour and the feelings that gave rise to the behaviour.

So the act of describing his feelings can be all that is needed to tell a child that he has been heard. As a result, more often than not this simple act is enough to curtail his compulsion to act out the emotion. A similar system can be helpful as he gets older and encounters problems outside the home, which lead to bad behaviour within it. Given a haven where they know that they are loved whatever their behaviour, children will frequently use it as an arena to act out misery or anger that has another source entirely. As the father of one eight-year-old puts it, 'Sally's teacher was telling us that there were no problems at school, but we knew perfectly well that something was wrong because her behaviour at home had deteriorated so badly.'

Obviously there is a need for children who act out in this way to be reminded of what they already know: that their behaviour is unacceptable. As emphasized, it is our experience that gifted children feel safest when the boundaries are strong and well defined. Gifted toddlers will test in very concrete ways the boundaries that their parents set: reprimanded for touching an ornament, for example, they may try touching all the other things on that shelf in an attempt to find out *precisely* what the rule is. Older gifted children will do the same thing, in effect, with more abstract rules, constantly pushing at the edges of what their parents have said. It may be that the strength of personality which often accompanies giftedness can feel quite frightening to a young child or adolescent. She needs her parents to hold and contain her, and part of this process will involve the boundaries of discipline.

How easy do you find it to talk openly about your emotions, or those of your child?

How able is your child to talk about his feelings?

More than this, however, the child who uses her home to act out her confusion or anger needs her parents to allow her to express them verbally instead. Although it can be hard to see at the time, when struggling with the behaviour of a child who feels out of control and beyond reach, these parents have already done something enormously beneficial in providing her with the security to treat her home as a haven in this way. What they need in addition is the courage to say out loud: 'We know that something is wrong. We can see that you feel angry and miserable. We're here whenever you want to talk about it.' Just as when she was a toddler, the feelings that are overwhelming her need to be acknowledged by putting them into words. If she is enabled to express her feelings verbally then she might not need to act them out in disruptive and challenging behaviour, or to hide still further by becoming withdrawn and silent, and adults can stop having to guess how she is feeling. Once she knows that her feelings are important, she can begin to trust others to value them and move towards expressing them in public. Only then can she begin to feel heard.

Parents in the wider world

Many of the problems that gifted children face in the world outside their family are duplicated, at a different level, for their parents. It is easy for the parents, too, to feel unheard; or for some, at a deeper level, to revert to the unheard gifted child they once were themselves. These parents share their children's need for a safe place to be heard.

Protecting the child in the wider world

One of the challenges that any parent faces is the need to protect his children in their dealings with the wider world. When children worry about things that they have observed or overheard, or just because of the deep questions that their minds have raised, it is the parent's job not only to resolve the issue to their intellectual satisfaction, but also to confine it within boundaries that feel safe. When children have, or are perceived as having, social difficulties the parent faces a struggle to discover the truth of the situation, to know whether his intervention is needed and, if it is, to decide what can be done.

These are issues that face all parents, but for parents of the gifted they can be made all the more pressing by their children's intense curiosity, perception and persistence, and by the extra problems that their children face as members of a minority. It is worth reiterating the fact that unusual children put their parents, by default, into a minority group as well. Just as most gifted children will meet few others like themselves in their everyday lives, so their parents will not normally be surrounded by others whose offspring are gifted. This difference can undermine parents' usual support networks, as acquaintances with similar-aged children may not be living through the same sorts of challenges that they are, and most parenting books or articles are understandably geared towards majority issues. As well as the feelings of isolation that this situation can engender, parents can feel helpless in the face of others' lack of understanding of their child's special needs. In addition, its very practical effect is that the parents of gifted children will often struggle to access advice or relevant experience when they need it.

> Has this been your experience?

Reactions to giftedness in the family: mixed messages

More than the need to guide and protect their child, however, these parents are challenged to find a way of dealing with other people's responses to his gifts. Knowing their child better than anyone else does, they often have a strong sense of his vulnerability. Unsurprisingly, this can give rise to an intense urge to protect him; to stand between him and the world. The pressures on parents in these circumstances are enormous, as they struggle to restrain the temptation to over-protectiveness at the same time as finding ways of coping with other people's reactions to the difference in their family.

From the earliest days of his life, at post-natal sessions or mother-and-toddler groups, parents can become aware of how much more advanced their child is than his peers. The range of feelings that this knowledge provokes will be directly influenced by other people's reactions both to the child himself and to their own adult conversations. Just like the child, their own more negative feelings can often result from the jaundiced or confusing ways in which other people have behaved towards them.

One of the more baffling attitudes that can be encountered is the fierce competitiveness of other parents, about everything from their babies' first words to their first teeth, from when they can wave to when they can begin to get dressed. We describe this as baffling for several reasons: because many of the arenas for these competitions are matters of pure physiological accident (no amount of parental encouragement or infant genius can affect the age at which she cuts her first teeth); because these sorts of people tend to relish the competition only when their children are the winners, and would prefer not to know that your child's development is incomparably more advanced than their own; and because they so often resort to blatant scepticism if a gifted child's parent does recount her achievements. Connor could not walk independently until he was 14 months old, but had been able to walk if he was holding an adult's hands from when he was just four months old: his parents just did not bother to tell anyone else what he could do. Their elder son, Patrick, had done the same at five months, and they had quickly learned to recognize the expression of disbelief when they mentioned it.

Questions raised by this phenomenon include: for what reason might a parent invent this sort of story? Yet if the story is true then why should it feel threatening to another parent? Why would someone invite you to celebrate her child's achievements, and then bridle when you reciprocate? Again, the message seems to be that pride in your child's abilities and achievements is universal and understandable, but only so long as they are not too high. If the child does *much* better than average, then open pride begins to feel like boasting about your own offspring and disparaging other people's, and it would be better to keep quiet.

The same sort of message can be read into the routine checks that health professionals make on children. The aim of these checks is, quite rightly, to determine whether the child is developing and progressing normally, or whether he and his family need additional intervention and support. All of this is positive and worthwhile, but it can feel to the parents of gifted children that something is missing. If you are asked at the nine-month review whether your baby can sit alone, and in fact he is just learning to walk; or if at two years you are asked whether you have any worries about how your child talks, when he can already chatter fluently, then it can feel as if your child's true abilities are of neither interest nor importance. The fact that these assessments are designed to find out whether a child can do X, rather than what he can do, is understandable but can be very excluding for some parents.

Much worse than the feelings of exclusion or dismissal, however, is the implication that giftedness is not worth identifying. The reality is that giftedness is a special need like any other, and that gifted children need support and their parents need guidance in just the same way as families with other special needs. It is bad enough for a parent who is aware of his child's gifts to feel that they are being ignored by the professionals. It is far worse for a child whose parents are *not* aware of her gifts, if the professionals also overlook her needs because they too are unaware of the difficulties that can surround giftedness. In both cases the message is that her gifts do not matter enough to pay them any attention, and once again the gifted child and her family remain unheard.

> How have other people reacted to your conversations about your child?
>
> What has it been like when your child has had a health check or similar examination?

Reactions to giftedness in the family: pressure to conform

In these circumstances it can be difficult for parents to form reliable relationships with other families. Hurtful reactions to their child can come even from quite close friends and relatives, perhaps because they feel threatened by his achievements. The status of these people as members of the family circle can make them feel able to share unwelcome judgements about how he should be treated: 'You shouldn't be pushing him to do so much,' 'I wouldn't be happy if my child spent so much time with his nose buried in a book,' and so on. All of this can conspire to make it feel easier, much of the time, simply to keep quiet about a child's giftedness.

This can involve a big personal sacrifice by parents. It is a rare parent who does not enjoy sharing anecdotes about her children, their achievements and the things that they have done to make her laugh. The parents of the gifted child, however, are hardly ever able to share their delight and pride in his gifts. There will of course be elements of a gifted child's behaviour that can be discussed quite innocuously with other families, especially relating to the things that he has in common with the other children concerned. With very few other families, though, will his parents feel able to share either their child's latest achievement or any uncertainties about how best to raise and provide for him. Once again they can find that even their usual support networks are undermined by the need to keep quiet about that aspect of their child. In a conflict with their child's school, for example, the disappointment can be intense if someone they expect to be an ally takes the side of the school: perhaps a relative is a teacher who is unable to step out of her professional role and see things from their point of view. The disillusionment with a friend or relative who lets parents down in this way can be lasting.

Even quite trivial conversations with other parents can be excluding for the parents of minority children. If the other parents waiting by the school gates are talking about their children's latest craze or struggles with school work; or if the general attitude to children's worries is that it is best to give them as little information as possible and they'll soon forget about it, then what contribution can a parent make whose child is not interested in the latest craze, finds the school work trivial and will not be distracted from questions about the things that worry him? Many parents resort, once more, to silence.

The combination of being effectively excluded from many of the conversations and activities that families often share, and of witnessing their child's isolation, can make it difficult for some parents to resist the societal pressure to conform. Bothered by teachers who have concerns about their child's social skills, able to see for themselves that he sometimes struggles in peer groups and desperate for him to be happy, parents can sometimes unwittingly add to the pressure on their child to fit in and be like the others.

> Have you sometimes found that other people make assumptions about what all children are like, and express surprise or disapproval of your child's differences?

At early birthday parties, for example, when their child prefers to stay with them rather than join in with the games, it can seem as if he is not enjoying himself. Additionally, it can make it difficult for his parents to mix with the other adults at the party, so that the child's behaviour is effectively excluding his whole family from the social situation. It can be hard to know how best to respond in circumstances like these, and the temptation is to shoo him off to be with the others. Obviously there is a fine line to be drawn, and sometimes a bit of encouragement is really all that he will need. Before he reaches this stage, though, a child who is perhaps not as socially advanced as his peers may actually need the support of his parents in a group situation like this, and genuinely not be ready to join in with party games. Here a better response might be something like, 'Why don't you sit here by Mummy, then, whilst I talk to the other grown-ups?' This suggestion offers support whilst also carrying the message that Mummy *does* feel able to join in, and is not willing to ignore the world for her child's sake.

Similarly, parents who are really concerned about their child's ability to make friends can help by inviting classmates home to play or have tea. This creates a one-to-one situation which the gifted child might find less threatening than the playground, and can give the other children an opportunity to get to know him in surroundings where he is relaxed enough to show himself at his best. Having begun to forge relationships in the home environment, he may then find at least those children more approachable at school.

On the other hand he may not yet be ready to socialize in bigger groups, even if his age peers all are, and he may even be the sort of child who will never really relish the crowded school environment. If this is the case, then whilst he might enjoy the home visits they will have little impact on how he behaves in a group; and that is probably okay *for him*.

What is difficult for the parents of a child like this is that although he may feel fine, they are still left with a child who does not conform. The irony is that their own efforts to support him in his difference can be very isolating for themselves, as it is often the case that the less your child has in common with his peers, the less potential there is for you to forge a relationship with the other children's parents. In some cases the situation is compounded by the fact that the gifted child is intensely demanding of his parents' company, and unhappy to be left without them. The net result is that these parents are often left with unmet social needs of their own.

> Do you ever feel isolated from parents of children a similar age to your own?

Parents of gifted children: a minority

The parents of gifted children can experience the same range of feelings and experiences as their children. Consequently they face the corresponding challenge: to find a way of living with their circumstances. For some parents this is doubly difficult, as in addition to the obstacles that they face as parents their child's problems have resurrected aspects of their own childhood. Even when uncomplicated by such personal issues, however, the challenge is not an easy one. Like the gifted child, the parent has to discover what sorts of people he can confide in and which are less understanding, and he has to find ways of coping when people react adversely to either him or his child. Like his child, this parent finds that he has something in common with minority groups in society, seeking somehow to reconcile the twin needs to acknowledge and value his family's differences, and to find a voice in wider society. Like his child, too, we believe that this is a process which must start with his *feelings*.

Parents of gifted children can slip into the habit of isolation without even realizing it. When they spend time in groups of other parents who do not appear to be thinking and feeling the same things as they do, the natural response can be to keep quiet, to hide their differences and to be reinforced in their existing feelings of being cut off from the majority. This leads to their replicating their children in withholding from other people not only any contribution that they might have wanted to make, but also the opportunity for those others to accept and value it. Like their children, too, at some level these parents can be drawn into a vicious circle which reinforces the belief that the difference within their family is therefore unacceptable to others.

A safe place to be heard

Like their children, then, what these parents need is a safe place to be heard. In common with all parents, they need the opportunity to share their fears and hopes for their child, to take open delight in their child's difference and to reveal their uncertainties and doubts. They need to be confirmed in their belief that their child is gifted, and honoured for their experience of the special challenges that this has brought to their family. Just being heard can be enough to start the healing process for these parents, for once there is a context in which they and their child are accepted, the implication is that their family is *acceptable*. Then they can begin to feel able to be heard in the sorts of circumstances when previously they felt compelled to keep quiet. Even when the reaction to their contributions is negative – when other parents resent their child's giftedness, or teachers doubt it – the value that the parents themselves have placed on their child's difference, simply by having the courage to speak out about it, can begin to alter their own perception of its worth and to change the ways in which they are able to respond to such challenging situations.

What sorts of circumstance can offer the parents of gifted children this much-needed safe space to be heard? The most fortunate will find a listening ear within their normal support network: it may be that they are on the same wavelength as their partners or spouses, or that they have a close friend or relative who is able to accept their child's giftedness and absorb their need to talk about it. Others might turn to an external source of help, such as a supportive health visitor, their child's teacher or a professional counsellor. When her health visitor asked Joan, in the course of a routine check-up, whether she had any concerns about her three-year-old firstborn, Joan replied, 'No. He seems perfectly normal to me.' Her health visitor smiled kindly. 'He's not perfectly normal, Joan. He is an extremely clever little boy.' This affirmation stayed with Joan throughout her son's childhood, reassuring her with its ring of spontaneous truth-telling at some very difficult times.

Another option is for parents to make contact with other parents of gifted children, through voluntary organizations such as the National Association for Gifted Children or similar local groups, where they can find reassurance in the company of people who have shared some of their most significant parenting experiences. Whatever the location and nature of the safe place where the gifted child's parents can be heard, the effect will be the same. Having experienced what it is like to be valued and accepted, they become more capable of valuing and accepting themselves, and of ensuring that they are heard by others outside that safe place.

As former counsellors ourselves, our hope is that this book will go some way to providing that safe space. By outlining many of the experiences and obstacles that unite gifted children and their parents, we hope to provide reassurance that there are others like you. In describing some of the thoughts and feelings that you yourself may have had, our hope is that reading this book is helping you to feel heard.

Summary

- People outside the family can respond in confusing ways to a child's giftedness. Gifted children often feel under great pressure to conform, to socialize, to be more normal.

- Some gifted children will never be comfortable in a crowd. Many adults also feel more at ease alone or in one-to-one situations. This is perfectly normal.

- If gifted children are not allowed to be themselves, and feel unable to make themselves heard, then they can lose confidence and self-esteem.

- The existence of just one person who allows them a safe space in which they can be themselves, and who values their contributions, can be enough to 'inoculate' gifted children against the potentially negative effects of other more difficult situations.

- Parents can also help their gifted children by enabling them to express their emotions.

- Gifted children's parents can often find that their experiences mirror those of their offspring. Other parents can respond badly to their children's gifts, and they can feel under pressure to make their children fit in with the others.

- Parents, too, can lose confidence, both in themselves and in their children's gifts, if they are never allowed to admit what the true picture is.

- Parents too need a safe place, where they can be themselves and be open about the reality of their gifted child.

Note

1   A comprehensive school is a non-selective state secondary school.

References

Mason, P. and Essen, J. (1987) *The social, educational and emotional needs of gifted children.* London: Cicely Northcote Trust.

Moore, J. (1996) 'Children's activities – why run them?' *Looking to their Future.* Spring 1996, pp.7–8.

Webb, J.T., Meckstroth, E.A. and Tolan, S.S. (1994) *Guiding the gifted child: a practical source for parents and teachers.* Scottsdale, AZ: Gifted Psychology Press.

Related contacts (see Appendix for full details)

United Kingdom
Anti-Bullying Alliance
Anti-Bullying Network
Bullying Online
Kidscape
National Children's Bureau

United States
American Academy of Child and Adolescent Psychiatry
National Education Association Bullying Awareness Campaign

CHAPTER 5

Giftedness and Schools

School occupies an enormously important place in the world outside a child's family. Unfortunately, for gifted children and their parents it can often prove significant for all the wrong reasons. In this chapter we try to understand why that should be, and what measures can be taken to ensure that things go right. What is it like to be a gifted child at school? What does the education of gifted children look like from their teachers' point of view? How can teachers and parents work constructively together for the benefit of these remarkable children?

What is it like to be a gifted child at school?

There are three separate aspects of school life which most impinge on any child: the work, the teachers and the other pupils. We have talked already about some of the social difficulties that gifted children can have, and of course school is often the main arena for these problems. Indeed, many of the problems that gifted children face at school are heightened versions of the sorts of issues that they can encounter in any walk of life, and they are therefore covered elsewhere in this book. Here we concentrate on the other elements of school, outlining the impact on highly able children of both academic work and the teachers who set it.

It is important to emphasize that school has positive as well as negative facets. Most teachers have a genuine interest in their pupils as individuals and many love to provide new challenges for the brightest ones. Many gifted children blossom at school, enjoying the work, forming mutually rewarding relationships with their teachers and establishing lasting friendships with their peers. No child will have a completely smooth ride through his education, but the high abilities of gifted children can make it easier for them to cope with the demands that school places on them. At the very least they can get by in most subjects without too much effort, and nobody would want to disparage the obstacles that face children whose abilities are at the opposite end of the scale.

Having said all this, it is equally important to give a voice to the special needs of the gifted child: they may not seem as pressing as those of children with learning difficulties but they are just as real. In both cases the children's needs may not be different from those of other children: to be given intellect-appropriate work; not to be bored; to be able to socialize with other children working at a similar level at least sometimes; and so on. The challenge for their teachers is to find *how* those needs can be met.

School can be difficult for gifted children from the very beginning, and indeed even from the stage at which they join a pre-school or nursery. It is not uncommon to find comments on the early school reports of highly able children to the effect that they are very demanding of adult attention, but in the circumstances this is unsurprising. Many able children have been blessed with a rewarding and stimulating home environment in which parents and older siblings respond to their curiosity, answer questions and read aloud to them regularly. As a result they may acquire basic levels of literacy and numeracy before they start school, and grow used to being nurtured in their enthusiasms and inquisitiveness. If when they start school they are confronted by a teaching system whose pace is slow enough to cater for the least able learners, then they may join a whole raft of gifted children nationwide before them, whose earliest school memory is of their teacher ignoring the fact that they were already literate and forcing them to 'learn' the alphabet again.

For many gifted children this is one of the most shocking and long-remembered early experiences of the sorts of problems that can be thrown at them by the world beyond their family. Here, for possibly the first time in his life, a child is being cared for by an adult for whom his welfare, and that of just one or two other siblings, is not her sole concern. For some children this experience will occur much earlier than for others, if for example they attend a day nursery from a very young age, but even then it is often the case that no real problems emerge until they move on from being allowed to play freely all day. It is at this stage that gifted children can begin to rebel against the structure and content of activities that are designed for a child with more average abilities, offering little space for the sorts of conceptual leaps and cross-curricular links that come naturally to them. It is at this stage that parents often begin to observe worrying changes in their children. Such changes stem from the emotional impact on a gifted child of spending several hours each day in the company of children with whom he has little in common, in the charge of adults by whom he feels unheard, engaged in activities whose content or structure is inappropriate to his abilities. Who wouldn't be adversely affected by such an experience?

For a highly intelligent child, lessons that go at the pace of even the average learner can seem repetitive and far too easy. If she is constantly moved from task to task every ten minutes, or whatever the assumption is about

> What was it like for your child when she started school?

the normal attention span of a child, then she may become incredibly frustrated. If she is given no room to stretch her intellectual wings then she can feel isolated in the level of knowledge and interest that she has in areas outside the school curriculum: there may be nobody with whom she can exchange ideas, or even share the fact that she *has* any interesting ideas. If her teachers ignore, or perhaps do not believe, the fact that she already has certain knowledge or skills then she will be forced to repeat work that she has already done. If, as a result of the ensuing boredom and frustration, she begins to make careless mistakes then she may be forced to do even more repetitive work, because by now the teacher (no doubt working under pressure, and certainly feeling uncomfortably accountable for everything in the current climate) will insist that there is no point in giving her harder work until she has stopped making silly mistakes on the basics.

These doubts about her abilities can be manifest in all sorts of ways. Good schools provide all kinds of opportunities for children to shine, from talking about their favourite subject in assembly to writing for the school magazine or newsletter. Unfortunately, at other schools it is not uncommon for gifted children to be accused of showing off when they try to share their knowledge or ask probing questions about a topic that interests them, or reprimanded for putting up their hands too often to answer questions, as well as for working too quickly.

Some teachers even accuse these children of cheating when they are able to work answers out in their heads without the aid of written workings, or of lying when they claim already to know about a new topic. Prisca's family moved house at the end of her Year 4, and consequently she started a new school at the beginning of Year 5, aged nine. She vividly remembers how, in her second term there, her teacher appeared one day with a new maths text-book for his pupils. It was the first in a series of four which she had been encouraged to work through on her own at her previous school, where the staff had been greatly supportive in nurturing her gifts. When she mentioned that she had seen Book 1 before, the teacher accepted her claim and gave her the second book in the series. When, however, she explained that in fact she had completed that one as well, along with Books 3 and 4, the teacher became angry and accused her of making up stories in order to show off. Lacking the confidence to protest further, Prisca simply began again at the beginning of Book 2.

Here once more we see a gifted child who is just not able to make herself heard, with all the attendant consequences for her self-esteem and ability to relate to other people. More than this, however, the area in which she is being doubted, silenced and failed is one of the subjects that really matters to her. Prisca's mind had relished mathematics from the very beginning. Her parents remember a family journey when she was three: as they drove into a local town her elder sister read a road sign – 'That number says 30, doesn't it?' – and as they left the town a few minutes later the silence was broken by Prisca's response: 'Half of 30 is 15.' A book of maths problems was to Prisca what a colouring book or video is to many other children: her way of relaxing and having fun. Imagine what it must be like for a child like this when the person whose role it is to teach and nurture her in her favourite subject chooses, instead, to ignore what she tries to tell him about her knowledge and abilities, to give her work so easy that it holds no interest for her, and to concentrate on her poor handwriting or silly mistakes to the exclusion of her gifts.

It is impossible to exaggerate the emotional impact on a gifted child of this sort of neglect or poor treatment in one of the areas where her gifts are focused. The emotional welfare of gifted children is intimately bound up with their intellectual abilities. Even as adults many very able people will report increased levels of restlessness, irritability, unhappiness or even depression if they are deprived of opportunities to pursue their particular gifts. As school children it is not just a lack of opportunity that troubles gifted individuals, but also the implication that the opportunity is lacking because the gifts are not real. School is inevitably the focus of the praise or criticism that children receive. It is hard for them to step outside the reality of their particular institution and keep their belief in their own gifts and worth intact, if they do not appear to be valued at school.

Max Lucado's well-known fable, *You are special* (1997), makes this point well. It tells of the Wemmicks, little wooden people whose prime aim in life is to give and receive stickers: stars signify their approval of each other's talents and behaviour, and grey dots their disapproval. Nobody can feel good about himself if he has more dots than stars, and our hero, Punchinello, has not one single star. He is covered in grey dots. Not until he pays a visit to the wood-carver who made him does he begin to see that other Wemmicks' approval or disapproval is not as important as he has believed. He is special no matter what the others think. He discovers that the stickers only stick if you believe that they matter, and this frees him from their tyranny.

Gifted children in a school environment can also feel trapped in a world in which other people's judgement – from the views of their peers to the opinion of their teachers, from their results in tests to their performance in group situations – is what determines their worth. Whether they are covered in stars or grey dots the effect of this will be harmful, for either way the implication is that their worth is determined by the approbation or disapproval that they receive from other people. The most powerful amongst those others, of course, are their teachers. It is they who determine not only the majority of the stickers that are received, but also the opportunities that are available for receiving stickers. When Michael's science teacher placed his exercise book beside his neighbour's and scathingly compared his poor presentation with the other girl's immaculate work, no mention was made of the fact that the content of Michael's work was about 60 per cent more accurate than hers. It is hard for a child to step back from this sort of situation and realize that he is still special, no matter what qualities his teacher decides are worthy of dots or stars. It is far more likely that he will begin to lose his sense of value as the grey dots accumulate and the stars are withheld.

For the mathematically gifted Prisca, matters only became worse when she moved to a middle school at the age of 11. Here she was actually held back, academically, by a teacher who allowed her dislike of individual pupils to stand in the way of their progress. This teacher had a system whereby pupils had to write their names in a list on the board if they wanted any help with a maths problem; they could then come up to her desk in turn, after which their names were erased from the list. When it came to Prisca's turn the teacher would often simply erase her name with the one above it, rather than give her the help that she needed. It is sadly not unknown for teachers to behave in ways that we would normally describe as bullying, although as the Education Editor of the *Daily Telegraph* put it: 'We know from Ofsted [The Office for Standards in Education, responsible for inspecting all schools in England] that many schools are bad at meeting the needs of the most able, but examples of teachers bullying their pupils are thankfully less common' (22 July 1998, p.19).

Much more common is a simple lack of awareness of the needs of the gifted. Even the best teachers can do little when many of them have received no training in provision for the able. Yet if gifted children are not given the emotional understanding and intellectual challenges that they need then the impact of poor teaching can be catastrophic. A child who is constantly told by one in a position of authority over him that he is not as bright as his parents are claiming he is, that he must have cheated to have achieved those results and that he is, in effect, a liar, must be a very mature child indeed if he can stand his ground and maintain his self-esteem. Motivation can be sapped by teacher accusations of cheating or unjustified boasting. A child whose teachers doubt his ability can easily begin to believe them and to share their implied belief that his parents are just pushy. Why not? His teachers are in authority over him, after all. Not all able children are capable of self-motivation, and dormant talents will diminish over time. It is sometimes easier for a child to fulfil a teacher's low expectations than to draw attention to himself by exceeding them. The resulting boredom and frustration can give rise to disruptive behaviour, truancy, switching off, aggression, attention seeking, withdrawn behaviour and even depression.

Moreover, without adequate teacher training the sorts of problems that can stem from a child's giftedness are not always mitigated even by her being identified by the school *as* gifted. Although some teacher-training courses do cover aspects of giftedness, there are also some that do not, and certainly it would have been missing from the training that many of our more experienced teachers completed. Lacking awareness of what it is like to be gifted, it is all too common for teachers to put their more able pupils into certain stereotypical boxes. Thus Uma was 'privileged' to be the narrator in her primary school play each year because she was so good at reading, whilst all her friends were busy dressing up in fancy costumes and parading on the stage; and Kiri never questioned until she was an adult the assumption that science was where she excelled – which was true, but she was also very witty and sociable, and nobody had ever seemed to recognize or care much about those bits of her character when she was a child.

> What have been the most positive aspects of your child's schooling so far?
>
> In what ways has your child been misunderstood by any of his teachers, or had experiences like any of the ones described above?

What is it like to teach gifted children?

This sort of tendency towards stereotypical views of the gifted is clearly outlined in the feedback that two of our group received from a group of teachers who had just completed a morning's training on the pastoral needs of gifted pupils. Asked to summarize the view that they had held of gifted children before the training, the teachers used words like *bright, confident* and *fortunate*. Asked how they now saw the same children, they used words like *vulnerable, complex* and *needy*. Asked how their approach towards their gifted pupils might change as a result of the training, the teachers referred to a higher level of awareness of these students' needs and possible isolation, to an increased sympathy and to a new desire to provide them with support in the classroom and time to express themselves.

Clearly these teachers were open-minded and warm-hearted profession-als who were prepared not only to absorb new information about a particular group of pupils, but also to allow that information to affect their attitudes and classroom practice. Why, then, had their professional training not enabled them to access that information any sooner, leaving them to fall back on ste-reotypes? *They* had been let down, as much as their gifted pupils, by a system that had left this gap in their training. There is no difference between the need for teacher training regarding gifted children and the need for teachers to be aware of the needs of particular cultural or religious groups within their school, of their dyslexic pupils or of those with learning difficulties. Only once such training is in place regarding the gifted can schools begin to recognize that the very able need the same level of special attention that the least able require.

The reality, all too often, is that teachers are either unaware of or simply overwhelmed by the needs of their gifted pupils. What is it like for a newly qualified teacher who has received no training in these matters, when he encounters a highly able pupil with special needs of a kind that he may never have come across before? Lacking not only training but also much experience of the norm for all children, he cannot easily take in the exceptional nature of the gifted. What is it like even for a more experienced teacher, who is aware of the nature and needs of gifted children but has also to cater for the rest of her pupils, as well as coping with the daily mountain of paperwork, marking and preparation, pastoral and administrative duties? As one primary teacher put it so succinctly, 'When I've done all the marking and preparation for 29 of my children, then I start on Harriet Proctor's work.' Teachers like these would love to be able to give more to *all* of their pupils, and are often all too aware of the ways in which they are failing to meet the special needs of the gifted, amongst others. Awash with new information and changes in doctrine or practice, they sometimes struggle just to keep their heads above water, never mind to find islands of time and space to devote to their gifted pupils.

Interestingly, there are parallels here with the experience of the *parents* of gifted children. Just as with your first child you have no context, no background against which to view his abilities and characteristics, so context and experience is vital for teachers in their understanding of a child. Identifying a pupil as gifted will be impossible for them until they are familiar with children who are average in ability. It is easy for parents, struggling to meet their gifted child's needs, to forget the gradient of their own learning curve over the first few years of his life. It is only fair that they should acknowledge the fact that teachers have not had these years to learn about and adapt to the particular personality of their gifted child. Teachers also lack any genes in common with their pupils, and this must make each child's characteristics seem much more impenetrable and confusing than they would to his birth parents.

This sort of background information can make all the difference to how a gifted child is perceived. Morag, then aged 14, asked one of her favourite teachers why pupils should be obliged to stand up when adults entered a classroom. 'I don't mind for you,' she conceded, 'because I respect you. But why should we have to stand up for someone we don't even respect?' Her teacher was good enough to give her a proper answer – he said that she was meant to be showing respect for a position rather than for an individual – but his sharpness of tone in reply was quite understandable. Clearly he had interpreted her motivation as teenage belligerence, and this, too, was perfectly understandable. Her parents, though, would instantly have recognized in her question the urgent need to understand a concept, to grasp it intellectually, before she felt able to accept it and act upon it. Her question was never intended as an attack upon the teacher. Indeed, she would not have felt able to approach him if she hadn't liked him so much.

> How do you think that your child's teachers perceive her?
>
> Which aspects of your own knowledge and experience of your child could be helpful to her teachers?

No matter how gifted the child, he is still a child, with a child's levels of tact and diplomacy. Yet the combination of unsubtle phraseology, and questions that can genuinely stretch the limits of many adults' knowledge of a subject, can make it easy for teachers, under great pressure already, to feel personally threatened by a gifted child's impulsive question or comment. Seven-year-old Tyron was delighted when his teacher announced that his class was going to do a project on mountains, especially when she said that they would start by looking at the highest mountain in Japan, for Tyron's father had recently returned from a business trip to Japan. When Miss Harris wrote 'Mount Fujiyama' on the board, Tyron was quick to correct her: 'You don't say that, Miss. It's Mount Fuji or just Fujiyama, not both.' The teacher's response was shocking and indefensible – 'Shut up, know-it-all' – but perhaps a little more comprehensible in the light of what has been covered in this section so far, than it would be if quoted without discussion.

Teachers are no different from other professionals in this respect: they work under a variety of stresses, to which they are called to respond with dignity and competence. Like all service professionals, they spend almost all of their working days interacting with other people. Under the weather, facing personal difficulties or exhausted by their own toddlers' disturbed nights, the option of retreating behind a desk or computer is not available to them. This much, as noted, they have in common with many other workers. What is unusual about teachers is that *their* ongoing and unavoidable interactions are with massed ranks of children. Each individual interaction is made in public, and every weakness or mistake ditto, with consequent effects on reputation and discipline.

This, then, is the context in which parents must see the teachers of their gifted children: against the background of all the usual pressures of their job comes the need to make additional provision for children who are potentially amongst the most challenging they will encounter, in terms of their personalities as well as of their academic needs.

> What do you think it is like to teach in your child's school?

One such difficulty is presented by those gifted children who make a very good job of hiding their abilities: it is clearly unreasonable to expect a teacher to read the mind of a pupil who deliberately and consistently underachieves. More than this, it can be a struggle for teachers to provide for *any* minority group within a class of 30 or so mixed-ability pupils: each lesson is limited in time; the curriculum is relatively inflexible and it is part of teachers' stress that their creativity has been so reined in; and the opportunities to tailor the teaching to each pupil's individual needs may be genuinely restricted. This can all be made even more difficult if some of the pupils exhibit challenging behaviour as well, as do many gifted children when they are characteristically checking that the boundaries are safely in place. And then there is the gifted child's need for constant stimulation, knowledge and clarification. As one parent described her child, 'No matter how tired or busy I am, she's always *there there there* with her questions and games.' This mother loves her daughter and would not have her any other way, but it is small wonder that such children can provoke negative or angry reactions from teachers under stress.

In these circumstances it can be hard for teachers to avoid being drawn into a battle of personalities with their gifted pupils, for the choice of teacher tends to be very significant for these children – and note that male teachers can have a very different impact from female ones, particularly for boys. Their own force of personality can be hard to resist for any adult. For teachers who have to find their way around the many challenges that the gifted present, *and to do so in front of the rest of the class*, this can be even more problematic. No matter how articulate, stubborn and demanding an able child might be, he is still a child. It is completely inappropriate for his teachers to react in the way that they would to a similarly articulate, and possibly unreasonable, adult. Easy to write. Easy for a hard-pressed teacher to put into practice under the watchful eyes of 29 other restless pupils?

> What do you think it is like to teach your child?

What is it like for parents in this situation?

Nevertheless, the day-to-day trials of a school and its teachers must be balanced, in the eyes of each pupil's parents, against the particular needs of their own child. The challenges that teachers face are genuine, and there are many good and caring teachers, and plenty of good schools which try their best to meet their gifted pupils' needs. But the reality is that there are also schools and teachers who remain unaware of those needs; or who retain stereotyped and inaccurate views of gifted children and their parents. There are some poor and even hostile teachers, and some schools which simply fail their gifted pupils. Whilst valuing and celebrating the excellent work that many teachers do in difficult circumstances, it is also vital for us to acknowledge and be open about the devastating experience that some gifted children and their families have through school.

For all parents the start of their children's formal education is a watershed in their family life. For parents of children with special needs it can be a particularly worrying time, as they strive to ensure that the school is able to meet those needs. For the parents of children whose special needs may not even be recognized, the experience can be traumatic, especially in the light of schools' claims to value individuality and teach according to needs. Nor might this be an isolated experience for the family, as transitions between schools (because the child has reached a certain age, or the family has moved, or the parents have decided that the previous school was unsuitable) carry a similar potential for conflict and difficulty.

Indeed preparation for schooling, and later for changes in class or school, is particularly important for gifted children. They may need to be introduced to the concept of a school timetable and to practise lesson structure in contrast to the freedom of family life. Similarly, it may be helpful to talk them through the idea of being one in a large group, and the need to speak to a teacher differently from how they speak to their parents. Later, as class changes are introduced, even the best schools' introductions to the coming academic year will necessarily be global, with scant individual focus. The families of gifted children may come to recognize a pattern of troublesome behaviour at the beginning and end of each academic year, as change is anticipated and absorbed.

It should be stressed again that school is only *potentially* problematic for these families, since the start of a new school can also be hugely positive for both the children and their parents. If the school is right for the child, whether it is her first school or one that she moves on to later, then the discovery that she is happy and her needs are being met can bring enormous delight and relief to both her and her parents. In the best of circumstances parents will feel that they are welcome in their child's school and that their concerns are taken seriously; it will be clear whom they should approach to discuss those concerns; possible strategies will be discussed with them before being implemented; they will feel involved in decisions about their children and confident that their own knowledge of their child is valued. All of this will help them in their turn to feel more able to discuss their concerns with the school without becoming hostile or defensive; to persist where concerns remain, while nonetheless recognizing the positives; actively to seek a positive relationship with the school and where possible to contribute to its life through a forum like the Parent Teacher Association or board of governors. This sort of fruitful home–school relationship will obviously be of huge benefit to all concerned, but especially to the child.

When the opposite is true, though, and school is a bad experience for children, it is easy to forget that this can also be extremely difficult for their parents. One of the most distressing aspects of this situation can be the changes that they observe in their children when they are miserable at school. Within weeks of starting a school that does not meet their needs, gifted children's parents report quite drastic changes in the behaviour and personalities of their offspring. From being an enthusiastic and intensely curious infant, a gifted child who is suffering socially and intellectually at school can quickly appear to have had her intellectual spark extinguished. She may become sullen and withdrawn, or her behaviour deteriorate to the extent that every conversation is a battle and her parents are suddenly faced with a torrent of rude, aggressive and naughty behaviour. Gifted children are by definition quick learners, and if a child knows that school is where she suffers most then she may well begin to refuse to go there, turning the morning routine into yet another battleground for the weary parents and miserable child. The frequent plea of the parents of gifted children who suffer in this way is, 'I just want to have my little girl/boy back again.'

If the poor behaviour is being taken into school as well as the home then it can be difficult, in a school where this child is not yet known very well, for the teachers to avoid focusing on her behavioural problems – in the parents' eyes, to the exclusion of tackling the frustration and social isolation that is at their root. The social isolation is actually more likely to be noticed than the intellectual boredom, however. If the teacher is not familiar with the special needs of gifted children then he can see a child who does not mix very well with her classmates as one who is simply lacking in social skills. Gifted children's parents often express their frustration with what they see as a school's obsession with this issue, and its insistence that their child should not be pushed academically until she has sorted herself out socially.

This situation will not be helped if the child is so unhappy that she is refusing to do her work properly at school, or perhaps simply covering up her abilities in order to try to fit in with the other children. By the time that she starts school a perceptive child can easily have picked up on the false modesty and antipathy to difference that is so prevalent, in British society at least. Intellectual ability has an appallingly low status in this country, in contrast to the kudos that is accorded to achievements in sport, and a child who wants to avoid being the odd one out might well hide her true level of knowledge and skills. In this case her bad behaviour and refusal to play with the others will be the only things that draw her to her teacher's attention.

The result of this situation, from her parents' point of view, is that their claims about her abilities may simply not be believed by the school. Parents entrust schools with the education and care of their child, and when they find that her needs are not being met then it is easy for them to feel that they have let her down. More than this, it is obviously humiliating and frustrating in the extreme to find that no provision has been made for your child because your claims about her needs are simply not believed. Rather, you are being portrayed as the dreaded Pushy Parent who refuses to accept the truth about your child, or perhaps as the Bad Parent who cannot instil acceptable behaviour or common courtesy in your child. Experienced teachers do know a lot about providing for the average child, and good teachers have thought hard before forming their views about what is best for all the pupils in their care. If their priority is conformity, however, and if in addition they perceive a parent as unrealistically ambitious for her child and perversely unwilling to accept guidance about his social and behavioural problems, then there is little chance of school and parents working together on her behalf.

Increasing the obstacles to this sort of cooperation is the defensiveness that both parents and teachers naturally feel when they have reason to approach each other about a child. Uncertain about what is coming; often

> What is your relationship with your child's school like?

uncharacteristically quick to infer that blame is being unfairly apportioned; protective of their own knowledge of the situation – the most reasonable of people can react badly in circumstances like these.

Acceleration

One solution that tempts many parents when their gifted children hit a crisis in their schooling is acceleration into a higher year group. How successful is this likely to be?

The brief answer is that it depends on the child, the school and the relationship between the two. For instance, it is not uncommon for people, whether parents or teachers, to dismiss acceleration out of hand as a result of their own disastrous experiences of it. If there is no long-term consistency in the school's approach to providing for its most able pupils then acceleration at this juncture may simply lead to repetition at a later stage. When Kai was at a tiny village primary school he was able comfortably to keep up with the work of pupils three academic years ahead of himself, and to do so unobtrusively because there were four year groups in the same class. The middle school was sceptical, however, and permitted him only to work one year ahead of himself in a couple of subjects, and by the time he reached secondary school he had effectively marked time for the three years that he had leapt at primary school.

It is also worth bearing in mind that even when applied consistently, acceleration into an older year group will not always solve able children's problems. It may do little more than diminish the differences between them and their classmates, as those in the year above may have a head start on the gifted child's age peers but this does not mean that they can work any faster than them.

For some children, though, acceleration works well and schools do need to keep an open mind about its possibility: many parents are keen for a bright child to move up a school year or two, and the children concerned will benefit greatly if the school is aware of the issues involved and can have an informed discussion with parents about the various options. Acceleration could of course be applied in some subjects but not in others: maths is among the most common. It is also possible to negotiate a fail-safe position so that the child can be reinserted into their age-peers' class if necessary.[1]

A useful rule of thumb regarding acceleration was suggested by Margaret Branch, one of the founders of the National Association for Gifted Children. She used to say that there are four aspects of a child's development – physical, social, intellectual and emotional – and that you need at least two and preferably three of these to be advanced, in order for acceleration to work well.

Obviously the home–school relationship is one of the keys to success for any suggested provision for the gifted. The problem for parents can be that they do not know how to ensure that the relationship becomes or remains strong. Hampered by a desire to avoid being labelled pushy, held back by the wish to be reasonable and not to ask for too much for their own child at the expense of others, and caught up in the emotions that arise from their own memories of school, many good and caring parents can feel impotent to do anything to help their child. What they need, then, are some practical hints for approaching schools in a way that is likely to increase their chances of reaching productive solutions, whether in response to a crisis or as part of an ongoing effort to manage their concerns about adequate provision for their gifted children. Only then are parents likely to be able *either* to embark on a fruitful relationship with the school, *or* to see clearly that this will never be possible and that some sort of change is needed.

> Have you ever wondered whether acceleration might work for your child?
>
> In which of Margaret Branch's four areas is your child advanced?

The parent–school relationship: some thoughts
Separate your feelings from your child's needs

Before they can even think about approaching their child's school, many parents will find that they need to address their personal feelings about education and teachers. If a parent was himself made miserable by lack of challenge and social isolation at school then his child's problems may well bring these feelings back to the surface for him. If in addition his own school problems were never resolved, then he will have no model for how things could have been improved. Indeed, at some level he may even believe that it is just not *possible* to do anything about situations like this. He was not heard when he was a schoolboy: his unhappiness was unacknowledged and his needs were not met. How can he now be expected to know how to help his child when she faces the same challenges?

What this parent needs is support for himself, in order that his daughter might have her needs met more effectively. The problem that can arise if his own needs remain unmet is that he might be tempted to try to be heard by his child, by discussing her difficulties with her at an inappropriately adult level. This can have three unwelcome consequences. First, the child herself is now burdened with her father's feelings of impotence and negative perception of the school, as well as with her own problems. Second, the father will in any case not really have had his needs met by this sort of conversation. Third, gifted children above all others will be swift to pick up on the dissension between parent and teacher, take sides and play off one against the other. Perhaps as a result of this, research appears to show that the more parents discuss school issues with their children, the less teachers seem willing to accommodate those children (Dorothy Reynolds, personal communication). Of course it is helpful for parents to listen carefully to what their child tells them about school and to provide opportunities for her to tell them more, but this is different from talking potential solutions over with her in an inappropriately adult way; or from encouraging her to think disparagingly of her teacher; or from sharing with her their concerns about the school's approach.

As a first step, then, parents may need to seek support for themselves when they feel enmeshed in their own bad memories and the feelings that these provoke, or even simply when they experience strong emotion as a result of their child's suffering. Without this support for themselves they are unlikely to be able to focus rationally on their child and her needs, in their dealings with the school that is the cause of her unhappiness. In a way, seeking this kind of personal support is actually something that they are doing for their child.

In summary: remember that this is about your child, not about your feelings. This works both ways. Just because you feel sick to the stomach, impotent and under attack the minute you cross a school's threshold, it does not mean that your child's teacher is anything like the people who caused those feelings in you as a child. Conversely, just because your feelings are more intense than those of some other parents in the same circumstances, it doesn't mean that there is not really a problem to be addressed. In either case the focus needs to be on your child, not on you.

Is any of this relevant to you?

Your child's needs should *be met*

Having turned the focus onto their gifted child, his parents must believe that what they are asking from schools – that the special needs of their child be met – is *reasonable*. When they approach a school for help in stopping their child's social isolation or bullying, or in ensuring that his academic needs are met, this is *not* being pushy or demanding.

In the US, gifted and talented education is entirely a state affair. There is no federal legislation mandating states to provide special services to their gifted and talented students. Around 60 per cent of states have mandates to identify and/or provide programmes for gifted students; around two-thirds of these allocate funding for this purpose.

In England and Wales, although there is no statutory requirement that schools make specific provision for their gifted pupils, what is statutory is that they have to cater for pupils according to their age, aptitude and ability. In the absence of statutory requirements, the Gifted and Talented team at the DfES use encouragement to influence schools to take seriously their responsibility towards gifted and talented pupils. Secondary schools from 2006, and primary schools from 2007, will be asked as part of their annual school census[2] to identify their Gifted and Talented cohort. More teacher training courses now incorporate Gifted and Talented in their curriculum; most Local Education Authorities (LEAs) now have someone with responsibility for Gifted and Talented provision; many schools have a Gifted and Talented Coordinator.

Whilst none of this means that most gifted and talented pupils have their needs met adequately, it does mean that the subject has a higher profile than used to be the case. Parents who raise it with schools can do so in the knowledge that there is now a lot of material available to support teachers in their Gifted and Talented provision. A lack of provision, whatever the location, is totally unacceptabel. When parents ask for their gifted children's educational needs to be met in school, they are after all only asking for their child to receive what schools are designed to give.

Parents should also feel supported by the hierarchy of people and institutions who are available to help when things go wrong. In the UK, schools have both academic and pastoral hierarchies of staff who can be approached if discussions with the immediate subject or class teachers are unsuccessful. Somewhere within this structure there may be a Gifted and Talented Coordinator, and at the top of the school tree is the Senior Management Team, led by the headteacher. Beyond the school there are the Governors, and one of them may have particular responsibility for Gifted and Talented provision within the school, or for the particular academic subject on which your concerns focus. State schools come within the remit of their Local Education Authority, and of course the ultimate recourse is your Member of Parliament. Very few families, though, will feel the need to go very far up this hierarchy (or the comparable hierarchy that applies in their locality). Most will find that carefully managed dialogue with the school itself will reveal whether or not a workable relationship can be forged with the teachers there.

Careful, honest record-keeping on the parents' part will help all involved in this process, whether or not any conflict has yet arisen. It helps the other party by ensuring that *you* remember things accurately, and helps you by building a consistent record of communications to which you can refer as needed. Again this is something that can come more naturally to people in other areas of their life than it does in their dealings as parents. Ideas that families have found helpful include the following. Build up a file in which you keep copies of all letters and emails, both sent and received. On the telephone, keep pen and paper to hand so that you can jot down the date and time of any conversations and the name of the other person, as well as taking notes as you talk; put this record into the file as well. You may or may not feel comfortable taking notes in a face-to-face meeting: it can be useful to spend a bit of time immediately afterwards, either filling in any gaps in the notes that you took or making the notes that you did not. Put these in the file too. It can also be good to send a letter straight after a telephone call or face-to-face meeting, putting on record what was agreed and checking whether your memory of the conversation accords with the other party's. Thus you will build up a consistent record of all that has been discussed and agreed, in case of any future dispute or deterioration in the relationship.

In summary: remember that it *is* reasonable to ask the school to meet the special needs of your gifted child. You may disagree about the particular ways in which they will meet those needs, but met they should be.

> How do you feel about asking for more from your child's school?

A gentle approach

Equally crucial is for parents to understand the teachers' perspective. Many teachers feel thoroughly embattled already, and as a result a parent can seem hugely threatening and challenging outside the context of the normal round of school parent-teacher meetings. This impression will be intensified if the parent herself behaves defensively, either because she is uncertain whether what she is asking is unreasonable or because of her own personal issues. Having turned the focus on to her child, and resolved her guilt about approaching the school in this way, a parent needs now to think carefully about how she should raise the issue with the school.

There are certain truths about confronting people: it does not have to be confrontational; you don't make yourself heard if you shout; being assertive is not the same thing as being aggressive. It is vital for parents to think about phrasing things in a way that avoids putting teachers' backs up. If your aim is for a situation in which you and your child's teachers are working together towards the same thing, then you need to tell them that. If your belief is that parents and teachers have different sorts of specialist knowledge about the same children, then this is worth mentioning too. We tend to focus on our own child, but it is worth acknowledging that the teacher has about 30 others to deal with as well.

Everybody responds well to empathy, compassion and appreciation, and professionals like teachers are no different, even in a work context. A good start to a meeting could be the parent expressing her appreciation of the teacher giving up his time for this extra meeting, and her understanding of the fact that he is responsible for many other children besides her own. She might even confess to how worried she herself has been about this

> Does this reflect your own approach to confrontation?
>
> Is there anything here that could be useful for you?

meeting: self-disclosure of this kind can be very disarming. Much of any first meeting will involve both parent and teacher learning about each other.

Good phrases to use during the meeting might be: 'Is this a realistic expectation of the sort of provision you can make? If not, is there any way that I can help you to achieve it?' 'Obviously you see a different side of my child from what we see at home. How does he appear to you?' 'I feel very worried about my child at the moment. Can you suggest anything that might improve the situation?'

In summary: remember that confrontation does not have to be aggressive, and that acknowledging the teacher's perspective can help to defuse tension in a meeting.

Getting it off your chest first

This gentle approach to a meeting may well be the last thing that many parents feel ready for, at the point when their child's situation has deteriorated badly enough for a meeting to be set up in the first place. Bowing to the professional judgement of a teacher whom you believe to have failed your child? Acknowledging the needs of the other pupils when it is *your* child whose needs are unmet? But the sort of approach that we are advocating here is not about being hypocritical or denying feelings like these. Rather, it is about tackling the situation in a way that is actually likely to produce the results that you want. To do that, you have to acknowledge the perspective of the other party to the meeting.

Your own feelings of protectiveness towards your own child, or of anger towards the person or situation that is causing her distress, are very human and may well be totally justified. Nonetheless, it has to be remembered that the teacher concerned is human too. She also has feelings, and these may include anxiety about what the meeting has in store; tension based on past experience of difficult meetings with parents; guilt that she has let down her pupil; fear of being reprimanded; anger about having to give up some of her free time; pride in her own professionalism; low self-esteem and associated defensiveness. If your approach to the meeting does not take into account any of these possibilities then the outcome is unlikely to be successful. Nobody responds well to overt personal criticism, aggressive confrontation or the feeling that her own expertise or point of view is being dismissed out of hand.

How can these two conflicting facts be reconciled? On the one hand the parents of unhappy gifted children have feelings and opinions that are important to them and which they need to off-load. On the other, the teachers of unhappy gifted children are unlikely to listen to the parents' genuine concerns if they are first barraged by all the feelings that the parents are jettisoning. The solution to this dilemma lies in the parents doing their off-loading *elsewhere*, before they attend any meeting with the teacher. Ask yourself the question, 'What would I really like to say to this person?' and then find an outlet for the answer. This might take the form of writing everything down, or of saying it all to your spouse or friend, or even of ringing an anonymous listening service like The Samaritans. Whichever way you choose, the point of the exercise is clear: unless you have dealt with your own feelings it is unlikely that you will be able to focus on your child and her needs when you talk to her teacher. Conversely, once you have got off your chest all the things that you would really *like* to say to that person, you will be better placed to decide how you *could* say that, helpfully and productively.

> Are there things that you would love to get off your chest, regarding your child's schooling?
>
> Where might you let off steam in this way?

In summary: remember that your child's teachers also have human feelings and responses. There are some things that might be better said elsewhere.

Careful phrasing

Having cleared some of the emotional baggage out of the way, it is time to sit down and think about exactly what you want to say in the meeting; what you want it to achieve; what questions you want answered; what outcomes you want to avoid. The most useful question to ask about how you might express yourself or the approach you might take is: 'How will this be heard?'

An example should help to illuminate the importance of this. Imagine that you receive a telephone call, unexpectedly, from the parent of another pupil in your child's class. As you read each speech that follows, all of which are attempts to convey the same bit of information, we'd like you to think about two things. First, how would you feel if somebody said it to *you*, out of the blue? Second, what is it about the way it is phrased which provokes those emotions?

1. 'Naomi came home with a big scratch and bruise on her collarbone today. She says your James did it. Do you know anything about it?'

2. 'I'm ringing about James. You've got to do something about him. Naomi came home all scratched and bruised today, and I know it's not the first time he's done something like this. I've heard other parents talking. I know you won't want to hear this, but he's turning into a proper little beast. You'll have to do something.'

3. 'I don't quite know where to start. I mean, I know it's not your fault, and I really don't want to fall out with you, but Naomi's just so upset I don't know what to do. I know James wouldn't have done it on purpose but I just had to ring. I hope you don't mind? It's just that *I'd* want to know if he were mine.'

4. 'Do you have a few minutes? There's something we need to talk about. It's really difficult for me to say this, but I think that James may have hurt Naomi at school today. She's come home with a nasty mark on her collarbone and says that James did it, but I'd really like to hear his side of the story. I'm sorry to ring like this, but I really wanted to speak to you in person, to see whether there's anything we need to do about the two of them.'

It is not hard to see that some of these approaches are more helpful than others. The first one sounds quite bland and factual, but is actually so blunt that it would come as a real shock to most parents who heard it. What's interesting about this approach is that the person who took it may well not be able to see why it made the listener so defensive: it isn't as though he attacked her in any way or blamed her for the incident; he didn't even say categorically that he blamed James. He merely stated, very clearly and succinctly, what the problem is. Yet it is so very direct and unexpected that the shock may well raise the other parent's hackles.

The third approach, in contrast, tries so very hard to tread an inoffensive path that this parent never actually gets around to saying what the problem is. There is a genuine effort here to see things from the other parent's point of view, and a reluctance to leap to conclusions, both of which are admirable – but this amount of preamble is likely, ironically, to undo the good work that it tries so hard to accomplish. By the time the listener has heard this much, his imagination will have taken him goodness-knows-where in his attempts to guess what his son is meant to have done. A gentle approach is good, but it must be an approach *to* something.

The second approach merits little discussion. It is very unlikely that this conversation will ever progress beyond the hissing and spitting of protective parents. Although the caller is doing no more than expressing her feelings about the apparent attack on her child, it is hugely unhelpful for her to direct this towards the parent of the alleged attacker. As mentioned above, these feelings need to be dealt with elsewhere before the call to the other parent is made.

Finally, of course, it is the fourth approach that is most likely to succeed, but its virtues deserve closer analysis. *'Do you have a few minutes? There's something we need to talk about.'* Here the caller acknowledges that his telephone call may have come at an inconvenient time, but also suggests that it is probably going to be important to speak to him quite soon. In other words, he makes himself heard by conveying the message that the conversation *does* need to happen, whilst at the same time making an overt effort to see things from the listener's point of view, by acknowledging that he has intruded into her space.

Next comes a bit of self-disclosure, which is a very useful technique when being assertive rather than aggressive: *'It's really difficult for me to say this, but…'* Sometimes we stop ourselves saying what we'd like to say because of fears, anxieties or any other uncomfortable feelings or concerns that we have around the issue itself or the communication of it. When we disclose these feelings or concerns up-front, it frees us to say the thing we are anxious about saying. It reminds us and allows the other person(s) to see that we are human, which allows for relatedness and supports understanding. It may also encourage the listener to disclose her feelings in return, thereby adding to the depth of communication.

The facts follow this rather gentle opening gambit: *'I think that James may have hurt Naomi at school today. She's come home with a nasty mark on her collarbone and says that James did it.'* At some point in the conversation the problem does have to be stated and this is a very clear and factual summary of it. On the other hand, it is also followed closely by the statement, *'I'd really like to hear his side of the story.'* The speaker has not jumped to any conclusions: there clearly is some sort of problem here, but he has not yet made up his mind what it is. Finally he re-emphasizes the fact that he sees himself as being on the same side as his listener: *'I'm sorry to ring like this, but I really wanted to speak to you in person, to see whether there's anything we need to do about the two of them.'* He regrets having to call her with this difficult news (more empathy with her point of view) and he wants to know whether there's anything that *they*, not just she, can do about it.

> If you reflect on conflicts that you have experienced or observed in the past, what sorts of approaches or phrases have you found most and least helpful?

No doubt this father has had to off-load his feelings of anger and defensiveness before he was able to make such a productive telephone call in response to the situation. Having done so, and having thought carefully about what he wants to get out of the conversation, he phrases what he does say in terms that are most likely to achieve his aims. Just as when a parent approaches a school, one of the key aims here is to maintain a workable relationship with the other party, and this is the reason why the off-loading needs to be done elsewhere and the phrasing chosen so carefully. It might feel better in the short-term to blast her with a few choice phrases, but what happens the next day and the day after that? In the long term it is vital to give careful thought to how your words will be heard by another person.

In summary: remember that you can say what you want to say in many different ways. Think carefully about what you want to say, *how* you can say it and how the other person will *hear* it.

Careful planning

It is worth re-emphasizing a point that has emerged from the last example: being clear about *what* you want to say is just as important as how you actually phrase it. Many parents find it useful to think about exactly which points they want to get across to their child's teacher, before they go into a meeting with her. Many even find it helpful to write down these points so that they are not forgotten in the heat of the moment. The same applies to questions that they want answered and even to background information like their own observations of their child, what they have learnt about the policy of their LEA or State regarding provision for gifted children, or anything helpful that they have read elsewhere. It may feel slightly awkward to refer to a piece of paper in the middle of this sort of meeting, but many parents have said that this was far preferable to coming home and kicking themselves for forgetting to mention something vital. Teachers, too, prefer parents to bring along a list, or at least to have ordered their thoughts before a meeting, as it saves time both during the meeting and later.

It may also be worth considering that parental observations of gifted children in the home can be a useful contribution to a conversation with their teachers. It has been our experience that gentle anecdotal explanations have the double advantage of providing verbal evidence of a child's abilities and of expressing this in a non-threatening way. When Siân became concerned that her six-year-old daughter, a gifted mathematician, had been misjudged by the school, she arranged a chat with Rhiannon's class teacher. In the course of the conversation she shared an anecdote about how much Rhiannon was enjoying learning how to knit: 'The other day she asked me to cast on 13 stitches. After a while I heard her muttering to herself as she knit, and realized that she was using the rows to work out her 13 times table.' At school Rhiannon was being set simple sums with the rest of the class. When the teacher heard this story it opened her mind to Rhiannon's true abilities and things began to improve. Good teachers greatly value the insight of parental observations of children, who inevitably behave differently at home from how their teachers see them at school.

One of the advantages of this anecdotal approach was that it freed Siân from the need to state openly her opinion that Rhiannon was mathematically gifted. Not only did this avoid any potential conflict with the teacher about the validity of that opinion, but it also freed Siân herself from the need to feel absolutely confident that the label 'mathematically gifted' was applicable to Rhiannon. All she needed to feel confident about was her genuine and in-depth knowledge of Rhiannon's behaviour and nature, and her ability to ask for help from the school to work together on Rhiannon's behalf.

Of course part of the success here was due to Siân's low key approach, but part was also due to the fact that she used this approach in order to convey a *particular* message. Nobody hearing that story could deny that Rhiannon was more mathematically able than the average six-year-old; nor indeed that she had a natural interest in the subject, rather than being the victim of pushy parents. Siân knew before she went into the meeting that this was what she wanted the teacher to learn from it. The anecdote was chosen because it conveyed that message effectively.

Another point to emerge from this example is that Siân had thought not only about what she wanted to say but also about what outcomes she wanted from the meeting: in this case, that her daughter be set more appropriate maths work. It may be worth writing at the top of your page of notes for a meeting what you see as the *point* of it. What is it meant to achieve, from your perspective, and what sort of compromises are you willing to make in that outcome, if any?

In summary: think carefully before any meeting with the school about what points you want to make, what questions you want to ask and what outcomes are your priorities. It may be worth making notes about all this, to take into the meeting with you.

> What, above all else, would you like your child's school to understand about him?

Practice

It may even be worth practising all that you have planned, before you go into the meeting. With a partner, a friend or even a mirror you could role-play the meeting and practise your responses to a variety of possible scenarios

> Would role play practice be helpful for you?

and reactions. Obviously it will not actually be possible to second-guess the content or outcome of the meeting, but for some people this approach can be helpful.

In summary: role play might also be a useful tactic.

In the meeting – some further ideas

Certain issues come up again and again in meetings between teachers and concerned parents. For instance, such meetings can feel so intimidating or unfamiliar to parents that they find themselves forgetting the sorts of conversational skills that would normally come naturally to them. It is therefore worth giving some suggestions which in other contexts are probably very obvious. (Many of the ideas in this sub-section and the next are taken from Treffinger 1988.) Do ask for further explanation when you don't understand what has been said, and be prepared to ask questions to clarify what actually happens in the classroom, in the playground or wherever the problems are arising. Conversely, do feel able to check the level of communication by asking the teacher to tell you what he has heard you say, and by being open about what you are *not* saying as well as about what you are. Do ask for a full explanation of the meaning of test results, marks, and so on. Don't settle for explanations that rely on vague opinions or generalizations ('all of the children love the art and craft work that we do'), but maintain efforts to see that the discussion focuses on *your* child.

Other tips that may seem obvious include the advice not to criticize past teachers to your child's current teacher. It may appear that you are comparing her favourably with them, but what are the implications about your views of the teaching profession, or about how willing you are to gossip about teachers, including colleagues who may also be her friends and mentors, and even possibly herself at some meeting in the future? On a more personal level, it is important to focus on facts and evidence rather than on what you infer to be the teacher's feelings about your child – always remembering that it is not his job to like his pupils, but only to teach them well without allowing his feelings to interfere with that process. Similarly, focus on your own concerns or observations ('I have some questions about Hari's reading books') rather than on what you suppose or believe to be the teacher's problems ('You are giving Hari books that are far too easy'). Be alert for opportunities to be positive about both child and teacher, and about their relationship with each other.

If you are a teacher yourself, be aware of the possibility that your child's teacher finds that fact threatening. Even if you are not a teacher, but a different sort of expert or professional, could your child's teacher be intimidated by his perception of your own knowledge and standing? In this case it will be especially important to acknowledge his professional experience and training.

It is particularly helpful to use inclusive language, talking about what *we* can do to help your child. For example, if you have an idea about a new form of provision for your child – that he be accelerated in a particular area, sit with different children, or whatever – then you might suggest that 'we give X a try, and monitor it for a few weeks'. In this way you demonstrate that your desire is not to prove the teacher wrong ('you've been doing Y, when all along I've known that X would be the thing'), but rather that you have an idea which we can try together. You value his input, and *we* are a team working together for the considerable benefit of the child. If it doesn't work then the outcome will be that at least *we* have tried it, not that one of you was right and the other wrong.

> Would any of these ideas be useful for you in approaching your child's teachers?

In summary: never forget that you know a great deal more about your own child than anyone else does.

After the meeting

Parents sometimes come out of meetings with their child's teacher kicking themselves for having forgotten to mention or ask something, or feeling slightly dissatisfied with the outcome. A useful tactic to use towards the end of these meetings is to suggest to the teacher that you would like time to think about the issues and will be in touch again. It may be that on further reflection there is no need to do this; you could let her know, with no harm done, via a quick note or a comment when you next see her. It may be, however, that there really are a couple of outstanding issues, in which case it will feel much easier to approach her for a quick follow-up chat if the ground has already been laid for this possibility. Similarly, if the teacher has proposed a solution to a problem or made a suggestion for some sort of change, then a helpful response might be to welcome the suggestion but to set up another appointment to evaluate how things are progressing. If it is you who has made the suggestion, then again you might suggest that you review its implementation together at a future meeting.

Most importantly of all, if you do still feel dissatisfied, unhappy or uncertain as the meeting comes to a close, then try to state as honestly as possible that you are still concerned, and why. If the teacher is herself uncertain about alternative resolutions then it may be necessary to ask to discuss the matter further, with more senior teachers, or to say that you will need to seek advice elsewhere before talking to her again. You could then seek

> How do you feel about suggesting such follow-up meetings? Have there been times in the past when this might have been a useful tactic?

help from a support organization, the LEA or State, or even simply from your partner or friends. The key is that even if the outcome is not what you would have wished, and issues remain unresolved, the end of a meeting should not signal the end of the opportunity to discuss that subject matter with that teacher or, worse, the end of your relationship with that school or teacher. Of course crises will sometimes happen, and you may decide on consideration that you *wish* to end that relationship, but in general these meetings should be seen as the beginning of a new phase in your child's education, not as the conclusion of all discussion of the matter.

In summary: bear in mind that the end of the meeting may not be the end of the matter, and be prepared to acknowledge that fact quite openly.

And finally...

Not for the first time in our book, it is crucial to acknowledge how much harder all of this is in practice than when it is written down on paper. It is not always possible to plan ahead. Unforeseen things do occur on a day-to-day basis and you do have to deal with them there and then – unless, of course, you feel able to say that this is something you need to think more about before you are able to respond to it properly. Such a response is perfectly reasonable, and may prove much more fruitful in the long run than a hasty or knee-jerk reaction.

Even when you do have time to plan and prepare – and we hope that at least some of our suggestions may support you in this – things are of course never as easy in practice as in theory. Shortly after writing the first draft of this chapter, one of us wanted to ring the father of one of her child's classmates, to clear up a misunderstanding that had cropped up between their children. She had plenty of time to prepare, and since the contact was made by telephone she could even use pre-written notes unobtrusively. None of this stemmed the flow of discomfort and apprehension as she dialled the number, although the outcome of the call was thankfully positive. In the same week, this person was unexpectedly approached by her child's teacher to discuss some recent poor behaviour at school, about which she'd had no inkling. Instead of having the sense to say, 'Thank you for letting me know. Can I come back to you this afternoon when I've had chance to think a bit about it?', in her own words she burbled senselessly at her child's (excellent, as it happens) teacher for five minutes, before the school bell put an end to her stream of consciousness. Still, she has stored this experience away in the hope that its recollection will help her to do better next time!

The private option

Around 7 per cent of pupils in the UK are educated in the private sector and it seems fair to assume that a disproportionate number of these pupils will be gifted, compared with the population as a whole. These privately educated pupils do not form 7 per cent but 15 per cent of all A level candidates. They make up not 15 per cent but around 40 per cent of the A level candidates who achieve three grade As or better. There is a similar picture in the US, where around 10 per cent of pupils are privately educated: these students make up around 18 per cent of those who have attained at least a bachelor's degree by their mid-twenties. Such statistics cannot fully be explained by the advantages of a family background in which education is highly valued, or even by the strengths of the schools themselves. The innate gifts of many of these pupils must be a contributory factor, particularly since many private schools are academically selective.

Fee-paying schools can hold many attractions for gifted children and their parents. Schools with sufficiently tough academic selection criteria contain few non-gifted children, and in them the minority disadvantages are at once reversed. A group of gifted children in daily contact can be relied upon to strike sparks from one another and to progress further and faster than almost any of them can alone. Most teaching staff will have chosen to work in this environment precisely because they enjoy the constant stimulation. Social isolation is not unknown, and neither are interpersonal difficulties with teachers, but the probabilities of either are greatly reduced, provided the right school place can be obtained. Because of the cost, what fee-paying schools rarely have is the child who really has no interest in learning, let alone a child

from a family with no interest in education. And pastoral care is often remarkably good, especially at boarding schools.

Paying stiff fees and passing stiff entrance examinations do not, of themselves, magically guarantee any child a good academic education, much less a
happy, nurturing one. A child whose family makes huge financial sacrifices to
keep him in a school in which he fails to flourish may suffer the life-long
effects of disappointment, unhappiness, guilt and insecurity. Nonetheless,
what willingness and ability to pay do confer on parents is a very much wider
choice of schools than is normally available to the state-school child, particularly if boarding is considered realistic. In this section we consider some of the
factors that parents may wish to take into account when selecting an independent school for their gifted child. Our suggestions are necessarily rooted
in the British experience, but will also be of some interest and relevance to
parents who are making these decisions outside the UK.

Whether or not the school selects its pupils on the basis of their gifts in
any field, what it is selling to parents is the much greater level of individual
attention only possible in small classes. It is the ratio of teachers to pupils
which largely determines the fees that a school will charge, because teachers'
salaries are normally the biggest item in a school's budget. Roughly speaking,
the smaller the classes the higher the fees – and this means that, as a rule of
thumb, if the classes are not much smaller than in the local comprehensive
then parents should ask themselves how good a buy this is. In general, it
should be noted that school fees tend to rise faster than inflation and that
extras, even beyond uniform and equipment, can seem endless. The cost will
inevitably mean that the private sector is not an option for every gifted child,
even if his parents wanted it to be. For those who cannot afford the fees there
are some possibilities worth investigating, often based at individual schools,
but these are increasingly few and far between. We know that it is a source of
distress to some parents that for their gifted child the private option is not
available, even though others would reject that option on principle. Whilst
acknowledging the position of both these groups of parents, we are also
aware that there are other families who do take the private option and who
would like some guidance in selecting the right school for their gifted child.

Few parents are experts in the specialist field of matching child to school.
If they have any doubts at all, they may feel that sound professional advice at
the right time is worth buying. This normally involves a full Educational Psychologist's assessment of the child, and then a consultation with a specialist
agency which has in-depth knowledge of the current situation of a huge range

of schools. Such agencies should take all known factors into consideration, including religious and other preferences, together with financial and other limitations, before coming up with a short-list of schools likely to be appropriate.

Alternatively, parents can approach the Independent Schools Council (in the UK) or other national listing organizations for information about their local schools or suitable boarding schools, and begin by requesting a prospectus from each. These will include a schedule of fees and parents will quickly notice that some schools charge far more than others, which may be a factor in their decision. Other factors may include preferences about a school's size, religious affiliations, single-sex or co-educational status, selective or inclusive admissions policy, and traditional or progressive ethic. Having collated a long-list of schools from which they have requested more information, parents will then be able to come up with a short-list of schools worth visiting.

Many parents will feel that it is wise to make a preliminary visit to these schools on their own, without their child. Most schools have open days that can facilitate a discrete preliminary visit of this kind. If parents feel reasonably happy about one or more schools that they have seen then they can take the child along on a later occasion. A good school will probably arrange to separate the child from his parents for a little while on such visits, to form its own view of him and to see how comfortably he copes in that new atmosphere. Received wisdom is that the more the child owns any choice of school the better things will probably be, although of course this will depend on the child's age and personality.

What factors should parents take into consideration when they are looking round an unfamiliar school? Its ethos or 'feel' is often the key to the right decision. The whole family needs to feel comfortable there. There are Armed Services children who flourish in Quaker boarding schools, and Sikh families who happily choose a Catholic school for their children, but this is likely to be because these parents feel a fundamental connection with the ethos of the school, despite their apparent differences in background. For instance, some parents of young children will feel at home in the junior department of a highly academic, traditional boys' senior school, and their children will thrive in its formality and intensity. Other parents will seek a co-educational school with a more recognizably primary-school atmosphere, less emphasis on academic results and more on the nurture of the whole child.

As part of their assessment of a school's culture, parents should not dismiss their feelings about how their child interacts with any teachers whom they meet. When Jonathan's parents were trying to choose his first school they were shocked by the differences in attitude to him as a toddler.

> One school went to the trouble of providing him with a box of toys to play with while we talked to the Head. They made him really welcome, drawing him into the activities of any class that we visited and eventually inviting him to join the nursery class for their afternoon break while we finished our tour of the school. At another school, he might as well have been invisible to all the teachers – except to the headmistress, for whom he was clearly nothing but a nuisance!

It is vital that parents do not ignore their own emotional response to a school visit, for it can be an effective indicator of any future relationship with that school.

Jonathan's parents are practising Christians who were also disappointed when this headmistress didn't understand their concerns about her claim that pupils 'celebrate' all the major religious festivals, rather than just learning about them. Other parents may share her view that this distinction doesn't matter very much, but for Jonathan's this conversation revealed an important failure in what that school could provide for their child. Similarly, the parents of some gifted children will be less keen than others on signs that a school sets great store by sporting prowess, suspecting that this could lead to some academically gifted children being teased and undervalued. Parents necessarily have a limited time at each school, even if they make more than one exploratory visit, and even such apparently small concerns should be examined closely to see what they might reveal about that family's compatibility with each establishment. It may turn out, upon analysis, that the concern really is too minor to influence the decision. If you didn't think much of the science block, for example, even though you had been impressed by everything else that you saw and heard, how indicative was this of the state of the rest of the school buildings?

Again we would urge parents to trust their instincts about how much this sort of thing matters to *them*, regardless of how other people might perceive it. A family's relationship with a school is like any other relationship: the unique product of interactions that will not be quite the same as the interactions which each party has with any other. It is this relationship which is the key to the success or failure of the child's time at that school, for it is this relationship which will ultimately determine how parents and school react to any problems that might arise.

Quite apart from the impact that a school's culture will have on the child, it is worth remembering that a fee-paying school will have a parent-population that has actively chosen it. If a school is the right choice for your child, therefore, the chances are that you will have something in common with many of the other families for whom the choice was also right. This feeling of the whole family being at home with a school is bound to enhance the parents' ability to work cooperatively with its staff on behalf of their child.

In addition to this broad exploration of the school's ethos and culture, the parents of gifted children may wish to raise specific questions about how the school caters for its more able pupils. This is a personal decision, of course, and some parents will not wish to draw attention to themselves and their child at such an early stage in their relationship with the school. Others, though, will openly be looking for a school which can cater for their child's currently unmet academic needs. A defensive, uncomprehending or dismissive answer to such questions will in these circumstances tell them as much about the school as the more welcome response which is relaxed, knowledgeable and discursive.

Parents who are seeking a highly academic school will often be drawn to those which select their pupils on the basis of an entrance examination. Most schools have fixed dates on which these are set, but many are also flexible in meeting the needs of pupils who for various reasons wish to enter the school at different points during the school year. Such exams may therefore be taken alone or with other children, who might be potential rivals or could be attempting to enter different year groups. It is not uncommon for children to be coached for these examinations. In the UK, preparatory schools are named after their traditional role in preparing children for the Common Entrance Examination, and against this background the families of state-school pupils may well feel that it is reasonable for their children to be coached as well.

Not all independent schools set entrance exams, of course. Although there may tend to be fewer gifted children in those which do not, it does not follow from this that such schools are less good at meeting each pupil's individual needs. Again this is a decision in which the child's personality will have to be taken into account. Does she need an atmosphere of academic competition and the company of similarly able children in order to thrive? Or would she be happier in a gentler environment with an emphasis on nurture, where she could for a while at least be a big fish in a little sea? Indeed, her personality might be so sociable that it would be too traumatic for her to be taken out of her local state school and the secure group of friends that she has made there.

Parents will differ in their views about how much her own wishes and prefer-ences should be taken into account when making these decisions. What works for one family would not be right for another. In this area, as in any other, parents need to have faith in their knowledge of their own child. They are the ones who best understand her needs, who care most about having those needs met, and who will be constant in their love and support if the decision does need to be reviewed in the future. No decision is irreversible, and by far the most significant contributor to their child's security and well-being is the value that they put on her unique qualities. Like any other parent, the parents of gifted children cannot do more than base their decision on the best of their current knowledge of the options available, guided by their feelings about what is most comfortable for them as a family.

Summary

- School can be great for gifted children, but it can also be an arena in which any potential intellectual or social problems are intensified.

- The usual speed and level of lessons can be highly frustrating for gifted children. Teachers' responses to their gifts can have an enormous impact on their own self-perception.

- Acceleration can be a successful solution for some children. Children develop at different rates in physical, social, intellectual and emotional terms. As a rule of thumb, acceleration will work best when the intellectually gifted child is also advanced in one or more of the other areas mentioned.

- Many teachers have had little or no training in meeting the needs of the gifted. Many teachers are giving all that they can humanly give already, and feel sad and frustrated because they are unable to offer more time and space to their pupils with special needs.

- The sorts of challenge that gifted children present to their parents are mirrored in the experience of their teachers. In their approach to schools, parents need to acknowledge their own steep learning curve about giftedness, and that their child's teachers may currently be at a different place on that curve.

- It is heart-rending for parents whose children are miserable at school. If in addition they believe that their family is being failed and misunderstood by the school then anger will be added to their feelings of sadness and anxiety.

- It is crucial for these parents to find somewhere to offload such feelings *before* they approach the school. It is much easier to avoid aggression and achieve a workable relationship with your child's teachers if you are able to be gentle and cooperative in your approach to any meeting with them, using careful phrasing rather than being perceived as attacking.

- Clarity is important, too, however. Careful planning is needed before a meeting to set out your message and your hopes for the outcome. It may help to take some notes with you.

- It can be useful at the end of a meeting to ensure that the door is open for a follow-up chat or review of any suggestions that have been made.

- If your child's needs are not being met then there is a hierarchy of people and institutions to which you can appeal. Careful record keeping will help you throughout this process.

- For some families private schooling will be an option which provides their gifted children with a more appropriate education as well as greater access to other bright children. In selecting a school, parents should trust their instincts about how well their family would fit into each school's culture and ethos, as much as their understanding of their children's academic and social needs.

Notes

1   Research which supports the acceleration of bright students is drawn together in Colangelo, N., Assouline, S.G. and Gross, M.U.M. (2004) *A nation deceived: How schools hold back America's brightest students*. Iowa: The Connie Belin and Jacqueline N. Blank International Center for Gifted Education and Talent Development. Available to download for free from http://nationdeceived.org

2   A data collection exercise by the Department for Education and Skills (DfES).

References

Lucado, M. (1997) *You are special*. Wheaton, IL: Crossway Books.

Treffinger, D. (1988) *Parent-teacher interviews*. Stafford, QLD: The Queensland Association for Gifted and Talented Children Inc. Available from: http://www.qagtc.org.au/parteach.htm#top

Related contacts (see Appendix for full details)

United Kingdom

STATE SECTOR:

Department for Education and Skills
Northern Ireland Education Department
Qualifications and Curriculum Authority
Scottish Executive

INDEPENDENT SECTOR:

Independent Schools Council (ISC)
Independent Schools Council Information Service (ISCis)
ISCis Ireland
Montessori St Nicholas Charity
SCIS/ISIS Scotland
Steiner Waldorf Schools Fellowship
WISC

OTHER:

Advisory Centre for Education (ACE)
British Mensa
Gabbitas
Independent Schools of the British Isles (ISBI)
National Academy for Gifted and Talented Youth
National Association for Able Children in Education (NACE)
Scottish Network for Able Pupils (SNAP)
Tomorrow's Achievers
Westminster Institute of Education

United States

Center for Gifted Education
Center for Talent Development
Davidson Institute for Talent Development
Duke University Talent Identification Program
Johns Hopkins University Center for Talented Youth
State Resources for Gifted Education
Summer Institute for the Gifted
US Department of Education, including:
    Jacob. K. Javits Gifted and Talented Students Education Program
    National Research Center on the Gifted and Talented

Australia
GERRIC

Books

Ashworth, Sherry (2002) *Disconnected*. London: CollinsFlamingo.

Novel raises important questions about growing up gifted and pressured in an educational system with emphasis on examinations.

Delisle, Jim and Galbraith, Judy (2002) *When gifted kids don't have all the answers: how to meet their social and emotional needs*. Minneapolis, MN: Free Spirit Publishing.

Offers practical suggestions for encouraging social and emotional growth among gifted, talented and creative children and youth. Includes first-person stories, easy-to-use strategies, classroom-tested activities, and resources for helping gifted students.

Delisle, Jim and Lewis, Barbara A. (2003) *The survival guide for teachers of gifted kids: how to plan, manage and evaluate programmes for gifted youth K-12*. Minneapolis, MN: Free Spirit Publishing.

Two veteran educators of the gifted give teachers information, advice and encouragement. Includes reproducible handout masters.

Leyden, Susan (2002) *Supporting the child of exceptional ability at home and school*. 3rd edition: London: David Fulton.

Overview of issues that arise at different ages with practical guidance and specific examples.

Pomerantz, Michael and Pomerantz, Kathryn Anne (2002) *Listening to able underachievers: creating opportunities for change*. London: NACE/David Fulton.

Based on discussion with secondary school pupils the contents include teachers communicating with able underachievers, thinking and learning for these pupils.

Porter, Louise (2005) *Gifted young children: a guide for parents and teachers*. Maidenhead: Open University Press.

Shows how to identify gifted children aged 0 to 8 years and how to challenge them without pushing too hard. Suggests strategies for ensuring their emotional and social adjustment, assesses strategies for educating gifted young children, and addresses issues faced by immigrant families.

Stopper, Michael J. (ed.) (2000) *Meeting the social and emotional needs of gifted and talented children*. London: David Fulton Publishers.

Topics include curriculum development; extension and enrichment programmes; the role of the family.

Teare, Barrie (2004) *Parent and carers guide for able and talented children*. Stafford: Network Educational Press.

Comprises three sections: effective communication with school, developing skills and recommended fiction.

CHAPTER 6

Gifted Children
and Home Education

No consideration of gifted children's education would be complete without mentioning the possibility of withdrawing them from conventional schooling and educating them at home instead. There are specialist organizations which provide information, support and contact for families who are considering or have embarked upon home education (see the end-of-chapter notes for details), and these organizations can inevitably offer much more comprehensive answers to your questions about home education than we are able to in just one chapter of this book. What we offer here is an overview of how a child's giftedness may impact on the decision whether or not to home educate.

As has been clear throughout our book, it is often the case that the choices and experiences of gifted children and their families are heightened or intensified versions of those of any other family. This will certainly be true of the decision whether or not to home educate your child. First there will be a range of concerns about the impact of this choice on the child himself and, second, there will be concerns about its impact on you as parents.

The gifted child

Some parents take the decision to home educate their child long before he reaches school age, as a matter of principle and positive choice. For many, though, this option will first be considered after something has gone wrong with their child's schooling. Some children, for example, experience the beginning of formal schooling as a bereavement: the freedom to explore and question at will from the starting point of their own interest and achievement is suddenly curtailed by the divergent needs of 29 others, in a curriculum set bewilderingly far below their needs. If there are no adequate compensations in the form of companionship, games, the acquisition of social skills, exciting projects or equipment, then school can seem like a prison or punishment. In these circumstances questions will inevitably arise about the impact on a child of keeping him in or removing him from the traditional school environment. Can his academic needs really be met at home? And what about his social needs?

Academic needs

Concerns about whether academic needs can be met at home may be less pressing for gifted children's parents than for the majority: on the contrary, gifted children's academic needs are likely to be the stimulus for removing them from a school environment in which those needs are being neglected. Their parents may well decide that home education will restore the freedom these children need to go at their own pace, if school is not allowing them to fulfil their academic potential but is rather inhibiting their intellectual drive and squashing any creative impetus, or if an unavoidable change of school when parents move home, for example, brings the child into a very different and unmanageable school situation. Consider the case of Sameen, who started in a school where her intelligence was recognized, tested and provided for by a differentiated curriculum, including liaison with the secondary school in subjects where she had advanced beyond the primary curriculum. When her parents moved house, her new school was rigid in its approach to the extent that the headmaster even refused her access to the juniors' library because she was too young. Her mother reported, 'It seemed that she was switching off and content to accept what was on offer: she believed she should only learn what she was 'supposed to know' and had given up any desire to discover for herself.' Having read up about home schooling, her parents decided to withdraw her from school and give her the opportunity to progress at a rate suitable to her. Within a short time she was back to her lively, enquiring self, working at widely different levels in different subjects.

Concerns may remain for parents who choose home education about whether they will continue to cover a broad enough curriculum in the home; about their own ability to provide a well-based and properly structured

> Do you ever ask yourself whether your child learns more at school or at home?

education; or about the long-term impact on whether their child will later be in a position to take national examinations and go on to university. It may be possible to have recourse to the occasional or regular use of home tutors, selected with care on the basis of their training and normal child-safety concerns. All such issues are routinely addressed by the various home-education support groups, and the fact remains that for some parents the key point is that school has failed to provide for their child's academic needs, whereas at home he seems more able to be himself and to learn at his own pace.

Social needs

Similarly, the parents of children who have suffered bullying or social isolation at school may well feel more positively than others about the social impact on their child of removing her from the school environment. For gifted children in particular school can, as we have already explored, feel very alien and excluding. Given the choice between lots of socialization with people who don't much like her, and the risk of her spending a bit too much time on her own, many parents could well view the latter as less damaging. Indeed, home schooling may offer a much more positive experience of social life to the child. Sunita, who took her daughter out of school at the age of nine, described it like this:

> A lot of the socialization that went on in school was not positive anyway. Sheetal was younger than the rest of her class as well as being the only non-white child in it. We were certainly not sorry to see the end of all the bullying and teasing. Obviously she is still different, but at least now she doesn't need to deal with that fact every day of the school year. She has a good friend who she sees most days after school and plenty of other friends round about. She is also naturally very sociable and enjoys going to various clubs.

Again, the various support groups provide guidance about the ways in which home-educated children can have regular access to other social activities. Mavis, a qualified primary teacher who decided from the start to educate her gifted son at home, took great care to enrol him in all sorts of out-of-school clubs and activities, from Beavers to gymnastics; she also made sure that there was plenty of contact at weekends with their large family of cousins. So when Frank moved into the formal education system at the age of nine, he was sociable and well-balanced and had little difficulty in adapting himself to it.

For the gifted or other minority children, a greater worry for their parents can be the knowledge that being home educated would put them into yet another minority group. Do they really want to add this extra layer of difference to their family? Obviously this is a decision that each family must make for itself, but it will be one factor amongst the many that have to be taken into account, not least because of the knowledge that minority families already have of the impact of difference on their relationships with those outside the family. It is important to acknowledge that for some children the feelings of difference may be more bearable than the experience of going to school. Natasha, who suffered a bad bout of bullying after a change of primary school, became seriously school-phobic, so that her mother was obliged to teach her at home. Despite great efforts by another, more flexible school to reintegrate her into the mainstream, she remains fragile and lacking in self-confidence, often needing to take time out at home.

The need for independence

More than this, however, the decision to home-educate will also have an impact on the relationships within a family. Although the educational and social benefits of school life at its best may seem few and far between in the experience of some gifted children, school does also provide an arena in which children can first live a life that is to a certain extent independent of their immediate family. No parent knows exactly what goes on in the classroom on a daily basis, precisely what happens in the playground, or the details of what is said in her children's conversations at school. Incidents, both positive and negative, which are considered too minor for the school to report home can, if the child so chooses, remain for ever hidden from his parents. This privacy and separation must inevitably be lessened if a child spends all day within the family. Another potential loss for the child is the opportunity to take a new role in the separate circumstances offered by the school environment. Paige, who was the youngest of four children, had readily taken up the role of baby at home: small, fragile and often dissolving into tears, which brought out protective caring in the rest of the family. At school she presented herself quite differently and was perceived as competent, confident and achieving.

> Thinking about the social side of school life, what would your child lose if he didn't go to school? What might he gain?

It may, of course, be a private world which the child is very glad to lose, if things have reached such a low point that his parents are seriously considering withdrawing him from it. They may choose instead to give him more limited doses of the separation experience, in weekly clubs or visits to friends' houses, and in this way he will also learn more gradually how to live with his differences in the world of the majority. School may well be an inappropriate arena for some gifted children to learn these lessons, especially if their social development lags behind their intellectual and even their chronological age. The need for children to achieve independence as they grow, as well as making intellectual or creative progress and enjoying some level of socialization, must though be another factor in their parents' choices about their educational environment. It is certainly a further burden on their parents to have to monitor this as well as all the other facets of their development.

At the heart of the decision whether or not to home-educate there lies a key question: what do you want for your child at the end of it all? Against the criteria according to which they answer this question, parents can judge the many individual facets of their decision about her schooling. How much does it matter to them that their child should achieve her full academic potential? Is it important for her to be able to take national examinations and go on to university? Do they think that she should follow a broadly balanced curriculum, or is it better for her to have the freedom to pursue a few subjects about which she is passionate? When it comes to the social side of education, how important is it that their child learns to fit in and mix regularly with a cross-section of other children? Do they care very much that he should feel normal? How important is it for him to have friends of his own age? All of these questions will be answered more easily if parents have first been able to identify what they want the outcome of their child's education to be.

> What do you hope your child's education will achieve?

The parents

There will be a fair amount of overlap between many of the factors that parents will take into account when considering home education, and the criteria against which they would judge a school. As noted above, the key to any such decision is the question which environment will best provide what they want their child to gain from his education. The home education option, however, brings with it an additional and crucially important factor: the decision's impact not only on the children involved but also on their parents. It is the parents who must sort through the pros and cons of each option, and the parents who have to balance their own and their children's sometimes conflicting needs.

If home education is beginning to look like a positive option for a child then the next question for parents to ask themselves is whether it is viable within their family. Parents of the gifted are all too familiar with their child's intense demands and hunger for stimulation. Inevitably some parents' personalities will be better suited than others to coping with these demands on a 24-hour basis, where the parents have taken on almost the sole responsibility for meeting their child's intellectual, social and emotional needs. It is advisable for parents considering home education to reflect frankly and realistically on their existing pattern of interaction with their child. What is it like at the weekends or during school holidays? How much external input needs to be built into each day or week in order to keep the child stimulated and preserve parental sanity? How relaxed and cooperative is their relationship with the child? Does at least one of the child's parents find that the strains or challenges of long periods of time in his company are far outweighed by the benefits and rewards?

How well does the child respond to educational input and discipline from the parent most likely to be involved? Does that parent, or both parents in combination, have a wide enough educational background to recognize the field in which the child is making explorations? For instance, if a four-year-old asks his mother to 'count until the counting stops', does her mathematical training allow her to understand that this is a question about infinity? It is useful, here, to draw an analogy with foreign languages, where a fluent speaker will probably use actively only 10 to 20 per cent of the words and phrases he can understand. This principle holds true in most subject areas: good, flexible, child-centred teaching, which is what home-school teaching at its best should be, depends not so much on the teacher's keeping pace with a child, as on her having a much wider passive vocabulary than the active vocabulary she is actually using. At the very least she should have a real understanding of where to gain access to knowledge and information that she does not have.

As with any parenting dilemma this may well feel like a situation in which parents are willing to make sacrifices for the sake of their child's well-being. Again, if the situation has reached the point where a family is seriously wondering whether to withdraw a child from school altogether, then the sacrifices involved may be eclipsed by the prospect of relief from existing tensions and misery. The important thing is for parents to be realistic about their ability to cope with full-time child care, which is what home education must involve in addition to any teaching and learning. It is crucial that they do not ignore any evidence about this which has already emerged in their family life.

This evidence may include the memory of what it was like when one parent gave up work, for however long, when the child arrived in the family. Is it practical for the family to lose one parent's income, and is a career break feasible for one parent? How did that parent cope in the past with not going out to work? How much did she enjoy her world being so firmly rooted in her child's routines and social networks? How confident does she feel about her ability to facilitate her child's education, and how able does she feel to seek support in so doing? What sort of programme can she develop, which in some way differentiates work time from family time? How will she ensure that there is a discipline of curriculum and assessment of progress in her child's work? These questions may not be relevant to all families, but most will have to take them into account.

Further complications will arise if there is more than one child in the family. Will they all be taught at home or, if not, what will be the effect on those who are and those who are not? Another consideration will be the knowledge of what it is like for that parent to be part of an existing community of parents at her child's school. How much would she miss the school-gate experience? How important is that social network to the family, and if it is important then how likely is it that it would be maintained if the child left the school? How much does it matter to the parents that they and their family be perceived as normal? As parents of gifted children already, do they feel very disheartened by the prospect of putting themselves into yet another minority, potentially isolating themselves from others who have made more conventional choices? For some people this will matter more than others.

> What would you find most personally challenging about home-educating your child on a full-time basis?
>
> What would you gain most from it?
>
> What would your child gain most?

A further question must be how long you think the home schooling will last and what might determine a return to formal schooling. Sunita reported that

> Sheetal is thriving on being at home, is much more settled in herself and less influenced by peer pressure. Best of all has been watching her

realize what she can achieve when given the opportunity without the confines of curriculum and classroom pressure. Sheetal has no desire to go back to school – ever! As for us, we are still taking things a year at a time and it may be in her best interests to go back to school at some point in the future.

This comment brings out the additional point that if your child's school experience has been negative and difficult, it may not be easy to facilitate the return. How confidently can you maintain links with your State or LEA? Especially if your decision is a short-term one, it is important to make sure that the transition back to school is as straightforward as possible.

For most parents, home schooling will inevitably be a compromise and generally a temporary one. The decision needs to be made with as much knowledge and consideration as possible and to be kept under regular review. It is bound to depend a great deal on the personalities, circumstances and relationships involved in a particular situation. If it is embarked on positively and confidently as the best option, it can make a world of difference in the development of a gifted child.

Summary

- It can be helpful for parents to ask themselves: what do I want my child to gain from his education?

- For gifted children, home education may be a more positive academic option than for others whose needs are more easily met at school.

- It may provide a sanctuary from the social problems that some gifted children face at school. A positive effort needs to be made to build in other social contacts.

- Home education will inevitably reduce a child's level of independence from her family, as well as altering the academic and social balances in her life.

- It inevitably changes the social and intellectual balances in the parent's life, just as in the child's.

- Home education involves parents in full-time child care.

- Each family's decision must depend as much on the individual personalities and relationships involved, as on the child's social and academic needs.

- The decision needs to be made with as much knowledge and consideration as possible, and to be kept under regular review.

Related contacts (see Appendix for full details)

United Kingdom

Education Otherwise
Home Education Advisory Service (HEAS)
Home Education in Northern Ireland (HEdNI)
Human Scale Education
Islamic Homeschooling Advisory Network
Schoolhouse Home Education Association

United States

Center for Gifted Education
Center for Talent Development
Davidson Institute for Talent Development
Duke University Talent Identification Program
Education Program for Gifted Youth
www.homeschool.com
http://homeschooling.about.com
Johns Hopkins University Center for Talented Youth
www.midnightbeach.com/hs/
Summer Institute for the Gifted

Australia

www.austega.com/gifted
GERRIC

PART 2

Special Talents
and Special Needs

CHAPTER 7

Gifted Children with Special Needs

Gifted children are of course not really the homogeneous group that this book has at times been in danger of suggesting. In reality they are as mixed a bunch as any other group of children, and in particular some of them are doubly exceptional, having other special needs in addition to their giftedness. Such combinations of needs can in themselves present obstacles to a child's development and happiness.

We have already observed the developmental gap that is often evident in gifted children: their disparate levels of physical, social, intellectual and emotional development. These disparities can be intensified when a highly intelligent child suffers from a disability. Giftedness can be masked by a whole range of physical, psychological, sensory and social problems, from a physical condition that leaves a child wheelchair-bound, through sensory impairments like deafness or learning difficulties like dyslexia, and less obvious conditions that nonetheless require hospitalization or long-term absence from school, to difficult family circumstances.

In these situations a gifted child may well spend a great deal of intellectual energy in simply keeping up with the age-related norm. So a physically disabled child with a very alert mind may concentrate on reasoning out ways to overcome the handicap, or a child with dyslexia might develop strategies to conform to the requirements made of the class. These and other disadvantaged/gifted children often achieve their aims so well that they manage to appear average in their attainments, and their giftedness therefore goes unnoticed. It can be hard for others to see that these children are using all their energies to produce a result that puts them on a level with their age peers, when in fact their minds are functioning at a much more advanced level. Their gifts are in effect being concealed by their disability, condition or situation, just as they are using their gifts to conceal their condition. They become, as one headteacher put it, 'retarded gifted' (Peer 2000).

If the disability is more acute, or less manageable by compensative reasoning, concerned adults may focus far more on the disability than on the potential. Thus children for whom a statement of special educational needs[1] is in place may be subject to the ceiling of being brought up to the level of their age peers, without recognition that this is a denial of their real ability. Tony's parents refused such a process for their dyslexic son because they believed that he would still be desperately frustrated and aggressive at the end of it. They wanted to set the target according to his IQ, not his year group, and that would have put him three years in advance. If the focus is always on bringing a child up to the level of his peers, then this can actually inhibit the understanding of his special needs.

The sense of being different that is easily generated in such situations often weighs heavily on these children. Some may release it in bouts of anger and rebellion, especially in adolescence; some may turn it inward in acute and ultimately self-destructive dislike, which can take the form of serious eating disorders or even suicidal tendencies. For them and for their families the worries and tensions involved are hard to manage and need a great deal of support and understanding. This may be achieved by a mixture of the groups and organizations that exist to support both gifted children and those with the particular disability or condition involved – a mixture that will differ for every family. Our point, in this very brief chapter, is simply to draw attention to the oft-ignored fact that there are families who experience the additional difference of having a child who is in a minority *within* a minority: gifted within the disabled, dyslexic or other special needs community; disabled or dyslexic or with other special needs within the gifted minority. We are not qualified to advise their families as to the best ways of dealing with their children's very complex layers of needs, but nor would we wish to be amongst those who ignore them.

Note

1   In the UK, a legal document issued by the LEA which describes a child's educational needs and sets out how they should be met.

Reference

Peer, L. (2000) 'Gifted and talented children with dyslexia.' In Michael J. Stopper (ed.) *Meeting the social and emotional needs of gifted and talented children.* London: David Fulton Publishers.

Related contacts (see Appendix for full details)

United Kingdom

British Dyslexia Association

Contact a Family

Dyslexia Institute

Dyslexia Institute Scotland

Dyslexia Institute Wales

Dyspraxia Foundation

First Steps

The National Association for Special Educational Needs (NASEN)

Northern Ireland Dyslexia Association

United States

Information Center on Disabilities and Gifted Education

International Dyslexia Organization

www.uniquelygifted.org

Australia

Australian Association for the Education of Gifted and Talented

Books

Boon, Maureen (2001) *Helping children with dyspraxia.* London: Jessica Kingsley Publishers.

Offers positive answers to questions commonly asked by parents and teachers about behaviour, causes, identification and assessment together with a range of possible therapeutic interventions.

Chivers, Maria (2001) *Practical Strategies for Living with Dyslexia.* London: Jessica Kingsley Publishers.

Frank, Robert and Livingston, Kathryn E. (2004) *The secret life of the dyslexic child. How she thinks. How he feels. How they can succeed.* New York: Rodale Press.

With his experience of dyslexia Frank Robert focuses on understanding the best ways to raise children's self-esteem and confidence.

Kirby, Amanda (2002) *Dyspraxia: the hidden handicap.* London: Souvenir Press.
Includes strategies for parents and teaches to encourage children to improve their social skills and develop a strong self-esteem.

Lovecky, Deirdre V. (2004) *Different minds: gifted children with AD/HD, Asperger Syndrome, and other learning deficits.* London: Jessica Kingsley Publishers.
Through recognizing the different levels and kinds of giftedness, this book provides an insight into the challenges and benefits specific to gifted children with attention difficulties.

Macintyre, Christine (2001) *Dyspraxia 5–11.* London: David Fulton.
Explains dyspraxia together with intellectual, emotional and social development.

Montgomery, Diane (ed.) (2003)*Gifted and talented children with special needs: double exceptionality.* London: David Fulton.
Written for teachers, students, educators, researchers and educational psychologists the practical text provides guidance on identifying highly able pupils with special needs such as ADHD, dyspraxia, dyslexia and Downs Syndrome.

Moody, Sylvia (2004) *Dyslexia: a teenagers guide.* New York: Vermillion.
Increasing confidence, dealing with stress, building on creative talent together with strategies for study, exams and improving memory together with the personal stories of a dyslexic and a dyspraxic teenager.

Neihart, Maureen, Reis, Sally M., Robinson, Nancy M. and Moon, Sidney M. (eds) (2001) *Social and emotional development of gifted children. What do we know?* Austin, TX: Prufrock Press.
For teachers, parents and researchers. Written by leading scholars in the field of gifted children, the book summarizes research on special populations, the learning disabled, gay and lesbian students. Covers learning disabilities, adolescents, academically gifted, underachieving, creatively gifted.

Palladino, Lucy Jo (1999) *Dreamers, discoverers and dynamos: how to help the child who is bright, bored and having problems in school.* New York: Ballantine.
Explains how parents can identify and appreciate the Edison Trait – intelligence, active imagination, and a free-spirited approach to life – and offers eight steps to help support its benefits and minimize its problems.

Reid, Gavin (2004) *Dyslexia: a complete guide for parents.* Chichester: John Wiley.
Written for parents and teachers to enhance their role in supporting children. Includes up-to-date research, first-hand accounts and suggests resources.

Riddick, Barbara, Lumsden, David and Wolfe, Judith (2002) *Dyslexia: a practical guide for teachers and parents.* London: David Fulton.
Realistic strategies for non-specialists and parents wanting to help their children.

CHAPTER 8

Gifted Children with Asperger Syndrome

One of the areas of special need in which our group does have some specialist knowledge is Asperger Syndrome. Here Peter Carter, a Registered General Nurse and Registered Mental Nurse, and the father of three children, shares the insights that he has gained not only from his professional training and research, but also from his efforts to understand his gifted son who has also (eventually) been diagnosed as having Asperger Syndrome.

Asperger Syndrome (AS) is currently much talked about and mentioned in articles, because it is a feature that is more widely understood than it used to be, and acknowledged as being a significant challenge for those involved with the youngsters who live within it.

Many children with AS are very bright or even gifted – and conversely many bright and gifted children may live without it being recognized. There is a danger, however, of putting a label too readily on children who are merely strongly focused: of interpreting some of the better-known presentations as definitive evidence of AS. A gifted toddler may well present AS-type traits like an obsessive concern for how things are done, an attention to detail or uncontrollable rages. None of these is necessarily proof of AS.[1]

On the other hand, as more and more books, articles and programmes have spoken of and tried to illustrate AS, so some adults have come to recognize aspects of its features in themselves and have gained a better understanding of themselves, and of how and why events in their lives, or their lives themselves have gone as they have. This frequently brings a relief to them: many illogicalities, the awkwardness, the frustrations, the ridicule, the rejections, the failures, even the successes, find explanations, reasons, logic and acceptance.

The science, understanding and management of AS life is expanding every year. It is probably about 20 years ago that AS was brought from some obscure concept first spoken of around World War II, into being recognized as an all-too-prevalent developmental feature needing careful consideration, acceptance and skill to deal with as a parent, as a teacher, as a law officer, as a colleague, as an employer, as a spouse and as the individual with it.

I personally have had to make this journey of gaining consideration, acceptance and skills for myself to assist my son in his life with AS. Just as people with asthma, diabetes, hearing impairment, epilepsy, cerebral palsy or visual impairments have to live with and within their obstacles, so too do those with AS. But AS is less recognizable; a more subtle feature to adapt to, or even to grasp as a concept. Once I had considered that AS might explain my son's behaviour, much of my previous 12 years' struggles and joys now fitted a picture. This was good because this period of childhood – the teen years – is such an involved, unpredictable, delicate time for a parent as well as a child, that having this other factor adds more than just one extra dimension to the experience and the reality.

In the world of psychology and medicine, Asperger Syndrome is described as being a developmental disorder. It is mainly classified as an Autistic Spectrum Disorder. Another description is that it is a Pervasive Developmental Disorder. AS has a whole spectrum of degrees of manifestation. There is no clear defined description. For a diagnosis to be made, areas including the social, emotional, intellectual and perceptual aspects of a child will need to be assessed. Slowly evidence is accumulating to demonstrate that the actual physical facets within the cerebral-biochemical complex of the brain have not grown or formed quite normally, or do not function quite normally. AS and other autistic patterns seem to be caused by damage or mis-shaping of certain genes, which makes cells grow wrong and thus causes imbalances amongst the chemicals that make brain cells work properly, and also the misforming and misdeveloping of neural synapses. In a few people medicines may help correct chemical imbalances. For most others the cells cannot be repaired or improved. The cells affected are all part of the very complex structure of the brain and affect behaviour in various ways in certain situations, or even all the time. Some people are affected more profoundly than others. It all depends on where, how and how many cells and nerves are involved.

So what does this mean? It means that AS people do not have normal development in aspects of social skills, of emotional experience, of intellectual functioning, of perceiving and responding to cues and clues in interactions with other people. For example, the concept of The Other Person mostly is not present. That a person has feelings, is affected by me, or needs allowing for other than as a physical object, does not occur to a person with AS. Words, phrases, sentences are processed in a literal manner: for example, 'feeling' usually is understood as a physical sensation of touch. Emotions are largely unknowns or just reflex reactions, e.g. anger which cannot be controlled or tempered. Thinking chains often have only right–wrong, black–white logic routes. It is fact-based, with just one meaning. Perceptions and responses are commonly dulled or highly accentuated. For example, a sound, a light or even a colour is either not heard or seen, or arouses intense interest or intolerance. Such perceptions can even be intensely painful, causing violent defensive reactions. Typically, AS children do not see expression on the faces of others, and they usually do not have expressions on their own faces. Hence their attempts at social interaction are frequently inappropriate and provoke negative responses or events.

AS affects one's ability to mix in, understand and really link with other people. Those with it tend to be loners, or most are alone; but they desperately want to be part of groups, with others. Social skills and emotional development are much slower or impaired. This leads to failure in understanding or caring about the complicated rules and patterns of social interaction, body language and non-verbal communication. As a result, the person tends to interrupt, offend, ignore or be intolerant of other people, which causes those others to feel annoyed and angry and not want to have anything more to do with him. Teachers, for example, often see this as being rude, argumentative and disobedient, and so unfortunately react accordingly, leading the pupil to react angrily and become obdurate.

Emotions and feelings are very difficult for people with AS to understand, and seem frightening and uncontrollable and irrelevant. They are much happier with facts and figures and practical things. They have different and sometimes amazing logical-thinking abilities which other people cannot easily follow. There are times when they understand and see answers or solutions to problems that other people do not, including teachers. When they try to show and explain their answer and no one gets it, they often feel frustrated or think everyone else is stupid. They often have intense interests, or things that they find really important, but which others find totally boring.

Equally they can be absolutely unconcerned by things that others see as great and important. Squabbles and arguing and fights all too often develop because of these different opinions. People with AS tend to be adamant and rigid in such situations. Their interests and activities can be notably obsessional.

Allow me to use my son as my model to conceive and understand what AS can be. He is not a highly affected individual but still he has been a highly fraught experience – for him and for me. We must always hold in mind that the experience is also difficult and exasperating for the individuals affected. They get no explanation of us and why we do not, cannot, follow or be like them. How we are, how we interact, is inexplicable, inconsistent, illogical to them, just as their actions can be to us.

What made our son gifted was essentially a powerful memory and speed of absorbing information and facts and theories. Encountered once, it was learnt. Maths, English, history, geography, science – all could be consumed, then immediately used and some very perceptive ideas and views formed and expressed. Even visually and acoustically he had a similar acuity of taking in and putting out. Sport was not strong; handwriting and presentation were notable weaknesses. Creative imagination was never strong or easy. He was never at ease in groups or with his contemporaries. He longed for acceptance and too often sought that of the dominant, pushy clusters – the rough mob – a likely defence from being picked on or bullied. He enjoyed the company of adults 'who know things'.

Our son was seven when his intelligence and difficult behaviour caused waves at school and bumped us up against the headteacher, followed by educational psychologists and the Statementing Process[2] and its annual reviews. On and off through first and middle schools things eased and relapsed. Suspensions and expulsions occurred for periods. Home tutors were used at those times. All of this was seen by us and by the professionals as part of the gifted child picture. He fascinated or he annoyed various teachers, although male teachers created many fewer waves and seemed to feel less threatened or perturbed by him. Clinical psychologists came into the flow to help with anger management. Several educational psychologists and clinical/child psychologists came and went. When he was 13, following a particular session with him one clinical psychologist raised for the first time the possibility of AS. She asked a paediatrician about it, and a specialist consultant colleague was asked to see him. About this time, some fellow-members of our local branch of the National Association for Gifted Children gave us a paper about

Asperger Syndrome and this seemed to reflect our son's situation. The consultant also felt that AS was a possibility, and invited us to bring our son for a proper assessment, which eventually showed a clear diagnosis.

Our son was now 14: not a good age to find out that one has significant obstacles in social functioning; just as one is struggling to find who one is amongst hormonal change and growth. So now some new help started, via the educational psychologist, which the school and teachers claimed to understand more fully and adapt more effectively. Then one day on the school bus he caused a particular ruckus using his penknife as a threatening weapon. So we met the police and LEA, and he was out of the school system. Next came solicitors, courts, magistrates and eventually the probation service, and home tutors again. Away went any chance of 12 GCSEs – high grades foreseen – four was all he would be able to take and achieve: the LEA would not allow him to be in with other pupils, so any subject requiring facilities was barred to him. Investigation, trial and probation ate up 18 months, and by then he was 16 and beyond the education services.

More positively, he was able to accept help and find more awareness of himself through the law route than he had through education or therapeutic services. It had a higher street credibility, for one thing. He is now nearly 21. He worked consistently for one employer for four years, before they went out of business. In this time he commenced an NVQ[3] which is continuing with a new employer, after a time in modern apprenticeship status. He has grown, has learnt, is still learning to be a functioning human being. Hiccups come…and go. Shortness of temper and anger outbursts occur. He still tends to talk at people and needs to dominate conversations. He has always needed to shock others by what he says, and the f-word is still very prominent. Our house doors do still occasionally gain new dents and holes, as they have over all these years. He spent seven successful and much-enjoyed years with the Air Cadets. He has maintained a steady relationship with a girl for over two years – ideal, smooth – not totally. But whose ever is?

I wondered how to illustrate this person who is my son, but I became daunted by the amount of text that I would have to write, with potentially repetitious phrasing. So as answer I offer the brainstorm in Figure 8.1.

Any combination or none of the text within Figure 8.1 could be the reality of any one moment. You never knew what to expect but often you could expect something. One came to interpret his aura or the environment and circumstances and anticipated something. But this in itself could be an influence on whatever subsequently occurred because it added to the tension,

Selfish
- Not listening (habitual activity)
- Habitual activity
- Speak to anyone
- Do not interrupt
- Strong opinion
- Talk at people

- Arguing
- Strong voice
- Ignores others
- Gets too close
- Needs reasons & logic

- Intolerant of lesser ability
- Cannot accept help
- Intolerant of criticism
- Curious and intent
- Awkward around authority
- No failure
- Questioning

* Drawn to adults
* Sarcastic
* Unpredictable
* Fragile
* Witty
* Impatient
* Indiscreet
* Pedantic
* Over talking
* Very intent

Clumsiness
- Reading
- Small accidents
- Great distress
- Talk / talk-alike
- Sweet face
- Cannot lose
- Kicking out
- Hitting out
- Perfection aimed
- Doing it at worst
- Always last/worst

Watches WW1 WW2

→ Cannot reflect on outburst
↗ Unaware of hurt feelings
↗ Outspoken - honest - frank
↗ Unforeseen occurrences
↑ Poorly accepted
↑ Amazing knowledge and paths of thought
→ Swap ideas/themes quickly

Swearing

- Frustration
- No eye contact
- Dead-pan
- Fascinating
- Sudden anger
- No sharing
- Strong privacy
- Hearing everything
- Throwing
- Push into conversations
- Everything is aimed at him
- Wants to please but tends to offend
- Stunning memory
- Cannot accept jokes or laughing at him
- Escalating intensity
- Precise of anger

Figure 8.1

the unpredictability of the whole scenario for him. Other humans are unpredictable to him because they do not have his process of being and pattern of processing stimuli and data and observation. It was always important (we learnt late) to inform him beforehand what, where, when, how, even why we would be doing something – whatever… Suddenly springing things on him was inviting a problem, crisis, outburst…or nothing. When a reaction or response should occur nothing did; when no reaction or response should occur one occurred. Life was walking on eggs. Small inconsistencies, tiny happenings sparked the most intense outbursts. If a cup handle broke; a knife dropped out of his hand; a pencil point broke; a fuse blew and the lights went out – wham! – fists hit the table, things were thrown and a torrent of obscenities and threats exploded. Bafflingly, in major crises – nothing. ·

One's idiosyncrasies, preoccupation, obsessions, laxities and pet hates got sorely exercised and highlighted. You had to be prepared to explain and justify your prejudices, intolerances, dismissals and non-reactions, not constantly but at inconvenient moments. All those things we attempt to keep obscured, avoided, camouflaged, dressed-up or private can be suddenly yanked into the forefront, thrown at you when you never thought anyone knew: this person thrusts them before whoever else happens to be present – the world. To him they are facts, and facts are for all to know. Everything was fact. It is or it isn't. No in-betweens. He had and has no place or concept for in-betweens, grey areas, maybes, yes-buts, let's-imagine-thats, or pretends. Our whole sanity, equilibrium, ability to exist as adults depends on in-betweens. So here we are obliged to guide, educate, live with an individual for whom in-betweens are threats or inconceivable.

As our son grew, people would at times ask me what AS was. I came up with this analogy which seemed to have some effectiveness: AS is like colour-blindness where colours may be reversed or not registered or the density of colour registered may vary. It is not easy to know just quite what is being registered and how that affects how that person interprets the world and what he does with this interpretation. We the other people only understand that something is wrong by the person's actions and reactions – or if they tell us, if they know. They do not know that they are being different until interaction with others has negative effects that cause problems, or in the case of children when parents, teachers or others make these observations and face the problems.

Now we have somewhat of an image of AS, what about responding to it? What can be done? It is possible to do more and more. More and more is being understood about AS and about how to manage and adapt to AS symptoms and characteristics. Our response to AS has two prongs. Neither can have the name of cure or treatment. Both involve understanding what AS is, and learning how to be with AS. First is the prong of The Others – the parents, the teachers and all who encounter, interact with the AS person: those whose role is to help him to live an acceptable life. The second prong is the person with AS who will need to learn how to increase his chances of avoiding or reducing difficulties, and then how his AS characteristics could be directed to his and everybody's advantage.

Gaining an awareness of what AS is, and how it affects people, are the main steps for most of us. The subsequent step is training ourselves to tailor our interactive skills to offer the most constructive approach and mode of exchange with the AS person (described below). It has become apparent to me that the style of interaction most useful with an AS person will actually be very effective with anybody, particularly when that person is in a stressful, challenging or uneasy situation. All people in any role of authority would gain from bringing into their interactions these facets of manner and conduct. Through my experience with my son, it seems to me that policemen and others involved in law and order need these skills very much. Of course the training of most professional or client-contact roles touch on these skills indirectly and, all too often, partially. More specific emphasis needs to be made to raise alertness to AS, if for no other reason than that people with AS are males (the male to female prevalence is around 10:1 for AS and around 4:1 for other Autism Spectrum Disorders); the most awkward time in AS life is the teen years, as the influence of hormone changes and social change is in full flood; most brushes with law and order involve males, with teenage or early adult males disproportionately prominent.

Interacting with AS people means very often putting instinctive reaction and manner of being on hold. One's own pride, status and authority must take second place if one desires a constructive and productive encounter and outcome. Vital to learn is that AS people are unable to manifest and understand the infinite subtleties of non-verbal communications and even much verbal exchange. The normal cues and clues, tones of voice, body stances, facial expressions, interpersonal space, gestures are all mystifying and baffling to them, causing uncertainty and defensiveness; leading too easily to an impulse to defend oneself powerfully by voice or action. It has seemed to me, seeing my son engulfed instantaneously in intense anger, that anger is for them like having an epileptic seizure beyond their ability to control. It needs time and space to run its course and abate before anything else can occur – even offering comfort! The understanding of this is vital.

So too is the principle that AS children's outbursts are not, and should never be interpreted as, a personally directed reaction. Such an outburst is almost exclusively a self-aimed response. This is a perfection and failure issue: an interrupted logic trail, which cannot find the next step, cannot be reconnected. Self is now in chaos and being threatened. This perception has its logic but it is not our (the average person's) logic… But it is not a false logic, it is a reality to the person living it. Until we allow or touch that reality no link, help or control will be able to occur. Once the person has re-established a logic trail the outburst or crisis ends and it will be as if nothing had happened. It will take skilled interchange to assist the AS person to reflect and examine the crisis so as to pick out what happened and why, with the aim of identifying how to manage any future similar circumstance more desirably. (We never really acquired this skill: for my son the attempt only ever seemed to cause a reliving of the turmoil and reactions, sometimes more intensely. What happened in his own head we never knew…) The real aim for parents, and teachers in particular, is to create circumstances where difficult situations do not arise or can be recognized early, forestalled or manoeuvred in order to reduce or contain the anticipated reaction. The ultimate would be building the skill to help AS individuals recognize for themselves their tensions, and to give them tactics and techniques to master such tensions. To find the logic trail, or another logic trail.

Something that can be very useful is to create a distraction. Here one exploits their great curiosity to divert attention and thought away from the difficult situation – starting another logic trail. Parents and teachers could develop a repertoire of possible distraction scenarios to use when crises threaten or occur. These might include a noisy accident like dropping a saucepan, or a loud shout or curse. Or, if you are near the person, to suddenly rush off or to call out loudly to someone else. For any such tactic to be really effective it is important to get to know and be familiar with the child's ways, habits, preferences and dislikes, so that one can notice minor changes and signs earlier. Showing an interest in his activities and giving recognition to his ideas builds trust and acceptance of you. Showing affection and appreciation, although physical contact can be uncomfortable for him, is necessary even if not instinctive.

Using particular aspects of AS people, one can draw them into gaining an awareness of themselves, and this can be used to help them to be aware of how other people read situations and react to particular cues. A particularly useful skill is to help them learn turn-taking in conversation, because they tend to monopolize it and to talk at people.

Another useful skill is for them to give a smile response. They often have to be taught how to smile, and also what various other 'faces' and looks mean. Their smile will always be quite stiff or exaggerated. Little pin-drawings of faces can be useful to illustrate different facial shapes and their meaning.

A most helpful thing in the daily life of AS people is a regular structure and a reliable system of cause and effect. But it needs to be explained and given a rationale. Agreeing a scale of sanctions with the child adds clarity and logic. Writing a day/week flow-chart can be particularly useful. Unspoken rules and conventions can be particular sources of trouble and difficulties. These are so common in school, and need to be deliberately pointed out and reasons for them explained, both in advance and as the situation arises. It is important to forewarn or alert the person with AS to any change of activity pattern or timetable well in advance so he can adjust his logic trail and complete whatever he is doing or create a prepared halt or delay. Changing year classes and schools needs extra preparation.

Keeping an even tone of verbal communication and calmness of speech is also very effective. Ensuring that one obtains the person's attention and directing the communication at him is necessary, as is getting an acknowledgement of the message from the person. Then allow time for him to compute message to action. Eye contact is very poor in children with AS; they seem most uncomfortable when making it so we have to allow for this.

Also significantly helpful can be offering time-out or away from the immediate situation when signs of tension are signalled or recognized or anticipated. Structuring this time-out as a helping task or a specific project with a defined duration can be remarkably effective: sending the child out of the classroom on a necessary errand, for example.

When conducting a disciplinary intervention it is much better to draw the AS person out of the presence of others and address the situation with him on his own, and to do so calmly and in an even tone and pace of speech, addressing one point at a time. Simple? Yes! But we so easily do not do it, forget or get overtaken by instinct and impulse!

These are all quite basic recommendations, but consciously following them consistently is important and reduces drastically the potential for difficulties and troubles.

Now, the second prong: individuals with AS. Most of them will be helped by therapies or lessons that give extra understanding and practice in the difficulties that they have. The aim here is leading them into gaining awareness of themselves; what they find stressful; recognition of the rising tensions in themselves. With these skills the person can then change activity or distance or withdraw himself from the problematic situation.

These lessons also show and teach them skills of being with and interacting with other people, for there are some things that AS prevents them from learning and using naturally: they tend to be vocally monotone and rather non-expressive facially, and because of this other people cannot tell what they are thinking or feeling, and conversely they do not recognize and understand expressions in other people's faces. Lessons can explain how other people react to each other, and help AS individuals to imitate that by using particular gestures, responses, timings and distance between themselves and the others. They can learn to modulate their tone and pace of speech, and learn to turn-take and allow others to express their thoughts and have a point of view. Also that a different point of view is not by definition wrong, and does not imply that *you* are wrong or unworthy. They learn to perform appropriate gestures or expressions for various situations so as to fit in or to trigger positive responses from the other person, or to avoid misunderstanding or offence.

Important also is to get to know the early sensations of tension and anger, so that the person can do something to stop further build-up or to reduce the tension present. One trick some children have learned is to have a reversible badge, or a 'tension thermometer' which they can discreetly extend bit by bit out of a visible pocket, to give a signal to their teacher. Thus the teacher can use tactics to alter the dynamics of the lesson, such as giving the child a task to do away from the existing situation or provocateur.

These children need help, usually the skilled help of a therapist, to enlarge such awareness of themselves. Luckily recognition of AS and knowledge and skill with managing it is enlarging, but perhaps more useful, it allows earlier recognition and interventions, when children are more open to input and less established in unhelpful patterns of reaction and thinking. More exuberantly curious! As for all children, time and experience are the principal tools for the child with AS...only more time and more bruising experience. Eventually a pattern of interests, behaviours, reactions, even thinking is found in which they feel safe, secure, comfortable and functioning, even constructive and fulfilling. Those around them can ease that prolonged evolution by simply being present, being accepting, being consistent, being clear and perhaps firm, by not admonishing, by giving space and listening, and by loving them for *who* they are.

Some children can extend self-awareness by reading on or around the subject. More books are now available in fiction form as well as factual and reference or self-help form. How these are brought into the child's or person's environment needs careful handling. For my son, it was best just to leave a book around. His hunger for reading just about anything was very strong, and was linked with a powerful curiosity about science, facts and explanations. Fiction was never a sound draw; it was often a put-off. So also were any attempts to suggest that a book or article might help him. Dismissing the significance of a text gave it a notable allure to this inquisitive mind.

Change, encountering new things, meeting new and more people, getting things wrong or things not working out are all very challenging to an AS person. No different from anyone else, do I hear you say? Well, no! But the response is likely to be stronger, more intense. More likely to be mystifying or perceived as threatening. Received more as a challenge to their thought and knowledge than as an addition to it. Having choices is often perceived as threatening because the choice made could be the wrong one – dilemma! Getting it wrong just does not, cannot, fit the process, the logic, the person. It is failure – imperfect. Leading on from this is the reality that being in a group, a crowd, a class there is more and more opportunity for getting it wrong, misinterpreting, encountering other views, answers, reactions. The person's mind rebels trying to compute all this into his logic patterns. It all has to fit – but it cannot – bingo, a defensive reaction – usually outburst. It is here that he needs that space; time; quiet support; presence of reliable, consistent others like parents or teachers. He needs his safe, private place and behaviours that help and allow anxiety to be practised, indulged, expressed or simply to exist until it fades or is contained and put aside.

Meeting or encountering other people with AS can be useful. Certainly having some friends is good; a small number is more likely to be more helpful than a whole gang, which they are very unlikely to want to be in because of the potential unpredictabilities and combinations, leading to alterations and change. AS people and children usually long to have a few friends and make much effort to obtain friendship – clumsy, overwhelming, even threatening efforts. Candidates for friendship all too often become uncomfortable, put-off, uninterested and bored by the one-sided, egotistical intensity of the AS person's way of interacting and being a friend. This is sad to witness and to live alongside, for parents in particular. These experiences can ensconce the person even deeper into negative perceptions, aloneness and blocking-out, even into depression. Conversely, positive social activity can be stunning to see: he can absolutely baffle and bemuse those around him with thoughts, knowledge, product and achievement when it goes well.

It is important to understand that none of these suggestions represent 'cures', but children with AS can be helped and shown how to adapt to the ways they live and react, to find a comfortable, happy, meaningful lifestyle. Parents, teachers, others: do not despair. Children with AS normally come through some way, somehow, some when, to a tolerable and liveable life. There will always be a degree of the different, of eccentricity about their aura, their presence. That is *your* challenge: to accept and to enjoy this and them. They have their individualities just as much as you have yours.

If you are a person with AS reading this – well done. Use this not only to help yourself but use it to help those in your daily life to understand what your AS does for you. What you feel and you do and you say influences what others feel, what they do or how they say. We need always to help each other to help each other.

Notes

1   If a young child never engages in pretend play, and if in addition he does not use his index fingers to point at things that interest him, as most toddlers do, then this may indicate that he is at risk for autism spectrum disorders like AS. Parents who are at all concerned about their child should contact their GP or Health Visitor (or relevant local health professional) for information, a diagnosis or reassurance.

2   The complex and often lengthy process of obtaining a Statement of Special Educational Needs in the UK: a legal document issued by the LEA which describes a child's educational needs and sets out how they should be met.

3   National Vocational Qualification: a work-related, competence-based qualification rather than an academic or theoretical one.

Related contacts (see Appendix for full details)

United Kingdom
National Autistic Society
NAS Cymru
NAS Scotland

United States
MAAP Services for Autism and Asperger Syndrome

Books

Attwood, Tony (1998) *Asperger's Syndrome: a guide for parents and professionals.* London: Jessica Kingsley Publishers.
Description, analysis, strategies and case studies for parents, teachers and non-specialists. Outlines clinical aspects and diagnostic criteria as well as a good sense of what it is like experientially for individuals with Asperger Syndrome and for those who interact with them.

Attwood, Tony (2003) *Why does Chris do that?* Shawnee Mission, KS: Autism Asperger Publishing Co.
Practical approach, managing children and adults with autism and AS.

Baron-Cohen, Simon (2004) *The essential difference.* Harmondsworth: Penguin Books.
Director of the Autism Research Centre at Cambridge University explores the difference between male and female brains and explains his 'extreme male brain' theory of autism. Includes descriptions of and insights into Asperger Syndrome.

Boyd, Brenda (2003) *Parenting a child with Asperger Syndrome: 200 tips and strategies.* London: Jessica Kingsley Publishers.
Mother of 13-year-old Kenneth Hall, author of *Asperger Syndrome, the universe and everything.*

Haddon, Mark (2004) *The curious incident of the dog in the night time.* London: Vintage Books.
Poignant, funny and fascinating novel.

Hall, Kenneth (2001) *Asperger Syndrome, the universe and everything.* London: Jessica Kingsley Publishers.
Diagnosed with Asperger Syndrome at the age of eight, Kenneth offers insights, struggles and joys. Parents, siblings, teachers and professionals.

Jackson, Luke (2002) *Freaks, geeks and Asperger Syndrome: A user guide to adolescence.* London: Jessica Kingsley Publishers.
Luke is a 13-year-old drawing from his own experiences – 'so many books written about us, but none are written directly to adolescents with Asperger Syndrome and their parents'.

Lawson, Wendy (2000) *Life behind glass: a personal account of Autism Spectrum Disorder.* London: Jessica Kingsley Publishers.
The author, who has autism but was initially misdiagnosed as schizophrenic, shares her understanding of autism in an attempt to bridge the gap between her world and the reader's.

Lovecky, Deirdre V. (2004) *Different minds: gifted children with AD/HD, Asperger Syndrome, and other learning deficits.* London: Jessica Kingsley Publishers.

Through recognizing the different levels and kinds of giftedness, this book provides an insight into the challenges and benefits specific to gifted children with attention difficulties.

Pyles, Lise (2001) *Hitchhiking through Asperger Syndrome.* London: Jessica Kingsley Publishers.

A parent's perspective with practical ideas on how to calm and help them deal with academic and social demands.

Willey, Liane Holliday (1999) *Pretending to be normal: living with Asperger Syndrome.* London: Jessica Kingsley Publishers.

Based on author's own experience. Appendices provide helpful coping strategies and guidance.

CHAPTER 9

Gifted Adolescents

For children who are gifted in any area, with or without additional special needs, the teenage years can throw their personalities and problems into especially sharp relief. In this they are of course no different from other teenagers, but the nature of their gifts often exacerbates any problems.

The business of adolescence is to make the transition from dependent childhood to independent adulthood, but the process is seldom as straightforward as that statement might make it seem. It is almost always a time of turmoil, see-sawing between advance and regression, accompanied by great intensity of feeling. R.S. Illingworth, Professor of Child Health at the University of Sheffield, described it as the period when a young person dismantles the construction of building blocks acquired during childhood and reassembles them in a way which better defines the emergent, independent self. The process is often slow to complete and subject to intense ups and downs of mood or wild changes of direction. Nor is it a single, once-for-all phase, but a life-long process which could probably be shown in a bell-curve distributed over the individual's life, peaking most commonly in the age-band 12–25 but recurring in a minor way as a normal response to any major life-changing event. It is healthy adaptation, dynamic as long as consciousness lasts.

Three aspects of adolescence

Three interrelated but identifiably separate aspects to the process known as adolescence can be observed. First, there is a process of spiritual, emotional and intellectual individuation, normally accompanied by more introspection than the individual is likely to practise at any other time and by the emotional variety characteristic of the stage. Second, there is a process of physical and sexual maturation, and recognition of one's personal sexual identity. This process often involves physical adventures and experimentation; both in terms of physically challenging sport or travel and in terms of learning about romantic and sexual love and the skills of pair-bonding. Third, there is the process of attaining economic independence and beginning to make a responsible and adequate contribution to one's society.

Most commonly, all three aspects occur at roughly the same period in the life of the individual, although occasionally, for a wide variety of reasons, a particular individual may go through the full process of adolescence in one or two of its aspects outside the normal age-band for such development. Each aspect is stressful both to the individual and to others close to him, and the combination of triple maturation is very stressful indeed.

A few people seem to stop developing and live to a full old age stuck emotionally in their teens. Almost everyone knows someone of whom this is true, but very little is understood about how or why it occurs. As Jean put it: 'I find many of my classmates, now all aged 64 or 65, take frantic and absurdly expensive steps to conceal, even from each other, that we are almost all grey-haired wrinklies.' It could be that in the fast-changing culture of the present era, maintenance of adolescent characteristics is a very valuable tool of social survival – however undignified!

Intellectual and emotional individuation

Adolescence is the time when the individual, consciously or not, faces the existential two-sided question: Who am I? And what implications does the answer to that have for what happens in the rest of my life?

The answers are normally at first defined by contrast and conflict: 'I am not...', often focusing on the minutiae of the behaviour of the family of origin. A significant part of this process is a transfer of loyalty from family to peer group, which may entail considerable experimentation (in which group do I actually belong?). Some young people manage by living their lives in different, non-communicating sectors, like Ravi, who hid his trendy party-going gear in a trunk in a disused garage because he knew his mother would confiscate it if he brought it home. Some are less clear about where they want to be: 'At times', said Tasha, 'I just want to merge into the crowd; at others I want red and green hair and a purple velvet cloak to make me really stand out.' Different arenas, where they can try out how it feels to inhabit a different persona, can be very helpful for arriving at a true definition of individual identity. The definition, however, is determined at least in part by negatives and exacerbated by some degree of anti-family reaction. 'I don't want to be like you: you are boring, predictable, irrational, snobbish' – or many other pejoratives which adolescents regularly throw at their families. Hurt parents may find it hard to recognize the positives in such attitudes: first, that the young person feels safe enough to raise such a rebellion; second, that adolescent idealism is essential to the human drive to make things better. How many lifelong commitments to reform or change are forged during the idealism of adolescence?

Reaching for opposites and extremes is often a part of the journey to arrive at a settled sense of the true self. Thomas, a brilliant all-round academic achiever, was for a while such a determined egalitarian and such a rebel against educational discipline that he rejected all ideas of further qualifications and insisted that he would leave school after GCSE and take a course at a College of Further Education. Having already been defeated in several arguments they had had with him, his parents decided to say nothing, although their concern must have been palpable. Avoiding open disagreement, which might have pushed him into an extreme position, they left it to people outside the family to persuade him to stay at school for A levels, after which he gained an outstanding degree. Nevertheless, his concern for social equality remained, and he chose to live among and work with people less well provided for than himself.

These life-long implications of the decisions made on the basis of the answer to 'Who am I?' may be self-evidently theoretical, or far from self-evident, and indeed often lengthy and painfully practical. 'I am a poet. Fine, what do I need to be a better poet? And in a world in which poets are not well paid for their work how, therefore, do I earn my living?' Viewed in this way, it can be seen that to tie the term adolescence to the years between 12 and 25 is merely a convention arising from the fact that the majority of people in our Western civilization do face these questions most acutely during these years. For teenagers in search of security, yearning to be sure of themselves more than for anything else, the recognition that the answers to 'Who am I?' can only be either trivial or else very tentative – that no answers can ever be fully definitive until the final one, 'Dead' – probably accounts for much of adolescent stress, and may even be a contributory factor in adolescent suicides. It is a moot point how far it actually occurs in all people and how far, in traditional societies where the main existential questions are already answered at birth, one's life being pre-arranged by one's ancestry, it hardly arises. But even within Western contemporary culture, in which adolescence is very widely acknowledged, this questioning process may occur at any age whatever, from 4 years to 70, and beyond.

Extremely delayed adolescence is perhaps most clearly demonstrated in the case of the woman who, having spent her entire life first as a daughter and then as a wife and mother, without independent career or developing strong interests of her own, is widowed once her children are independent adults. She then faces, in the biggest possible way, the adolescent questions, 'Who am I? And what does this mean for the rest of my life?' Many such a widow has startled and both amused and horrified her concerned adult children by displaying a huge range of the symptoms of adolescence which they themselves negotiated several years previously. It can occur in a lesser way following any life-crisis, but is more usual when this crisis involves a lot more leisure than was previously possible. Few women adolesce introspectively in response to the challenge of a new baby; but many men do just that when coping with redundancy, for example. Such major changes in attitude and approach can result in drastic tensions for the family. If Dad is driven by outside circumstances to align himself with, or even go further than, his adolescent children, perhaps adopting a more anarchic, anti-authoritarian position than theirs, then who holds the security in the family?

Gifted adolescents

What is true of adolescents in general is often more acutely the case for the gifted. Their perceptions of truth, justice, rights and rationality are particularly intense, their belief that they know what should be done has probably been hitherto unchallenged. Added to that, their intellectual discussions are often fuelled by strong emotional undercurrents. This argumentative sparring has a deeply personal content, for the gifted adolescent has a particular investment in his cleverness, which may be his passport both to outside affirmation and to self-esteem. So ambition and the natural desire to change conditions for the better may well be turned into rebellion against the rules, structures and expectations currently in place, wherever these can be demonstrated to be irrational or out of date. Very little remains acceptable unless it is personally subscribed to or agreed with. It was only after Helen had experienced and been frustrated by the argumentative chaos of a whole-community debate that she began to modify her contempt of hierarchical committee systems.

Suffering under a confusion of conflicting needs and mixed messages, gifted adolescents may reach maturity by very varied routes, and at varied times. The clarity of their thinking may be constrained by acute sensitivity to other people's needs, making them reluctant to rock the boat. Their over-sensitivity to criticism, especially from their peers, may put severe constraints on their capacity to think and respond divergently. Their speed of perception, which quickly reaches the core of an issue, and their high motivation may give them an arrogant air of over-confidence and impatience with those who are slower to follow their arguments. Generally this is a protective outer shell which conceals a deep need for affirmation from those who have gained their respect. In the face of their critical assertiveness or their apparently wayward adoption of extreme principles, it is sometimes hard for those around them to be patient and accepting. Preparing a special meal for a young friend who argued fiercely with you last year in favour of his vegetarian idealism, it is not a pleasant shock when he tells you airily that he 'gave that up a long time ago'. But even if they are short-lived, we need to recognize that these and similar ideas are seriously undertaken as part of a trying-on-for-size and have their function in defining the emergent, independent person. The ease or difficulty of finding acceptance for their ideas and attitudes will make a considerable difference to how comfortable this stage of growth will be.

Further pressure is experienced by young people who have been isolated up to this point by their difference from their peers and their difficulty in making friends. The transition to emotional autonomy may be much harder without the support of friends of their own age; the isolation and confusion may continue to undermine their self-esteem. It is often only when they reach university that they find themselves in sympathetic surroundings and can at last be more open about their own ideas and feelings. In the meantime, the companionship of an understanding person outside the immediate family may offer a half-way house by giving some degree of separateness. In his last few years at school, Will spent more time with a neighbouring family than with his own, coming and going quite unpredictably. For him it was an opportunity to see how a different family functioned and to experience a different set of attitudes and expectations. His mother made it clear to him, however, that she was not prepared to cater for him separately at all hours, but would simply leave his food for him to have when he came in. This exchange allowed him to take responsibility for his decisions without his mother's worrying about whether he was starving or making too many demands on his friends: being out late at night would mean a cold or reheated dinner, but allowed him the choice of staying on where he was comfortable and interested. The autonomy he was able to build by this and similar instances gave him a true sense of individual identity, where a more rigorous approach ('The meal is on the table at eight o'clock and you must do your mother the courtesy of being there for it.') might have driven him into an extreme of rebellion.

For other gifted young people the social and emotional developmental stage that we call adolescence may not actually coincide with the teenage years at all. Some might work through it between the ages of eight and ten; for many others it will be delayed until they are adults. Very early spiritual and emotional adolescence is probably usually precipitated by some kind of catastrophic breakdown in the child–parent relationship, and it is probably more usual, in the very small proportion of children in which it occurs, among the more intelligent. It is kick-started by an absolutely essential re-evaluation of the child's understanding of his place in the world, at that age substantially defined by the parent. If a trusted parent catastrophically betrays the value-system which that same parent inculcated in the child, even at pre-school age, then the child may be catapulted into the sense of individuation, isolation even, and criticism of his own family which is one of the central attributes of adolescence. If he is lucky, he will almost at once become unusually dependent for the emotional nurture which he needs upon his peer group, again typical of adolescence. If there is no adequate peer group he will seek nurture as and when he can find it, no longer fully trustful of his family of origin. This is of course dangerous: so dangerous that some premature adolescents repress the whole catastrophe, to deal with it at a more traditional age...and with the damage brought about by the repression also.

It seems probable that with the increasing divorce rate amongst families with young children, the extremely-early emotional adolescent will become commoner, and therefore, it is to be hoped, better understood and supported.

Conversely, there appears to be a variety of reasons for a delay in adolescence. Young people may feel restrained by their high moral standards, even when tempted to rebel, or feel pressure to conform in the face of a sibling's extreme rebellion. If they have always had a tendency to question and challenge intellectually, then gifted adolescents may not experience rebellion as such a separate stage as some other young people do. Many gifted people are very good at making intellectual challenges, but not ready to make emotional challenges until way beyond their teens. This will be exacerbated if they have been so busy taking inappropriate responsibility for managing a difficult family situation that they cannot see beyond it until much later; or if they are embroiled in acting out their parents' unresolved issues. A more positive possibility is that the family has always provided a haven for the gifted young person in an otherwise hostile world: in these circumstances it can be especially painful to question, challenge and move away from the family's norms and influences.

It may also involve much more of a personal sacrifice for gifted children than for others, when they begin to transfer their allegiance to their peers, away from their parents. If they can see, for instance, that it is socially desirable to be a member of the 'in' group then they may also be able to see that the only way to achieve this social status is by failing to achieve any academic status. Adult disappointment in the 'waste' that this represents will then be added to the pressures in their lives. Some other gifted children, with different person-alities, choose deliberately to stay on the edge of the crowd. Others will keep pushing, if they don't encounter any boundaries, until they hit the ultimate boundary of the law. As in every other aspect of their lives, for gifted people these choices are made more acute by their heightened awareness of all the factors and ramifications of the decisions involved.

Towards economic independence

The need to be independent and in control, so constantly reiterated through adolescence, lies uneasily with a recognition, probably only semi-conscious, of some degree of continuing dependence on the family, even if only practical and financial. For some highly sensitive young people it creates a potentially damaging, self-destructive conflict. It is not surprising, in this context, that disproportionately many young people with eating disorders are reported to be highly intelligent. While comfort eating may represent a self-pampering response to stress ('I love me and give myself treats even if nobody else does') bulimia and anorexia represent a subconsciously self-destructive approach whose root position is 'I really don't deserve to be alive.'

In contrast to the teenaged adolescent who resents her continuing dependence, many orphaned or otherwise parent-deprived children, throughout history, have been forced by harsh circumstances to premature economic independence. Children from poor economic situations who are forced to undertake such adult tasks as mining, carpet-manufacture and brick-making very often have foreshortened lives, and in those lives much of the normal play-element of growing up may be replaced by the use of narcotics. Children who are thus forced into premature responsibility will, as soon as they get opportunity, have such a drive that one may consider it an actual need to become irresponsible youngsters, even several decades on.

Working as a Child Care Officer among West Indian families in Birmingham, one of our group found during the 1960s and 1970s that numerous girls from the age of about nine years were habitually left to care for younger siblings. The parents were out at work or out at play for most of everyone's waking life. On investigation nearly all of the hard-playing mothers had themselves been left to raise younger siblings at a very early age. They had no time whatsoever for fun: they ran their households and cared for the little ones, struggled with their school work – success in which was very highly regarded in their communities – and almost always dropped exhausted into bed late each night, with very little personal pleasure or satisfaction in the day's doings. For them, growing up meant becoming big enough and tough enough to seize their proper share of fun.

Physical and sexual maturation

The infamous adolescent mood swings are generated in part by physical changes and the often confused self-consciousness which comes from developing sexuality, but sexual or relationship maturity also occurs in a much wider age-range than is commonly supposed. Their progress into equal pair-relationships may well be slow, painful and mistake-ridden.

As a very rough rule of thumb every school-teacher knows that the more academically gifted the child, the greater the likelihood that 'romance and sex and all that stuff' will be delayed, often by conscious willpower, until the youthful academic has leisure to attend to it, but many a potential professor has had his or her academic edge blunted at a critical time by inconveniently raging hormones! It is not at all uncommon for both men and women of high intelligence to delay serious pair-bonding and procreation until early in their fourth decade, despite having been in most cases physically capable of reproduction for over half their lifetime. A few are simply too fascinated by other matters to develop that aspect of their lives at all, and in that particular sense bypass adolescence more or less completely.

Adolescence and the family

If adolescence is confusing for young people, it is also confusing for their families. Demands on them may see-saw in utterly bewildering ways: 'You never listen to me' / 'Why can't you leave me alone?'; 'Why don't you support what I want to do?' / 'Stop interfering with my choices [of friend, course, leisure activity]' and so on. At the same time, paradoxically, parental authority and all the shortcomings and illogicality of parental attitudes and behaviour are often fiercely challenged. The thinking skills developed by gifted adolescents often make those challenges very threatening. Working on the assumption, learned in their own growing up but up to now unquestioned, that parents set the rules and children keep to them until they leave home, Vijay and Sara were taken aback by Shantha's logical demolition of their position. Because they felt obliged to maintain the rules for the sake of their younger children, they suffered an atmosphere of scorn and hostility from Shantha until she finally left to go to university.

The confusion and disappointment is even more upsetting when what is being criticized has been undertaken for the sake of the children themselves. Rick and Jodi took their three children on camping holidays in Europe as often as they could afford it, to introduce them to as wide a variety as possible of western culture. 'Boring!' snorted 15-year-old Ben dismissively, 'We never stop anywhere long enough to get the feel of what it is like to live in a place.' Rick and Jodi felt really hurt. Opportunities for foreign travel were rare when they were growing up, so they had hoped that their expenditure of money and energy in planning an extended tour of France and Spain would be a real treat for their children. Instead it seemed to be thrown back at them as yet another example of their getting it wrong. It was quite hard for them to stand far enough back from the situation to recognize that, even so, they were providing an invaluable opportunity for Ben, in allowing him to assess what was happening and consider how he would like to change it. ('I don't want a superficial look at these places, concerned with museums, art galleries and buildings. I want to know what it is like to live and belong in these communities.')

The situation is further complicated when there are younger children in the family as well. Could Rick and Jodi afford to keep patiently quiet about such attacks if they felt it would undermine their upbringing of his younger siblings? How much should they insist on general family rules, not simply of politeness and consideration but, more importantly, of safety and health? It is much harder to avoid confrontation if Mum and Dad are aware that their 8- and 11-year-olds are listening in to the argument about being back home by a set time or always letting them know where they are going. It is not always easy to balance the freedom demanded by an older child against the security needed by younger ones. When Francesca's brother started planning to leave home to take a training course, she was desperately upset at what she perceived as the break-up of the family; at the age of six, she had assumed that they would stay together for ever. It took time and patient explanation from her parents before she could accept that the emotional link with her brother was still in place even if the physical link was broken.

Sometimes a rebellious adolescent can seem very like a larger, stronger and more articulate version of a toddler in a tantrum. And it is indeed true that the discrepancy between intellectual and emotional development which we have already noticed in gifted children may still be in play, giving rise to sharp contradictions between a demand for complete independence and an urgent need for protection. If their parents can manage not to demand consistency, but respond as well as possible to the current situation, then they may manage the transition to integrated adult more easily.

By contrast, sensitive and mature young people may find themselves at an embarrassing advantage in social understanding. Bella, living in a small house with her widowed mother, made a habit of getting up early to take her mother breakfast in bed. Although she gained gratitude and approval for being so considerate, she was very uncomfortable at knowing that she really did it because she wanted her own space in the morning. To be praised for her thoughtfulness when she recognized that she was manipulating the situation to her own advantage gave her a distorted sense of her own power.

In the face of the emotional, social and intellectual turbulence which their adolescent children are going through, it is important for parents to maintain their own independence and sense of values, even while recognizing that they can no longer impose them. It is for the young people themselves to decide which parts of their upbringing they accept and which they need to move away from. It can also be very reassuring for a volatile young person to find that his parents represent a fixed point in a confusing world, holding specific standards and expectations, welcoming him with warmth and concern while respecting his right to autonomy.

Sometimes it helps to step briefly out of the parental role and remember one's own adolescence. Sometimes referring back to an older generation will show a reassuring pattern of development. A grandmother who talks about rebelling against her mother can give a sense that this is part of a natural progression rather than a terrible failure of parenting. As Martin Amis remarked, you only learn to forgive your parents when you become a parent yourself. There is a school of counselling called Transactional Analysis and this, astonishingly, has room for parent, adult and child as perpetual parts of the mature individual, but makes no overt role for the perpetual adolescent in all of us. It is from people of any age able to contact their own inner adolescent that the richest and most complex intergenerational relationships come, very often to the profound delight and satisfaction of all parties. The inner adolescent within the parent is both a source of strength and a tremendous danger in living alongside adolescent offspring – and vice versa.

In general parents need to recognize that it is not their role to be companions and friends for their adolescent children, who need their affirmation from people outside the family and closer to their own age. It may sometimes seem, indeed, as though the parents' role is simply to be wrong and to provide a force to react against. But in the longer term, even if sometimes this process may take 20 or 30 years, the balance will redress itself as the parents learn to let go of their children and accept them as adult individuals, and when the young adults come to recognize how much they owe to the family they grew up in.

Related contacts (see Appendix for full details)

United Kingdom
@ease
Contact Youth
Muslim Youth Helpline
NAGC YouthAgency
National Academy for Gifted and Talented Youth
Rethink
Rethink Northern Ireland
Samaritans
Young Minds
Young NCB

United States
American Academy of Child and Adolescent Psychiatry

Books

Adderholdt, Miriam and Goldberg, Jan (1999) *What's bad about being too good?*
    Minneapolis, MN: Free Spirit Publishing.
Explains the differences between healthy ambition and unhealthy perfectionism and gives strategies for getting out of the perfectionism trap. Gives adults insight into how their behaviour and expectations can contribute to perfectionism in teens they parent and teach.

Apter, Terri (2002) *The myth of maturity: what teenagers need from parents to become adults.*
New York: Norton.

Common adolescent issues: lack of freedom, concern over physical appearance, irritability.

Armstrong, Thomas (2002) *You're smarter than you think: a kid's guide to multiple intelligences.* Minneapolis, MN: Free Spirit Publishing.

Helps kids understand Gardner's theory of multiple intelligences, what it means to them, and how to make the most of their own abilities and potential.

Delisle, Jim and Galbraith, Judy (1996) *The gifted kids' survival guide: a teen handbook.* Minneapolis, MN: Free Spirit Publishing.

Written with help from hundreds of gifted teenagers, includes facts about giftedness; IQ tests; how to take charge of their lives and their education; how to build healthy relationships.

Waddell, Margot (2005) *Understanding 12–14-year-olds.* London: Jessica Kingsley Publishers.

Practical advice for parents to help them relate to and communicate with their child.

CHAPTER 10

What is it Like to be a Gifted Linguist?

In contrast to the compound problems of gifted children with special needs, in this chapter and the two that follow we explore the very particular issues that crop up for children who are gifted linguists; those who are more multi-talented; and those who are especially creative.

From birth Wesley was very sensitive to sound and rhythm, responding to speech, singing and silence according to mood. This had its disadvantages: he screamed at the buzz of his father's electric razor, and even when he was four his mother was obliged to wait until he was out of the house before she used the vacuum cleaner. But at 15 months he came home from the child-minder's and produced a lengthy pattern of apparently undecipherable sound. Listening carefully, his family realized that this was a complete rhythmic rendition of Baa baa, black sheep. His delight when they joined in was palpable.

From then on, new words enchanted him. He was happy to repeat that an object with six sides was hexagonal or that his beans had gone down his oesophagus. By the age of three he was enjoying counting from 1 to 20 in French as well as English, and when his family went on holiday to France he enjoyed using basic French phrases. One day a little later he heard his mother singing an Italian song. 'What does 'no, no, no' mean?' he asked. It was the Italian for no, she replied, 'So now you know how to say no in English, French *and* Italian.' Wesley's next question was, 'Yes, but how do the French say the Italian for no?' He was already working, it seems, on the transferability of meaning, an idea that is essential to any accurate rendering of one language into another.

Obviously, children who grow up in a situation where they are exposed to more than one language, living in a foreign country or with parents who have different first languages, are at an advantage here. They can learn very early that there are different ways of saying things according to the language being used and that there are barriers when people do not understand what is being said.

Freddie, born in South America when his English parents were working there, learnt Spanish as his first language and determinedly kept to it on their return to England 18 months later. As he gradually picked up English, he found he was better able to converse with his grandparents who, it seemed, didn't know his mother tongue. One day his father came into the room when his grandparents were talking to him. Courteously the three-year-old turned and translated into Spanish for his Dad: 'Yayo dice que...' [Grandad says that...]. Later, when his father had a posting to French-speaking Africa, Freddie was somewhat resistant to learning French. Trying to encourage him, his grandmother remarked how odd it was of the French to call toes 'foot fingers'. 'Oh,' he said, brightening up, 'that's just how they say it in Spanish, too.' So the idea of closely related families of languages became a reality to him, and he was able to manage very well at the age of six in a French-speaking school.

In some immigrant families the children actually become translators, especially for their mothers, at an early age. This and the burden of bridging two different cultures may put considerable emotional pressures on them or bring about heightened family tension in adolescence. Which culture do they actually belong to, and what compromises can they make?

On a more positive note, the knowledge that such varied ways of speaking exist and can be applied more and more subtly offers all sorts of possibilities to bright young people. A secret code, like Molly's private diary which was written in Greek characters, kept her schoolmates from deciphering her personal writings. Codes fascinate many gifted children: Russian, Chinese and so on have the attraction of having difficult writing systems. More demandingly, the accurate use of another language in transferring ideas between cultures may become a fascination. Indeed the delight of producing a polished and precise translation may be life-long. Even at the age of 80, a professor of chemistry took great pleasure in making elegant translations of an Italian poem into German, French and English.

There is a sense in which scientific precision meets cultural understanding and creative problem-solving in the work of a linguistic translator. Certainly the learning of different languages demands close attention to meaning, both in formal structure and in idiom, requiring accuracy of thought as well as expression. In general contact with other people this may turn out to be a disadvantage, since gifted youngsters may resist saying anything in a foreign language unless they know it to be correct, thus making for a very restricted exchange when they are abroad. On the other hand, knowing precisely what you want to say and saying it clearly, whatever language you are using, is an extremely valuable skill. Many gifted young people say that they have only come to understand the use of English grammar after learning a foreign language where the grammar is formally taught. By contrast, many British pupils who were introduced to Latin through the Cambridge Latin Project have spoken of their bewilderment at not being allowed access to conjugations and declensions at the start. Only after the curious endings of words in different situations have been explained as, for example, a genitive plural or a future third person singular, has the mystery suddenly become available to analysis and reuse.

Language skills, however highly developed, should be recognized as a technique or vehicle, similar to good draughtsmanship or technical expertise in playing a musical instrument; they are no more than a means to an end. Without a living content, creative or communicative, they are little more humanly satisfying than solving a complex crossword puzzle.

CHAPTER 11

Managing the Multi-talented Child

In contrast to children who have specific gifts like a linguistic talent, which may not be matched in some other academic areas, some children are identified at school as multi-talented: their outstanding performance covers most aspects of the curriculum. Quick to absorb ideas and methods, they seem to acquire an instant command of almost every subject put in front of them. Their early reasoning skills, coupled with a real excitement about ideas, open doors to them across the whole sweep of the school day. Similarly, their acute sensitivity to people and situations often gives them an understanding of and access to the heights and depths of human experience from a very early age.

These characteristics offer a broad base from which they are able to pursue virtually any subject. When curriculum options come into play, these children often face acutely difficult decisions. The choices they make may well depend on both temperament and chance. Those who are more absorbed by the mental discipline of rational argument may be inclined to specialize in history, philosophy or theology. Literature and drama may, on the other hand, be more appealing to those whose sensitivity to human concerns is the main driving force of their personality. The excitement of building hypotheses from precisely collected data, an absorption in the wonders of the natural world or a fascination with the orderly logic of number draws others into science or mathematics. On the other hand, there is no hard and fast division between these positions. This means that an inspiring teacher, an unexpected opportunity or simply increasing emotional maturity may bring about a change of course or choice.

There are indeed people who continue to change course or focus throughout their lives. Professor Joseph Needham, a brilliant biologist, became in later life the foremost authority on the history of science and civilization in China. At a more day-to-day level it is not uncommon for undergraduates to feel the need to move out of one course into another. As Keri put it, 'I'm really glad to have changed from chemistry to history of science, because I so much enjoy writing essays again.' Setting out in detail a considered argument had always been a pleasure to her, but she had been persuaded to choose a science degree course by one of her schoolteachers whom she much admired.

In reality she could successfully have steered either course, and chose one over the other simply on the perfectly understandable basis that a mentor advised it. A different personality might have reacted more contrarily to the same circumstances, as father and daughter Joe and Gwen both did, in turn, at school. Joe was taken aside by his physical chemistry teacher before confirming his sixth-form[1] options: despite the fact that Joe was far and away the strongest student that this teacher had at the time, he counselled Joe very seriously to consider a change of direction towards the arts, where he felt that Joe's true talents lay. Joe, raised in the culture of a boys' grammar school[2] in which science was perceived as the superior intellectual option, dismissed his teacher's advice out of hand. Then, in his thirties, after a successful spell as a civil engineer, he bought a small business and went on to demonstrate what a gifted entrepreneur he also was.

During this period, he unknowingly had a life-changing conversation with his seven-year-old daughter, Gwen: 'Daddy, what's a university? [Joe explains.] Are there lots of universities? [Yes.] Which is the best? [Joe opines that traditionally Oxford has been seen as the best for arts subjects, and Cambridge for maths or science.] Well then, I shall go to Cambridge to do maths.' Gwen never wavered from this decision, and when making her own sixth-form choices she utterly rejected both the advice of her religious education teacher to move towards the arts, where he felt that her true gifts lay, and the implorings of her English teacher to do that subject at A level. Only once she had realized that her school did not offer the further maths that she would need for Cambridge did she decide that the place was more important than the subject, and switch her ambitions to philosophy, a subject in which she gained a very good degree.

Clearly, motivation is often the key in such decisions, and from a very early age. At three, Sasha was insistent that she wanted to learn the piano. Finally her mother sat her down to show her how to finger a simple tune. Sasha was contemptuous: 'Teach me a scale!' So Mum taught her C Major. 'Next, I want to learn B Major,' demanded Sasha, 'and then A Major', thus correcting her mother's alphabetically irrational starting point. But why such urgency to learn scales? Because it was the pattern she regularly heard when her elder sister and brother did their practising, so she believed that it would save her from being classed with her one-year-old sister, as a baby. The early impetus stayed with her, and after gaining a good degree in history she became a professional musician.

What shines out from cases like Keri's, Sasha's, Gwen's and Joe's is that such multi-talented individuals can in fact be highly successful in, and gain great enjoyment and satisfaction from, any one of a number of fields. It just does not seem accurate to say that Keri got it wrong when she made her initial decision to study chemistry, that Joe should never have gone into engineering, that Gwen wasted her time on mathematics or Sasha hers on history. What all these young people had in common was a highly unusual level of focus, applied quite successfully to a particular area for a particular time, from which each gained much in the way of experience, skills, self-knowledge and indeed enjoyment. Later they all changed their focus, not because they had got it wrong in the first place, but because their gifts were equally applicable in a very different area.

Thus it is vitally important for such multi-talented children to keep their curriculum as broad and their options as open as possible, in order to allow them the freedom to discover all of the different areas to which their gifts might be applied. They need a wide spread of subjects to enable them to make the links and juxtapositions that illuminate or emphasize a new approach to a problem. What matters for such young people is not so much the subject-specific data as the acquiring of sound thinking skills, the organization of material for an argument, the ability to identify links or trends and to make conceptual or creative leaps. Their thinking skills need affirmation, nourishment and challenge to enable them to check their data, for example, before developing an hypothesis.

This last point highlights once more the vital distinction between giftedness and emotional maturity. One A level student became very distressed by Nostradamus's prediction that the world would end at the millennium, until it was pointed out to him that the current hypothesis rested on a mistranslation of the original into English. What continued to be a preoccupation for him, as it is for many adolescents, was the urgent desire to transform a world in which he saw so much to be at fault. Idealism, the desire to create a brave new world, needs careful fostering while it measures itself against the realities of living, for being gifted does not guarantee that a young person will know at 13, at 16 or even at 21 what is the best way of using his abilities. The more creative of them may need a hard-earned emotional maturity before they can accept the acute personal risk of exposing their highly original and creative ideas to the external world.

Notes

1   Sixth form is the equivalent of grades 11 and 12 in the US.
2   A grammar school is a selective secondary school.

CHAPTER 12

Giftedness and Creativity: Some Pointers

Once giftedness has been identified in a child, there is often a strong impetus to seek constant achievement. This is regularly characterized as 'stretching him' or 'helping her to reach her potential'. Of course there are important motivators here. If parents have campaigned, struggled and made sacrifices to provide what they believe to be an appropriate education for their child, then they may well need the reinforcement of being proved right by brilliant results. If schools or individual teachers have worked hard to offer provision for their gifted pupils, over and above the demands of the general curriculum, then they may need to see such extra effort translated into results which reflect credit on the school. Having made so great an investment, both parents and teachers can be frustrated by what appears to them to be day-dreaming or time-wasting by the child in question.

In a culture in which the strongest emphasis is placed on setting and monitoring ever more demanding targets in standards and productivity, the prospect of a brilliant young person staring out of the window or lying on the sofa switching television channels may seem an affront to those who have worked so hard to open up opportunities for progress. The knee-jerk reaction is to deal with it by scolding or by the provision of even more activity. But it might be wise to try and find out a little more about what is going on behind that apparently abstracted façade. 'You're not listening to me, are you?' said the doctor to six-year-old Lim, who had come to the clinic for a crucial audiology test. He was staring out of the window at the rain-drenched car park. 'No', he replied. Very quietly, she continued, 'What are you looking at, then?' For the first time, Lim looked at her directly. 'I'm trying to work out what will happen when a car drives through that great big puddle by the gate.' Thus, at the eleventh hour, she established that he did not need to have his adenoids removed and grommets fitted in his ears.

Similarly, it can be frustrating for parents when their children respond with mischievous creativity to work that is too easy for them. Especially when parents are involved in what feels like a battle with the school to have their child's giftedness accepted, it can be maddening in the extreme when a bored child plays games with the work set, rather than aiming to do as well as possible. Five-year-old Henry had an eye for spelling: once, when he spelt 'aeroplane' correctly without prompting, his father's congratulations were greeted with the scathing response, 'But I've *seen* it written down, Daddy.' He created his own fun with the spellings that his teacher gave him to learn (two and three-letter words, week after week), by pretending not to know the answer and seeing how many ways he could get each one wrong. Distraction can arise as easily as abstraction from the needs of a creative mind.

In this way, apparent inactivity can often conceal a mind at work on ideas or concerns that may have little to do with the current curriculum. On the occasions when Aaron, generally conformist and a high achiever, became very distressed at the idea of going to school, his mother negotiated that she should be allowed to keep him at home. His 'sickness' was the urgent need to write down the music which flooded, quite unpredictably, into his mind. By the age of 12 he had already produced five string quartets and a cello sonata worthy of public performance. He was fortunate in having a mother and a school who recognized the need for creativity to be allowed space or quiet gestation time.

As well as space, however, creativity needs contact, because it is essentially communicative. What is created is not complete until it is in some way acknowledged or received. This interaction inevitably produces a series of tensions between the creating individual and the perceiving receiver; between novelty and frame of reference; between discipline and freedom; between being different enough to be interesting or enlightening but not so different as to be incomprehensible.

The first need is for a secure and culturally rich base. Breadth is essential because it is in the nature of creativity to be diverse and divergent: what is central for one pupil with one particular interest becomes peripheral for another with a different focus or talent. In secondary schooling, with its range of subject specialisms, such diversity is easier to offer than in primary schools, where it would be unreasonable to expect teachers to be conversant with all the likely enthusiasms of lively-minded 10- and 11-year-olds. In any case the ethos must surely be not to know more than the highly creative pupil but to know where to find and offer access to more.

Cultural richness must include access to a wide variety of material, instruments and equipment: artistic, musical, scientific, technological and sporting. It is a serious question how to ensure that these are available to the whole population, not just to those whose families have sufficient financial and cultural advantages to offer opportunities outside school or within the right independent school. It must be true that the best way to develop a climate in which creativity is acceptable is to offer appropriate creative opportunities to the whole school population.

For many children the tension between achievement and acceptability is intolerable. The stark choice is to be isolated and creative or join the crowd and suffer frustration. True differentiation, which celebrates each individual child's achievement in relation to his own aptitudes and abilities, is undoubtedly the best strategy for avoiding the worst of such distress. A combination of affirmation and challenge is likely to be the most successful approach. Knowing how and when to offer either is a creative skill in teaching, as is recognizing when a pupil needs internal space rather than pressure to achieve. A dangerous trend in current education policies is the heavy emphasis on end-products. The best creative enterprise defines its own end-product rather than having it pre-determined.

But for such processes teachers also need their own space to reflect on and integrate their reactions and understanding, before deciding what is the most appropriate action. How does one assess the productivity of time spent on thinking? The current tangible-result-orientated ethos militates against it. If education is genuinely to foster creativity then it has to be an open-ended process which enables the individual to reach outwards from a secure base. Some pupils will find fertile enough ground outside formal education, but this can in no way be seen as adequate provision or enabling the whole school population. Without opportunities and a sub-culture that celebrates diversity, there is limited scope for pupils to realize their creative potential. Although equipment and resources play their part, the prime requirement is for time, for both teachers and pupils to be in touch with their inner selves. Busyness, in terms of an overcrowded curriculum or an excess of administrative work, is one of the worst enemies of this process.

CHAPTER 13

Musically Gifted Children

Amongst our group we have been privileged to have a music counsellor of immense talent and insight, the late Michal Hambourg, an Honorary Fellow of Trinity College of Music. A distinguished pianist in her own right as well as being the daughter of the pianist Mark Hambourg, Michal came from a family that rejoiced in a rare depth and breadth of musicianship and creativity. She was once described as the last living link to major nineteenth-century traditions, having spent her childhood in the daily presence of great composers and performers. As a performer herself she appeared at the Proms and during the war at National Gallery recitals, as well as on the BBC as soloist and in radio dramas.

The contents of this chapter are taken from a combination of a talk that Michal gave to The Guild of Pastoral Psychology on 4 February 1993, 'Living in Music', and an article that she wrote for the Incorporated Society of Musicians' Music Journal, *'Crisis at 21 or Earlier', October 1985, pp.107–10. We are grateful to both of these organizations for allowing us to reproduce Michal's words here, as it allows us to hear Michal speaking in her own voice about the needs of musically gifted children. This is a subject to which she brought a unique discernment and level of personal experience, which would be lost if presented in anything other than the most personal terms. The only comment that we would add is that parents of children whose gifts lie outside music will nonetheless be able to see, from her words, that the same thread runs through all areas of giftedness: the need to be valued, to be understood and to be heard.*

For many years I have been working with talented musicians and their families, with age groups 2 to 20 onwards. I am very much interested in all areas of musical education for everybody. I want as many people as possible to love and enjoy music, and fortunately there are many areas today in which their interest can be encouraged. My own special field is in maintaining those who are born with an unusually high quality of talent. Contrary to the opinion that these children will achieve under any circumstances, they need a degree of caring and understanding which is not always available and which, in my opinion, must be offered in order that they can be given the confidence to achieve, instead of losing heart and giving up.

So, I am going to talk to you now of the true world of music, of human communication in this world, and of the pressing needs of our young and talented musicians for certain kinds of musicianly encouragement.

I would like to tell you how I came to be involved in this particular branch of music, as it bears some relevance to the nature of my work. I had a most privileged and nourishing musical childhood, in a large and distinguished musical family. My father's eight brothers and sisters all had a high degree of talent, and on his side of the family there have been musicians for many generations. As a 15-year-old boy, my father himself was toasted by Brahms: 'To the talented boy we have heard tonight. He will go far.' My mother was a pupil of the great Ysaye and came from a background of accomplished musical amateurs all involved in various kinds of music-making. From my earliest memories, our home was full of music and musicians.

As the fortunate possessor of an inherited musical talent, imagine the bliss for me! I had the exhilarating experience of living and learning in an environment which was totally congenial and stimulating. Many of the great musicians of those days were my parents' friends, and they actually had time for me! – very small and aspiring who played Bach and Mozart to them and was showered with advice, criticism and occasionally a word or two of praise. Those evenings were vibrant with a special kind of conversation, centred around a great tank of inherited musical ideas, many of which were handed down from artist to artist since the time of Beethoven. This cornucopia of ideas is sometimes called the living link and forms the basis of all my own offerings in music. In getting to know the core of great musical masterpieces, those who preceded us had endless experiences to offer us, and we can learn endlessly from their musical concepts.

I want to say here that all musical children should have the widest available experience of hearing great artists both past and present. Sadly I have heard it said that it is not a good idea to listen to interpretations other than one's own, on account of the temptation to plagiarize; I say here with some vehemence that music is a vast and great art. It is only by hearing and digesting every possible interpretation and combination of sound, including the voice, that one grows into making an interpretation of one's own; this also will alter through the years, as the experience of music broadens and deepens.

The standards of my own childhood world were exacting. It was taken for granted that practice, and the working disciplines allied to it, were a part of everyday life. I spent many hours perfecting technique and learning the notes of the masterworks composed for my instrument. The motivation was powerful as everyone in our home had one central purpose: to interpret great music to the best of our ability, and to share the enjoyment and love of this marvellous art whenever we could and with everyone who wished to listen.

How incredibly fortunate I was! My present work for young people has brought home to me that giftedness is usually associated with loneliness. Owing to those early days music is still the most powerful and exhilarating force in my life. It is a great, vital and potent art. I speak about it in these terms because I have noticed, with some sadness, that for many of us it has become trapped in stereotyped fashions which have become rigid and un-nourishing.

For me, as time went on and I grew older, the constant travel and public performance that is associated with a life in music began to get exhausting; also I began to hear the 'deeper note' within. I needed to be silent for a while and to wait. In the silence I began to consider the needs of young musicians, and of musical people, and to wonder if I could make a contribution to them. I quote here from an article by Martin Turner, Educational Psychologist, which influenced me at that time (Turner 1982):

> In his later years the philosopher Karl Popper put forward his scheme of 'three worlds'. Events are of three kinds and may occur in the three different realms proper to them. 'World one' is the physical world of objects and energies, the world studied by physicists. 'World two' is the psychological world, the world of human potentialities and dimensions, and 'World three' is the arena of culture, the world of ideas, theories, cultural artefacts and creations. In place of the ancient blood-letting, our ideas – our cultural creations – stand and suffer in our stead, our theories bear the attacks of criticism, and truth is born – or dies.
>
> Giftedness is an event in 'World two'. It is a human psychological potentiality. Without its rebirth into 'World three', without transformation into cultural achievement, it is of no more value than the gleam of Narcissus in the pool. We infer from giftedness in children an achievement in prospect: we acknowledge giftedness in adults by achievement in retrospect, regardless of what unprepossessing children they once made!

I went to hear many concerts, and became aware of a trend in musical performance which caused me to feel very anxious about the future of serious music and serious musicians. I heard many concerts presented by young artists of excellent technical expertise – notes were not a problem – but musical communication and its life-giving message was not present. The effect was of a series of mathematical problems, brilliantly presented by the players as evidence of considerable physical skill and mental agility.

I began talking to children and young people about their music-making and their work in other fields of education. I come from a large family and have two sons of my own, so that it was possible to talk with these young people in an informal way in my own home, or wherever we happened to meet. What I heard gave cause for deep concern, and I resolved to try and share my own experience as best I could, particularly to inspire confidence in the *personal* and imaginative quality of interpretation.

My place, I felt, was to be a part of the everyday musical scene, available to children and their families in my own home and anywhere else that was needed. I have always lived and worked amongst artists of outstanding gifts; I know them to be difficult, complex, prickly and suspicious, and I love them very much! I though that if I could manage to communicate with children of this nature, and from the earliest age, I might then be in a position to understand the failure of many such children to realize their musical potential and vision.

In view of my findings, I am not going to talk about techniques, for it appears to me that much of the practical aspect of musical talent is well catered for. We have splendid youth orchestras and excellent provision in schools and colleges for learning the necessary disciplines. It is the creative area of our music that we need to consider, and here I am going to quote from an article by the outstanding musical educator, Gladys Puttick (in Simpson 1976).

> The philosophy underlying my principles is based on the conviction that music can be taught, learnt and used as a language for the expression of musical ideas. As the 'mother tongue' is absorbed in early years, much of it 'caught' rather than 'taught', so can the language of music be similarly absorbed, whereas to separate its elements into isolated theoretical exercises produces a false division in the pupil's mind between musical literacy and practical music-making. In the musicianship class the materials of music are presented in logical orderly sequence, but in a

creative context, in which the student is encouraged to express his musical ideas in response to stimulus provided by the teacher. This response is guided in such a way that literacy develops almost unconsciously in the course of attempts to express musical ideas and make them intelligible to other musicians. The creative satisfaction resulting from an approach which encourages imaginative expression is felt by both student and teacher. Indeed, in adopting these principles, the teacher finds his own musical imagination stimulated in a way that allows him to continue to develop as a musician – important both as a personal fulfilment and in the imaginative guidance of his pupil's work.

I feel that this enlightened approach is particularly significant, in view of the needs of the young people who come to see me. During my sessions with the children many touching and interesting things have been confided to me, and from these confidences I will now discuss some of the ways in which we can alleviate the problems.

We all need assurance of our worth from the moment of our birth, and a great deal of early turn-off stems from our lack of attention when children attempt to share their ideas with us. We *must* be open to them, and remember that talented persons aged four are capable of conversation and discussion about everything in which they are interested. Babies aged three or four months respond to rhythm, one of the basic elements of life. Young children who listen to music cannot stand loud sounds, perpetual noise or continual background music. They love to sing and dance and try to play instruments; these activities should be encouraged but not pushed. In the early development of creativity the artist is born, and the first awareness of music is an intensely private and exploring experience. Opportunities to encourage the sharing of this experience must be made, but at this stage nurturing affection and interest are the first requirement.

Most musical children are ready to begin lessons around the age of five; their hands and muscles are very small and delicate and there must be a minimum of tension in this early work. These little ones like to know the 'why' of everything; they need us to answer their questions so that they can relate the information to their own ideas. These small children are very serious in their attitude to learning but it *must* be related to their own world. Many gifted children are aware from the earliest age of the difficulty of communicating. These children tend to disguise themselves in order to conform. They often develop quite a high degree of technical skill and then get bored by it. They all enjoy improvization and exploration of chords, and relating little phrases to each other. I cannot emphasize too strongly the importance of a rich and varied musical experience for them, as I have met several talented eight-year-olds who have refused to continue as they are so 'bored'!

I do feel it would help to have a panel of concerned and experienced musicians whom parents could consult and who would advise on individual needs. The true musician will not be able to keep away from his instrument, and he may need to experiment before he finds the one which is truly for him. What is essential is the opportunity to listen and become familiar with all kinds of music. Musical children need musical libraries. When a child is truly talented he will read music very soon; it is often easier for such a child to read music, which has immediate meaning, than words. I remember when I was about eight years old reading the Preludes and Fugues and Inventions of Bach, trying the early sonatas of Beethoven and Mozart, playing anything I could find. This was my fun, quite separate from my daily practice, which was the beginning of my musical disciplines and which received careful help. Children of seven to eight should not work for more than one hour daily divided into two periods. In developing the powers of concentration great care should be taken to avoid fatigue. Another necessity is time for quiet. Young musicians need a quiet place where they can think about music, or listen to the radio and hi-fi on their own. I call this growing up in music; it is a basic part of the musical way of life, and talent is inhibited when the need for this is not acknowledged.

When children grow older, they enjoy being taken to concerts and especially to hear other young people. In musical children the quality and concentration in listening is deeper than average and they can become exhausted or over-stimulated by too much exposure. For them music is not a drug and *must* remain full of meaning. To musically sensitive children the powerful sounds of the orchestra can be unbearable. When music is the centre of emotion in their lives they sometimes find that they cannot endure the things that music reveals. I particularly remember a little girl aged five who simply could not listen and burst into tears, because she said that music made her feel so dreadfully sad.

Gifted children are *not* popular. We all feel threatened by them, mainly I suspect because of their incredible energy, their infinite capacity for absorbing information, and the originality of their concepts. But we must be open to their amazing insights and ideas; we must listen to them and bravely enter into their world, and give them confidence in it. Then they will feel trusting enough to become a part of ours.

It is a revelation to hear a musical child talking confidentially about music; the inner world of such a child is vibrant with colours and sounds, very often special notes and keys to which they relate personally.

Music is a vast conversation piece for these children – keys and notes becoming dear friends, very often before the age of six! As I sit in my room with a child, seemingly glum and subdued, we begin tentatively to talk about music starting with the making of sounds and the use of our arms and fingers to explore the different intervals and suddenly I find myself sharing in an extraordinary private world of musical ideas where there can be real communication irrespective of age grouping. It is very clear to me that we should offer and *must* devise creative musical exchanges from earliest possible times for these children; I know it is not beyond us to make a bridge by listening seriously and caringly to musical ideas, thus reinforcing confidence by admitting to their existence.

Many gifted children are outstanding in all fields. When they begin their primary education they tend to disguise their abilities in order not to seem different, but they often feel able to express some of their ideas in music. When I see these children, I am careful to try and discover the best possible place in their timetable for their musical education, and particularly to avoid any form of early specialisation. When we respect the creative element of music in the development of such children, they are better able to cope with the academic pressures which tend to be their lot. We must be careful to keep options open, and not to mistake facility and skill for talent rooted in musicality. This is a delicate area, as so many young people can only see their career in music as performers. When I tell you that these children show great brilliance, memory capacity and speed in thinking, you can see how easy it is to point them in the wrong direction. If you ask what the criterion is for making decisions in such a sensitive area, I would say as a predominant factor, evidence of the capacity to listen to yourself whilst playing. This capacity is an integral part of true musicianship – it is difficult to describe. It is as if an internal monitor, part of the self and intensely involved, is communicating as part of a homogeneous process. When we are focused on technical reproduction, this monitor cuts out and performance is centred on the notes, producing a mechanical expertise, thus losing the inner meaning.

Specialist musicians who come to see me suffer from various forms of aridity, mostly arising from the dichotomy of intellect from emotion; musicians in the 12 to 20 age group have many anxieties. They dry up on stage or in examinations. They suffer from terror and nightmares related to insecurity and loss of memory. They can't concentrate – they don't feel like practising – they are doing their GCSE and A levels and feel exhausted! But above all – and I hear this so often – 'the music has no meaning'. This is a cry from the heart and cannot be ignored or fobbed off. Here is a talented musician saying *help*.

Let us consider the meaning of this great art in which we all have the honour to be involved. In serious music we recognize and experience our deepest longings, aspirations and feelings. We touch upon love and suffering and majesty, on the human condition, and the amazing natural world. No wonder that my young musical friends are distressed at feeling separated from such a source of nourishment! Learning to play an instrument, to write music, to read notation and scores are essential parts of our musical disciplines, but we cannot use these as we should unless we respect our musical selves and allow them living space. In adolescence a whole new set of problems occur, centred on an extending range of feelings and emotions. As we know, very young children rarely suffer from nervous anxiety when playing to audiences. The majority love performing and showing, in a delightful way, what they can achieve. Almost overnight around the age of twelve, young people begin to feel nervous. It is as though a new awareness was thrust upon them. At this time they really should not be exposed to frequent concert playing: they need and want to say more, and to say it more ably. They are becoming aware of a much deeper approach to musical life. Something in them realizes that there is a far wider musical perspective before them, and that they are going to interpret a whole world of ideas and emotions, which as yet they do not know.

Provided that there is real affection and encouragement, these young musicians do love to work and learn. We know that a tremendous amount of study and dedication is necessary in order to achieve, and when other people are listening they add an extra and stimulating dimension. It is important to play to friends and family and selected audiences, but public performance in big concert halls is a testing experience and in my opinion, during the adolescent years of study and preparation, it must be very carefully planned. Another life-giving area of communication lies in talking with others who know and love music.

Differences can be explained in sound which might take years to explain in words! We *must* talk to our young musicians about many subjects, musical and otherwise. We have to help them to realize the responsibility of becoming the bridge between music and the listener. To foster this understanding, we must foster their confidence as *individuals*, encouraging them to express musical thought, and above all to listen to the phrasing as they play. *Artists spend a lifetime in perfecting this intense form of concentration.* When a musician is under stress, it is most destructive to 'play out the feelings' in music. It is a negation of interpretation. The therapy is to be helped to find the way back to the return of musical integrity via consideration of the composer's ideas, and thus to the revival of creative activity.

These thoughts are the outcome of many confidential and lengthy talks with young and musically gifted people over many years. Nearly all of them have brought a problem relating to creativity, and the need for richer curriculums. I offer a few final suggestions which I hope we can all consider in the light of my findings.

First it is helpful to discuss the best deployment of practising time, and to do this frequently so as to become aware of the beginnings of early tensions.

Second we must frequently discuss and listen to the great masterpieces, and when the pupil is ready to learn them explain the available resources to be called upon, relating these to the composer's ideas, to style and to the period when they were composed.

Third we must be particularly careful not to present gifted and sensitive young artists to the public in situations of stress, and in working conditions which are beyond their power to sustain. Amongst these I mention the highly publicized competitions which are a feature of musical life today. I was happy to have been one of the group of concerned musicians who worked together on the ESTA Report, *Music Competitions.* You see, I think it is appalling that some of these competitions (which are as tough as anything which took place in the contests of the ancient world) are part of the battle of the television ratings, impossibly trying to compete with successful soap operas! How can we judge musical talent by first, second and third placements as in the Olympic Games? Music *cannot* be about winning places – surely it is about communication in depth. The whole crisis of musical young people is poignantly summed up by Stevie Smith in the lines, 'I was too far out, all my life, not waving – but drowning.'

I know that the thoughts I have been sharing with you concern areas with which we are all familiar. I have brought them to your notice as it appears to me that we are inclined to neglect pastoral care and the deeper musical levels, and to concentrate on specifically specialized training at the expense of the whole person. It is my conviction that we need to provide a more balanced approach, in order to develop in our young artists the necessary resilience to maintain and enjoy a very taxing profession, and to develop into maturity.

We have a wealth of talent in this country and we must nurture it in all dimensions so that the great message of music remains vital and alive for us all. I myself work daily at the piano in order to keep always in touch with the great dimensions and the proportion of truth in music. My main concern is to find the place of music in the lives of all those who love and need it, and to encourage them to be brave and open to patterns of creative musical thought.

References

Simpson, K. (ed.) (1976) *Some great music educators: a collection of essays.* Borough Green: Novello.

Includes an article by Gladys Puttick, a pioneering spirit at Junior Trinity who championed creative musicianship at a time when it was not fashionable. We are grateful to Anne Cassal for helping us to track down the source of Michal's quotation from this article by Anne's late mother.

Turner, M. (c. 1982) 'Still gifted at nineteen?' *Newsletter of the National Association for Gifted Children.*

We are grateful to Martin Turner for helping us to track down the source of Michal's quotation from his article, which appeared in the NAGC's Newsletter in the early 1980s.

Related contacts
Trinity College of Music

Junior Trinity
King Charles Court
Old Royal Naval College
Greenwich
London SE10 9JF
Tel. 020 8305 4328
email junior@tcm.ac.uk
www.tcm.ac.uk

Creative musicianship classes for 5–18-year-olds. The students explore music as a personal language.

Other courses are offered at:
Birmingham Conservatoire

Tel. 0121 331 5901/5902
www.conservatoire.uce.ac.uk

Guildhall School of Music and Drama
Tel. 020 7382 7160
www.gsmd.ac.uk

Royal College of Music
Tel. 020 7591 4334
www.rcm.ac.uk

Royal Northern College of Music (RNCM)
Tel. 0161 907 5264
www.rncm.ac.uk

Royal Scottish Academy of Music and Drama (RSAMD)
Tel. 0141 832 4101
www.rsamd.ac.uk/juniordept

Specialist music schools include:
Chethams School of Music
Tel. 0161 834 9644
www.chethams.com

Dublin Institute of Technology Conservatory of Music and Drama
Tel. 353 1402 7815
www.dit.ie

Purcell School of Music
Tel. 01293 331100
www.purcell-school.org

St Mary's Music School
Tel. 0131 538 7766
www.st-marys-music-school.co.uk

The Yehudi Menuhin School
Tel. 01932 584403
www.yehudimenuhinschool.co.uk

CHAPTER 14

Effective Communication: The Way We Say It

Of all the issues that affect gifted children – those with special needs or specific talents; both within and outside the family; at school or in home education – perhaps none has such far-reaching consequences as the problem of communication. How can they and their families most effectively communicate, with each other as well as with the outside world? In this chapter Catherine Shaw visits communication in relation to giftedness. She relates her knowledge as Interpersonal Communication Skills Teacher, Assertiveness Trainer and Community Mediator to her experiences of counselling gifted children and their families. Using case studies she shows how effective communication has made a difference to individual experience, and explores a ten-step checklist of key communication assets. Communication itself is a huge subject: it is visited in this fashion here in order to show the impact of effective communication on experience and outcome with respect to gifted children's needs.

We live in a world where conformity and uniformness have great influence and where those who do conform may receive apparent, short-term benefit. There is a cost however, and the cost can be high – on the individual, the family and society as a whole.

The needs of the gifted child and the needs of parents of gifted children are different from the norm and although there may be pressure to fit in, whether in the long term or the short term, no-one benefits if it is fitting in at the cost of a loss of self-worth.

Although being different can be a double-edged sword and can be a decidedly positive experience, it may also be a cause of isolation and disconnectedness and can lead to fundamental needs remaining unfulfilled.

This can have an impact on self-esteem, ideas of who we think we are, the choices we make, how we experience our lives and how we live in the world. In a nutshell being different from the crowd can be stressful and challenging.

The manner in which this difference gets expressed can cause confusion and unhappy experience, or it can generate satisfaction and inspiration. Sometimes children may need encouragement to express their experience, and they may need to have reassurances of safety and acceptance first.

There is an innate value in difference and individuality; we are not all the same. To use a culinary analogy, compare the stir fry to the same ingredients being liquidized into an unrecognizable mush. The stir fry allows the richness of diverse colour, texture and taste to be recognized and appreciated. Each element, clear in its uniqueness, contributes to the richness of the whole.

Within the world of the gifted – as individuals, young people, parents and others concerned to support our children – the aim is to define our voice, to allow for our richness to be expressed and to satisfy the personal need for happiness.

When a child sees differently, is aware of more or other than he is normally expected to be aware of as a child, it can be a painful and confusing experience. The child may also have expectations, conscious or unconscious, of others around him, which may bring up a sense of powerlessness, isolation and fear, particularly if the person involved is an adult or person in authority. Validating the child's experience, perception and feelings can be a gift we can give to the child to help growth, understanding and moving on. It can be difficult to do this as a caring adult, if one is feeling stuck oneself.

Each person has her own internal map of the world which is a basic design from which we live our lives. It is made up of our beliefs, interpretations, perceptions, knowledge, experience, interests, focus, drives, frames of reference and so on; basically what we consider to be in the world, how we think the world operates and ourselves in relation to it all.

When internal maps differ from person to person, group to group, difficulties can arise. The gifted child's internal map very often differs in aspects that others don't have at all in their frame of reference, and therefore there is no intrinsic awareness or understanding of the gifted child's experience or needs. The challenge is to share territory in a way that generates understanding and is respectful of all. It can be met through effective communication.

For some meeting this challenge may be natural, while for others it may entail developing skills and practising different or new styles of communication.

Sharing territory successfully entails a dance between connecting with ourselves, or helping our children to connect with themselves, and connecting with others. All of the following steps are involved in connecting with self and connecting with others.

The topics are intended as an introduction, pointers, or as suggested areas to explore in greater depth as required or desired. They are not covered in fullness here, but please refer to the Related contacts at the end of this chapter for further resources.

Step 1: Identify needs

We may not always be aware of what our underlying needs and the needs of our children are. Sometimes when we are aware, we don't always know how to express them in a way that others can understand. Sometimes, even with our best efforts, we may not be heard by the people we want to hear us. Sometimes it might be necessary for us to help others hear us and help them understand our needs. For a mutually satisfying exchange it is necessary to offer recognition of the other person's needs too.

Underlying needs are universal, such as the need for respect, understanding, support, authenticity, self-worth, peace. Talking through issues with someone you trust and feel safe with can help clarify the underlying need. In attempting to recognize and identify needs, it is likely that feelings will be involved as well. Most feelings arise in response to needs satisfied or needs unfulfilled.

Step 2: Recognize and acknowledge emotion

Emotions are a natural aspect of human experience and expression. It hinders the process to criticize or judge feelings, so practising acceptance, allowance and validation facilitates the moving on process.

Identifying the feeling helps the communication flow.

John, a gifted seven-year-old unhappy at school, hit the nail on the head for himself when he expressed the pressure he felt to conform: 'They want me to be an oak tree like the rest of the trees in the forest but I'm not a tree I'm a frog, a big brown, jumping frog who has lots of ideas and needs to jump around a lot.' John, who had a natural charm in his style of expression, took it upon himself to tell his teacher how he felt. The teacher was sympathetic and with the added support of communication between parent and school, and new appropriate strategies in place, John was able to settle in himself. Later he decided actually he was a mountain. Through expressing himself and sharing his feelings he arrived at the enlightened awareness that no matter what anybody else thought of him, he had the power to define himself. John's frustration had partly been that he felt expected to be like everyone else; realizing that it was okay for him to be different, and that he could communicate with the appropriate person who could hear him and accept his difference by taking on board his needs, gave him a sense of value, place and freedom to be.

Step 3: Listen

Be aware of when you are genuinely able to listen and when you are not. Are you listening to yourself? How are you listening to others? When listening to others, rather than just hearing the words they are saying, listen for the feelings they are expressing, and listen for their needs as well as hearing their words. Listening in this way helps cut to the core of the issues and enables understanding. If you miss the mark it usually doesn't matter, as often the person will appreciate your effort of connecting and will clarify for you.

Step 4: Include awareness of non-verbal expression

We communicate through our facial expression, body posture, gestures and so on, as well as through use of language. When listening to others, include listening to and observing their non-verbal signals. Be aware that we sometimes leak out expression through non-verbal channels. If the leakage is not congruent with what we are saying verbally, it can cause confusion and possible breakdown in communication if it is not clarified. So, for example, if you are feeling uncomfortable about saying something, it may be helpful to disclose this is how you are feeling, so the other person is clear and then doesn't misinterpret any non-verbal signals you may be displaying unawares. Non-verbal signals can give clues about what a person may be feeling.

Step 5: Express understanding

In a mutual dance of sharing territory, it is helpful to express your understanding of the other's experience, viewpoint and need. When you have listened effectively, reflect back to the person what you have heard and understood, including perceived feelings and needs. Phrases such as, 'Can I tell you what I've understood from what you've just said…?' or 'Let me see if I've understood you…' can lead you into the reflection. If you are checking out your perception of their feelings and needs, remember to ask rather than tell. For example, say '*Are you* feeling frustrated because you have a need to complete your work?' rather than '*You are* feeling frustrated…'

Mark, a gifted six-year-old, told his mother that he didn't want to go to school any more. His mother felt exasperated, as she thought she had successfully negotiated with the school regarding Mark's academic needs, which had caused unhappiness previously and now seemed to be fulfilled. She felt at a loss. Her frustration made it difficult for her to enter into Mark's world of experience at that time, and explore what was going on for him. She was aware of not being able to help him and fortunately was able to ask me for help.

It seemed to me that he was in turmoil. Sometimes it's helpful to make simple observations and make tentative enquiries as to whether what we see is accurate. 'I see you smile when you talk about your homework and I saw your head turn away when you said you didn't want to go to that school anymore, and I am wondering whether there are some things that you are happy with at school and some things you are unhappy about, and it is difficult to feel both at once. Is that right?'

Having his feelings validated and understood enabled him to express his unhappiness in more detail. It seemed he felt angry particularly with the headteacher, and felt choked up with things he wanted to say to her but couldn't because he was fearful of her being bigger than him.

We got a teddy out and put it on the sofa and I asked him to imagine teddy was the headteacher and he was allowed to say exactly what he wanted and do exactly what he wanted. With gleeful expression he told teddy/headteacher that she shouldn't have that job and should leave and let someone else come who was better. He expressed anger and frustration at an incident where he had perceived the headteacher treating another pupil in a way that offended Mark's feelings and need for someone in an authority role to treat others with respect. Telling the teacher just what he thought of her in a safe way gave him a release, and he began to wonder why the teacher had behaved that way. I suggested he might ask teddy that and imagine what the headteacher might say. He came up with the suggestion that the teacher was tired and was having a bad day, and that although he didn't like what had been done he could understand tiredness and bad days. Thus he came to an acceptance of his own feelings and realized that the teacher was human and he could allow her to have off-days too, although he would prefer to have someone in charge who didn't hurt his feelings. Offering understanding and expression of feelings was enough for Mark to resolve things within himself without having to communicate with the offending party. Mark returned to school relieved in himself; he had come to terms with the situation and was subsequently happy.

Step 6: Ask for what you need and want

Making clear requests increases the likelihood of needs being met. Ask for specific actions. For example, asking teenagers to put their shoes away when they come home is more specific than asking them to clear up after themselves. Remember that asking for something is just that – asking – it is a request, so phrase it in terms of a request, for example, 'Would you be willing to…?'

A request also allows the other person the freedom to choose their response, which creates respect. The response may well be a yes, or it may be no or an expression of their own related need, such as a need for relaxation. When you make a request and don't get an immediate yes, welcome this as an opportunity to deepen your understanding of the other person's needs, and an opportunity for mutual fulfilment; be willing to explore this with them. What sometimes appears immediately as a conflict in needs can usually be negotiated in a way that allows for mutual satisfaction (see Step 9).

Step 7: Use clear language

When expressing yourself use the word 'I'. For example, 'I feel delighted'; 'I need a rest.' There is a phrase adopted in common usage: 'you make me feel…' Avoid using this. It can sound like blame and impedes respectful communication. When we own our feelings and needs, others find it easier to hear. There may be all kinds of causes for our feelings. If you want to relate your feelings to something another person has said or done, it can be more useful to say 'When you… I feel…because I have a need for…' This can then be followed by a request: 'Would you be willing to…?' Avoid using the word 'should': this implies no choice, which can be disempowering. It can be replaced by the word 'could' or 'would'.

> At 14, Sam was happy with his friends at school, happy with the level of work he was being given for his high academic needs, yet also very depressed and was beginning to have complaints come home from school about his aggressive behaviour to certain teachers. He was struggling with the fact that he felt certain teachers weren't acknowledging his need for respect of his opinions and views. He expected teachers to be more aware than him and be able to behave in a way he was struggling to behave himself. He felt a lack of role models and guidance and understanding in people he expected to know better, and felt powerless and frustrated. Validating his feelings and experience allowed him to be open to my coaching him about how he could express himself differently. He felt unsafe about expressing his vulnerability to a particular teacher, whom actually he quite admired, and yet

he felt let down because this teacher wasn't able to help him in the way he wanted to be helped. We explored how he might express his feelings differently to the teacher, and practised specific communication styles and skills including taking responsibility for his feelings, expressing his needs clearly and making clear requests. When he was ready to ask the teacher for a tutorial he was able to carry through and communicate in the ways we had explored, calmly and openly, and as he was also able to share his sense of vulnerability, the teacher's attitude to him changed. Sam felt listened to and noticed the teacher being more understanding of Sam's struggle; little by little trust developed between them, and the teacher who Sam had previously had most difficulty with became the person Sam turned to, to talk to and share his frustrations with, and ultimately became Sam's mentor.

Step 8: Ask others what they need and want

If others aren't forthcoming with expressing their needs, ask them. Don't assume you know what is important to other people – ask them. Ask them what they need, what they want, what they would like to happen, what is important to them in regard to the situation. This allows them the opportunity to reflect if they haven't already, it allows them to clarify and it creates a sense of equality in an interchange where you may be expressing your needs and wants.

Step 9: Believe and act in accordance with a win/win outcome

If we allow ourselves to be influenced by the competitive lose/win, or win/lose approach in our communication, then relationships and desired outcomes suffer. Respecting oneself and respecting others and communicating in a way that creates an outcome that satisfies both parties is not necessarily an easy art when we are dealing with different internal maps; however, it is possible through the practice of win/win orientated negotiation skills. In a nutshell, this involves clear self-expression of feelings and needs; a willingness to hear and accept others' feelings and needs and motivation to create mutually satisfying solutions.

Step 10: Express gratitude and appreciation

When we are having difficulties it is easy to focus on the challenge and forget to give attention to what is already working and what we are happy about. Remember to express gratitude and appreciation. Let others know when your need has been fulfilled by their words or actions. For instance, 'When I reflect

on [the action of the other person], I feel…because it fulfils my need for…'
Focus on the positive: what we focus on expands.

> At six years old, Isaiah was an exceptionally talented drawer. He loved to draw buildings that demonstrated perspective way beyond his years, yet his work was never displayed at school and his mother, Maya, felt he was being ignored in class. When she had been to talk with his teacher previously she had come away feeling frustrated and dismissed and nothing changed. When we reviewed the conversation Maya had had with the teacher, Maya realized she had been fearful of not being taken seriously and recognized that she may have come across as demanding and determined to get her own way, with little consideration of the teacher's viewpoint. Maya attended a subsequent meeting where she was careful to ask for the teacher's view and to listen to it and reflect; this opened up discussion where it came to light that Isaiah was struggling to speak much English at all (English was not his primary language) and consequently the teacher was herself struggling to meet Isaiah's basic educational needs.
>
> On understanding this, Maya took it upon herself to give some regular time with Isaiah after school helping him improve his English. The teacher, for her part, clearly took on board Maya's points, as Isaiah began to return home excited about new friends, with a growing confidence about his schoolwork and pride in his artwork now displayed around the school. Maya was so delighted with the change in her son's demeanour that she returned to express her appreciation to the teacher. By the end of the term Isaiah had led the 'Care and Share' assembly by showing his favourite drawings, and Maya enjoyed the new sense of partnership she felt with the teacher and school.

A voice for the needs of gifted children has begun to be defined, which heralds the possibility of living with those needs met. As gifted children, parents of gifted children or as people involved with working with gifted children in any way, we are part of the river of change. We can use our voices and encourage our children to use theirs in a respectful and effective manner that honours all difference. It is not always easy being at this stage. It means we may also be part of the struggle, which can be frustrating when it is natural and understandable to want everything to be sorted now so that your child could benefit from different awareness. If that were the case we would be living in a different world. So, frustrations are understandable. The above skills can take time to practise and master. They are worth the effort, for they are transferable skills in all situations in all aspects of life. They contribute to making the journey easier and more satisfactory.

PART 3

Conclusions

CHAPTER 15

Living with Giftedness

We opened our book with a question: how does it feel to describe your child as gifted? The emotions involved may well be very different, depending on whether your child is to be called gifted in private or in public. It may be that a parent is able to admit to himself that his child is gifted, and that this admission brings with it feelings of pride and happiness as well as some fears and uncertainties. Indeed we hope that our book has gone some way towards helping you to feel more comfortable about making this admission to yourself. What has become apparent in the course of the preceding chapters, however, is that it is often much more difficult for parents to admit openly to others that their child is gifted, or even to feel certain whether or not they wish to make such an admission. We want to end, therefore, on a note of optimism: it is possible to find a comfortable place for your child's giftedness, in your own life as well as your child's.

Hostility towards giftedness

It is not difficult to find the root of the obstacles that face gifted people and their parents when they find themselves in a situation where they might be prompted to talk about their own or their children's gifts. The greatest obstacle is fear of the reaction that could be provoked: jealousy; rejection; being judged as boastful or arrogant. 'Oh dear,' said a shopkeeper to four-year-old Wayne's father when the little boy correctly read some notices in her shop, 'You'll not be popular when he goes to school.' Nor did shop assistants always respond kindly to his habit of telling them how much change Daddy would need, before they had even totted up the items in his shopping basket. But why should they have had such a hostile response?

There is amongst the British in particular a peculiar inverted snobbery in which academic prowess, or indeed unusual success in any non-sporting field, is seen as elitist. As a result it is seen as acceptable and even admirably anti-elitist to mock people who are different in these ways. Negative stereotypes like the mad professor, the perpetual student and the pushy parent go unchallenged in a way that would be unthinkable if applied to other minorities. Yet how can gifted individuals and their families begin to connect with wider society when such images persist? If being gifted really meant being deprived of a childhood and social skills, having no common sense and using academia as a substitute for gainful employment, then who would want to be put into that box?

Perhaps even more inhibiting than such stereotypes is the risk of being seen as a threat; as being supposed to think oneself better than them. From the first occasion on which gifted infants are seen to reach milestones early, their parents pick up looks and hostile responses from others with children of a similar age. Kelly was her parents' first child and so they had no idea that her behaviour at ten months was unusual; but they soon found out from other parents' reactions to Kelly's sitting up in her pram looking meaningfully at a book, turning the pages and making noises of recognition. It wasn't long before her mother started to take Kelly's books away if they were going to a toddler group. The parents of Patrick and Connor, who could walk when holding an adult's hands from the ages of five and four months respectively, have memories of physically pinning them down in order to avoid fielding the reactions of parents whose similarly aged children could barely sit up without support.

These are not pleasant memories: their parents can recall feelings of isolation and of wanting at all costs to avoid being thought boastful. They remember the rush of protectiveness that led them to want to hide their child's gifts, to make the other person feel better and to ease a difficult social situation. We must be open about the fact that there is a genuine problem here with parental competition and jealousy. As parents, particularly of our first child, we are often acutely aware of when our children should have reached certain milestones and we want our child to be the one who reaches them first. The problem is that when we fail to acknowledge these feelings, we can end up resenting other people's children when they attain certain competences early.

> When have you experienced or feared these sorts of reactions to your child's gifts?
>
> What effect did it have on your own behaviour at the time?

Jealousy is provoked when one person, or a group of people, has something that another desires, such as wealth, power or fame. One of the things that parents desire is for their children to be seen as doing well, which means, implicitly or explicitly, a bit better than other people's. From a very early age, our babies are measured against a set of common criteria which are very clear-cut: your child either walks earlier than mine or she does not; she can sit up first or she cannot; she has more teeth or fewer than mine. More than this, in the West at least these are not just common criteria but supposed *standards*: your baby is later than she *should be* in sitting up; my child is an *early* reader; and so on. At this crucial stage of development, both for the babies and for us as parents, we find that our children are constantly being judged against others – and that we care very much about the outcome.

Why are some gifts more acceptable than others?

In this context it is worth reflecting on the fact that not all differences provoke the same sorts of emotions. If Tessa's nephew has shown from an early age the potential to be the next Brian Lara or Sol Campbell, but her own same-aged son has no aptitude for sport and she has little interest in it either, then she may feel quite at ease about this difference between them. Conversely, if Tessa's nephew consistently reached infant milestones before her son and has continued to outstrip him academically throughout their school careers, then she may care very much about this difference between them: it might cause her to feel resentment, jealousy and hostility towards her nephew and his parents. Sport might not be Tessa's little boy's thing, but how can her nephew do well at school without the implication that his cousin has done not so well? If both are playing the same game, then one cannot win without the other losing: if most infants are expected to walk at around 12 months old, then it can be hard to avoid the conclusion that the one who walked at 10 months is better than the one who walked at 14 months.

Yet it is possible for us to accept with insouciance some quite extreme differences between ourselves and others, or between our children and theirs, if they are differences in areas about which we do not care, or if they are differences that we perceive as non-threatening. Successful footballers, famous pop stars or celebrity gardeners are admired and idolized rather than resented; whereas successful businessmen are fat cats, famous politicians are derided and 'intellectual' is rarely a compliment. Why should this be? Perhaps because money, power and brains are seen as possessions to be coveted because they give someone an advantage over others; whereas great sporting or musical talent is seen not only as unattainable by the majority, but also as something quite separate from most people's daily lives.

Of course in every area there will be some people for whom others' achievements are painful: if you long to be able to paint the perfect picture, to be a famous actor or to become a judo dan, then you might well resent the talents of great artists, the adulation that film stars receive or the skills of world-class judoists, even though most people feel neutral about these things. For the majority of people, these activities are so distant from their own lives that others' successes in them offer no threat.

The crucial distinction, then, is between what other people *have* and what they *do*. I am jealous of what you *have*, because it feels as if your ownership gives you an advantage over me. In contrast I am able to admire what you *do*, because I do something different, so we are not in competition with each other. Thus Tessa's nephew's footballing ability is acceptable to her because her son doesn't do that; but his intellectual gifts are not, because they give him an advantage over her son. For the same reasons, celebrities can simultaneously be admired by many people for their sporting or musical achievements, and resented by many more for their wealth and fame. The former set them aside from ordinary people whose jobs are unrelated to football or singing; the latter give them unfair advantages over those same people.

What, then, of intellectual gifts? Into which category do they fall: possession or skill? Unfortunately for gifted people and their families, the common perception is that intellectual gifts are possessions: giftedness is something that they *have* which gives them advantages over others, just as some people have unfair amounts of money or power. Being clever isn't like being good at sport or music: it's something that we're *all* meant to be able to do; something that we all want for ourselves and our children. More than this, it is something that is constantly measured, from birth throughout childhood, and all mainstream children are measured against the same scale. If your child can chatter in paragraphs before mine can put two words together then it is hard to deny that this attainment gap represents an advantage over mine – and into that gap creep the first tentacles of my resentment.

> Do you think that anyone has ever felt jealous of you or your child because of her gifts?

Conversely, just as we have to be open about the fact that many parents feel jealous of gifted children, so we must admit that the parents of gifted children can find it well-nigh impossible to avoid comparing their child with others. Sensing that their own child has reached the key milestones early, copes with key tasks more easily, or is simply brighter than the other, they begin to feel invaded by other people's reactions to these differences: to feel the need to protect and compensate for the other person; to take steps to avoid being seen as bragging; to show that they do not think themselves any better than the norm.

Responsibility and choices

Part of the problem here is that these parents are taking inappropriate responsibility for other people's feelings. First, it must be said that the other person may not be feeling any of the things that the gifted child's parent is projecting on to her. Second, even if she is feeling inadequate and resentful, the gifted child's parent is not responsible for those emotions. Rather, they are a product of that individual's reaction to the differences between the two children, which may itself be at least partly the product of the British climate of inverted snobbery. The gifted child's parent has no control over any of these things.

When Martin joined in with a dinner-party conversation about restaurant hygiene he mentioned two contrasting Chinese restaurants in Oxford, and was momentarily floored by the bitter reaction of one of the other guests, a woman whom he barely knew: 'So is that where you went to university? Well – that must look good on your C.V.' Clearly Martin had done nothing to provoke this woman's bitterness, which was something that she had brought to the conversation and over which he had no control. Fortunately, he was able to realize that since he was not responsible for her feelings, nor was he responsible for soothing them away or trying to compensate for them. After a pause to collect himself, therefore, he merely smiled and moved the conversation in a different direction.

What Martin's experience shows is that although he had no control over this woman's response to him, he did have control over his own response to her. He could have given a provocative reply, or alternatively he could have denied the advantages of an Oxbridge degree and engaged in a futile attempt to bolster a relative stranger's self-esteem. Instead he chose to avoid the issue altogether; and this is always an option.

What is also clear about Martin, though, is that his decision about how to react was rooted in a very secure self-image. He was able to make a choice about the nature of his response (combative vs. apologetic vs. moving-swiftly-on) because he knows that he is a highly advantaged person and takes no pleasure in other people's feelings of inadequacy or jealousy about that fact. Thus he might engage with similarly confident people in a robust debate about the merits of automatically awarding MAs to Oxbridge graduates, or stress the very real value that he puts on his sister-in-law's gifts as a carer, in contrast to her own feelings of intellectual inferiority; but prefers not to be drawn into conflicts arising from other people's hostility to his gifts and achievements.

Parents, too, can make choices about the ways in which they respond to other people's emotions and behaviour. There are three separate elements to any social interaction in which their child's giftedness might be raised. First, there is the fact of the matter: their child is gifted, which makes her different from most other children. Second, they bring to the conversation their *own* feelings about this difference. Third, the other person's reaction will stem from *his* feelings about it. It is vital for these parents, if they are to make helpful decisions about their responses, that they are able to distinguish between the elements for which they are responsible and those for which they are not.

Obviously they are not responsible for the situation itself, but it does help if they can be clear about what is happening. Like Martin, they will only be in a position to see and choose between their potential responses to other people, if they first have confidence in their own assessment of their child. How can this confidence be attained? Parents can be aided in their quest by what, in Chapter 4, we described as a 'safe place' in which they and their children can be heard: a situation in which they feel that someone has listened to their point of view, taken it seriously and helped them to check it against reality. Gifted children's parents might find this safe space with a partner or friend, or they might feel able to seek a safe place with a professional listener, or to make contact with other parents of gifted children. If they do not feel heard – if on the contrary they feel undermined, doubted and isolated – then it is much more difficult for gifted children's parents to make real choices about their response to others. Instead they may feel driven to attempt to convince others of her gifts; or conversely to conceal them as much as possible in a defeated silence.

Ultimately, then, it is their own feelings about the situation which will determine how these parents communicate about it. Only for their own feelings, not for the situation and certainly not for other people's emotions, do they bear any responsibility; and only once they are secure in their own understanding of their child will it be

> You know your child better than anyone else does. Have you recognized him or her in the descriptions that our book has offered?
>
> How confident do you feel about your understanding of your child's differences?

possible for them to make choices about how they deal with other people's reactions to her gifts. As parents, then, they must learn to trust their own instincts about their child. It is our hope that parents who have recognized their child in the descriptions or case studies that our book has offered – whose family's experiences have been reflected here; whose gut tells them that there is something different and exceptional about their child – will feel more able now to accept a private, internal description of their child as gifted, exceptional, highly able, very clever or whatever phrase feels most comfortable.

The power of language

Armed with confidence in their own understanding of their child's differences, parents are more able to stand back from other people's reactions to those differences: to see that it is not their job to change or compensate for other people's feelings of hostility, jealousy or inadequacy. Their only job is to decide how to respond to the behaviour that results from those feelings: both how to lessen their chances of provoking them in the first place and how to deal with situations in which they are unavoidable.

Not everyone will care very much about the sorts of feelings that they provoke in others. Some gifted people and their parents will feel able to say with conviction that other people's emotions are their problem: whilst not wishing deliberately to upset anybody, nor are they prepared to treat the whole world with kid gloves. Clearly, the degree to which other people's behaviour impacts upon our own feelings and reactions will be different for each one of us. There are many other people who will wish to avoid conflict of this sort, and to this end one of the most powerful tools available to gifted children and their families is language. Many gifted people, both children and adults, are in the privileged position of having command over a variety of conversational registers and the ability to choose between them. They will be greatly aided, in selecting from a variety of potential responses, by an increased understanding of what sorts of emotion each option is likely to provoke. In particular, it can be useful to understand the difference between a *comparative* and a *descriptive* use of language.

If I use broad labels for my child, like gifted or even clever or talented, then it will be hard for you to avoid hearing, by implication, a comparison with your child who is *less* gifted or clever or talented than mine. If, on the other hand, I use specific descriptions of what my child is like, such as 'good at reading' or 'really keen on football', then I leave space for your specific descriptions of your own child. No comparison need be implied, because the areas in which I am describing my child may be irrelevant to yours.

As with any other minority group, this is not about denying the differences. 'Gifted' is still a useful shorthand for all the varied characteristics and idiosyncrasies that have been covered in our book, and there are real differences between what is normal for a gifted child and what is normal for the majority of children. As noted, admitting this fact – accepting the differences in ourselves or our children – is a crucial first step towards finding a place for those differences in our lives and deciding how to communicate about them. Similarly, seeing giftedness as one amongst many societal differences can help people to acknowledge that it *is* a gift: not earned, and certainly not a virtue – think about what horrors can result when high intelligence is grievously misused.

The aim is simply to focus on what each of us *does* rather than what each of us *has*. People who have a great deal of something, be it money, intelligence or anything else, are only at an advantage in the areas to which that thing is relevant. If what you do is different from what I do, then it is unimportant that I am at an advantage in the things that I do. You don't do those things, so what does it matter?

Realism and optimism

Obviously it is important not to over-simplify the complex issues involved here. There is nothing to be gained from pretending that intelligence is not advantageous in most situations. Jealousy of others' advantages is a natural human reaction and not always avoidable. The point is, rather, that we do have choices about how to communicate, and the non-comparative option is one that is less likely than others to provoke such hostility.

Thus, just as two mothers can have a perfectly equitable conversation about the fact that Jack plays hockey and Jill plays netball, so it should be possible for them to share that Jack loves Lego and Jill loves reading, or to say about their toddlers that Jill's a chatterbox and Jack can't stop climbing. These sorts of descriptions about what children *do* (reading/building) are far less likely to raise hackles than are statements about what they *have* (intelligence/dexterity), or labels about what they *are* (gifted/talented).

Again it is important to emphasize that this is not about denying the differences between children. In some circumstances it will be useful to pin a temporary label on a child, for how are we supposed to find useful sources of information about our children if we are not allowed to admit that some are gifted, some autistic and some both? What we are talking about in this chapter is the circumstances in which such global labels become obstacles to communication with others, and in which it is more fruitful to use specific descriptions instead.

Imagine a conversation between two mothers at the school gate whose children are in the same class. Julie remarks that her son, Seb, is finding Year 1 quite a struggle: he is a reluctant reader and really misses all the craft-work and free time that the children had in Reception. She thinks that perhaps the school is expecting a bit too much of the children, as she knows that several others in the class are also struggling; lots of them were upset because they got several spellings wrong in the recent test. She wonders whether Clare's son, Jonty, is having the same experience. How is Clare to respond? The reality is that Jonty is not only relishing the challenges of Year 1, in contrast to his frustration with all the colouring and playing in Reception, but made no mistakes in his spelling test, which was based on a set of more complex words than the ones that the rest of the class were given.

> How would you describe what your child does, rather than what he is or what he has?
>
> Would it sometimes be helpful for you to use these sorts of descriptions, when talking about him to other people?

One option, of course, is to state this quite baldly: 'No, not at all. Jonty finds the Year 1 work pretty easy. In fact Mr Wiseman set him a harder spelling test than the others last week, and he got ten out of ten.' It is not hard to predict the feelings that this response would provoke in Julie. Clare might as well have said, 'My son is cleverer than your son.' That may well be true, but it would be a very rare parent who could react with equanimity to such a claim.

Assuming that Clare doesn't want to lie ('Absolutely! It's a real nightmare.') or evade the question completely ('Sorry, Julie – I must catch Louise before the children come out…'), what other options are available to her? If she chooses to focus on what the boys *enjoy* rather than what they *are* (clever) or *have* (intellectual gifts) then the conversation may be able to proceed more fruitfully. She could say something like, 'No – in fact Jonty really struggled in Reception because art-and-craft just isn't his thing. He's much happier this year because he loves reading and writing. Isn't it funny how different they all are?' All of this is true, and yet by separating the two boys' interests Clare has avoided making a direct comparison between their abilities in the different areas. If she is confident in Jonty's abilities, with no pressing need for affirmation on that score, then she will probably feel fine about the fact that she has not actually shared with Julie the extent of his achievements. Instead, her focus has been on maintaining her good relationship with Julie, although not to the extent of being dishonest.

The conversation might then move on to a discussion of which other aspects of Year 1 their children are enjoying or finding difficult: perhaps Jonty is struggling with the swimming, or maybe they both love the football. Alternatively, Julie might persist with a more specific line of enquiry about Jonty's progress in reading, and then it would be silly for Clare to pretend that he has not moved much more quickly through the reading scheme than Seb and most of the others. This information may feel less threatening to Julie, though, when cushioned by the knowledge that reading is Jonty's thing and art or sport is Seb's. Against that background, too, it may be possible for Clare to ask whether Julie is really worried about Seb's reading, and to try to find a way of supporting her if she is.

Of course it is not possible for parents to banish jealousy altogether, just by choosing to avoid comparative language. There will always be occasions on which children are competing or being compared with each other and one will outshine the others. It may be that sport is Jonty's thing as much as reading is, and that as well as romping ahead in the reading scheme he is consistently chosen over Seb in football. Julie may care so desperately about these facts that she is unable to see past them when dealing with Clare and Jonty. Clare may have to accept that, for now at least, she is unable to connect with Julie.

Clare's ability to cope with this situation is bound to be enhanced, though, if she can understand that she is not responsible for Julie's *inability* to cope with it. The fact of the matter is that Jonty has certain advantages over Seb in areas that are important to them both. Clare has done her best to present these facts in terms that do not focus on those advantages, but in the end she cannot control Julie's response to the differences between their sons. She can be content that she has done her best not to exacerbate any potential problems, but that is all she can do. Julie's feelings and behaviour are her responsibility, not Clare's: Clare's job now is to decide what to do with them in the context of this particular relationship. She may choose for a time to avoid all but the most shallow of social chit-chat with Julie. In different circumstances – if Julie were her sister, say, and the boys cousins – she might not be so able to avoid the potential for future conflict: the ways in which the situation were handled would then probably be shaped by the family's historical ways of dealing with difficulties.

What matters most is that Clare should not allow her response to be dictated by Julie's emotions. The parents of gifted children, like any other minority group, are sometimes confronted by prejudice. Prejudice, it is said, is simply a feeling about difference. Overcoming prejudice is not, therefore, a matter of denying or destroying the difference, but of changing the feeling about it. There are occasions on which this is just not possible, and then the minority group is obliged to deal with the behaviour that the feelings provoke.

The outcome of these difficult situations is not always necessarily negative. Indeed, those who are personally comfortable with their own or their children's gifts can do a great deal, where the opportunity arises, to change other people's reactions to it. For example, a parent who is active in taking an interest in other people's children, in affirming the many positive characteristics or skills which these children have, can begin to build a wider understanding that intelligence is not an unmitigated advantage. A conversation on equal terms about the good and bad scenarios and situations in two families may lead to unexpected reactions. 'Goodness, how I envy you having your evenings undisturbed after 7.30. It seems like a dream to me.' 'Now that I see the demands it makes on you, I'm actually pretty relieved that my child isn't gifted!'

Being gifted is not a problem. The challenge is for each individual, or his parents, to understand what it means to be gifted; to accept it as part of his nature; and to live with other people's reactions to it.

Our hopes: priming the parents

We hope that parents and all who care for gifted children will have found some companionship in our book, and some sense of fellowship with others in this scattered minority. Not only as former counsellors, but also as former gifted children and as the parents and grandparents of gifted children, our experiences have nourished in us a great respect for this group of carers.

Gifted people often have an urgent need to grasp a situation intellectually before they feel able to cope with it emotionally. It is our hope that this book will help parents better to understand their own or their children's giftedness, and thus enable them to feel more emotionally at ease with it.

We hope very much that our book might act as a primer, not only as an introduction to the subject of gifted children, but also in detonating a great explosion of confidence in parents to ask for their gifted children's needs to be met, to live more comfortably with giftedness in their family lives and to resist the pressure to deny that part of themselves or their children.

If gifted children's parents are not able to acknowledge their gifts or to communicate about them, then how can the children themselves learn the place of giftedness in their lives? It is vital to give gifted people the opportunity to find a voice and speak with it, because they have so much to offer. Without their contribution, their ability to move things on with their intellect and perception and vision, humankind would be greatly impoverished.

> We must be open to the amazing insights and ideas of gifted children. We must listen to them and bravely enter into their world, and give them confidence in it. Then they will feel trusting enough to become a part of ours. (Michal Hambourg)

Related Contacts

United Kingdom
Advisory Centre for Education (ACE)

1c Aberdeen Studios
22 Highbury Grove
London N5 2DQ
Tel. 020 7704 3370
Advice Line 0808 800 5793
email (for admin. only) enquiries@ace.dialnet.com
www.ace-ed.org.uk
Independent advice centre for parents offering information about state education
in England and Wales for 5–17-year-olds.

Anti-Bullying Alliance

National Children's Bureau
8 Wakley Street
London EC1V 7QE
Tel. 020 7843 1901
email on website for general enquiries
www.anti-bullyingalliance.org
Brings together over 50 national organizations to work together creating safer
environments for children.

Anti-Bullying Network

Moray House School of Education
University of Edinburgh
Holyrood Road
Edinburgh EH8 8AQ
Tel. 0131 651 6100

email abn@mhie.ac.uk
www.antibullying.net
Established by the Scottish Executive for teachers, parents and young people to share ideas about how bullying should be tackled. Priority given to requests for information that come from within Scotland.

@ease

c/o Rethink
30 Tabernacle Street
London EC2A 4DD
Tel. 020 7330 9100
email at-ease@rethink.org
www.rethink.org

For young people under stress or worried about their thoughts and feelings. Part of Rethink, which provides practical advice, support and information to everyone affected by severe mental illness.

British Dyslexia Association

98 London Road
Reading RG1 5AU
Helpline 0118 966 8271
email helpline@bdyslexia.org.uk
email admin@bdyslexia.org.uk
www.bda-dyslexia.org.uk

Promotes early identification and support in schools to ensure opportunities to learn. Helpline free and confidential.

British Mensa

St John's House
St John's Square
Wolverhampton WV2 4AH
Tel. 01902 772771
email gtprogramme@mensa.org.uk
www.mensa.org.uk

Developing British Mensa Gifted and Talented (G&T) Support Programme.

Bullying Online

9 Knox Way
Harrogate
North Yorkshire HG1 3JL
email help@bullying.co.uk
www.bullying.co.uk
Registered charity providing wide range of online advice for parents and pupils, together with links to other organizations.

CHI (The Support Society for Children of High Intelligence)

PO Box 21461
London N6 6WW
www.chi-charity.org.uk
Acts directly on behalf of individual children whose intelligence level is above the 98th percentile with aim of helping them to achieve their potential.

Childline

45 Folgate Street
London E1 6GL
Tel. 020 7650 3200
Helpline 0800 1111
www.childline.org.uk
Free 24-hour confidential helpline for children and young people in the UK. Trained volunteer counsellors give comfort, advice and protection. Publications for parents, carers and young people include family, bereavement, bullying and racism, crisis point and child abuse.

Childline Cymru/Wales

9th Floor, Alexandra House
Alexandra Road
Swansea SA1 5ED
Tel. 0870 336 2935
Provides a bilingual service.

ChildLine Northern Ireland

1st Floor, Queen's House
14 Queen Street
Belfast BT1 6ED
Tel. 0870 336 2946

Childline Scotland

18 Albion Street
Glasgow G1 1LH
Tel. 0870 336 2910

Contact a Family

209–211 City Road
London EC1V 1JN
Tel. 0207 608 8700
Helpline 0808 808 3555 (freephone)
email info@cafamily.org.uk
www.cafamily.org.uk
Provides support, advice and information for families with disabled children.

Contact Youth

139 Ravenhill Road
Belfast BT6 8DR
Tel. 028 9045 7848
Helpline 0808 808 8000
email info@contactyouth.org
www.contactyouth.org
Northern Ireland's voluntary organization for the provision of youth counselling services. Youthline available to young people between ages of 11 and 26 years. Free confidential helpline for 8–18-year-olds.

Department for Education and Skills

GTEU Dept 4E, Sanctuary Buildings
Great Smith Street
London SW1P 3BT
Tel. 020 7925 5716
email info@dfes.gsi.gov.uk
www.standards.dfes.gov.uk/giftedandtalented
The Standards at the National Programme: Gifted and Talented site provides latest thinking on current gifted and talented initiatives, practical guidance and advice.

Dyslexia Institute

Head Office and National Training and Resource Centre
Park House
Wick Road
Egham
Surrey TW20 0HH
Tel. 01784 222300
email london@dyslexia-inst.org.uk and info@dyslexia-inst.org.uk
www.dyslexia-inst.org.uk
Educational charity founded 1972 for the assessment and teaching of people with dyslexia.

Dyslexia Institute Scotland

74 Victoria Crescent Road
Dowanhill
Glasgow G12 9JN
Tel. 0141 334 4549
email glasgow@dyslexia-inst.org.uk

Dyslexia Institute Wales

14–18 City Road
Cardiff CF24 3DL
Tel. 029 2048 1122
email cardiff@dyslexia-inst.org.uk

Dyspraxia Foundation

8 West Alley
Hitchin
Herts SG5 1EG
Tel. 01462 454986
email admin@dyspraxiafoundation.org.uk
www.dyspraxiafoundation.org.uk
National charity offers contact with other members both locally and nationally.

Education Otherwise

PO Box 7420
London N9 9SG
Helpline 0870 730 0074
email enquiries@education-otherwise.org
www.education-otherwise.org
UK-based membership organization provides support and information for families
whose children are being educated outside school.

First Steps

1 Taylor Close
Kenilworth
Warwickshire CV8 2LW
Tel. 01926 864473
Helpline 0845 120 2916
email first.steps@btconnect.com
www.first-steps.org
Registered charity which aims to help, in a practical way, people who suffer from
phobias, obsessional compulsive disorder, those with general anxiety, panic
attacks, anorexia and bulimia, and those who wish to come off tranquilizers,
together with help for their carers. Also help, advice and support for the carers of
those with borderline personality disorder.

Gabbitas

Carrington House
126–130 Regent Street
London W1B 5EE
Tel. 020 7734 0161
email schools@gabbitas.co.uk
www.gabbitas.co.uk
Consultancy specializing in independent school education. Guidance for parents,
students and schools in the UK and worldwide.

Gabbitas

Tel. 020 7734 0161
email admin@gabbitas.co.uk
www.gabbitas.net
Provides a directory of the United Kingdom's independent schools and specialist
schools, as well as links to other websites.

Home Education Advisory Service (HEAS)

PO Box 98
Welwyn Garden City
Herts AL8 6AN
Tel. 01707 371854
email enquiries@heas.org.uk
www.heas.org.uk
Established 1995, offers advice and practical support, including legal aspects.

Home Education in Northern Ireland (HEdNI)

email info@HEdNI.org
www.hedni.org
An inclusive organization for all backgrounds, religious beliefs, races and culture
to support rights of families to choose for themselves what suits them best.

Human Scale Education

Unit 8 Fairseat Farm
Chew Stoke
Bristol BS40 8XF
Tel. 01275 332516
email info@hse.org.uk
www.hse.org.uk
Established 1985 to promote small human-scale learning communities within state
maintained and independent sectors of UK education.

Independent Schools Council (ISC)

St Vincent House
30 Orange Street
London WC2H 7HH
Tel. 020 7766 7070
email office@isc.co.uk
www.isc.co.uk
Represents interest of associations and member schools and promotes choice,
diversity and excellence in education.

Independent Schools Council Information Service (ISCis)

ISCis Central
5 Barby Road
Rugby
Warwickshire CV22 5DT
Tel. 01788 570537
email central@iscis.uk.net
www.iscis.uk.net

Regional offices throughout UK provide services to parents. Help with finding school fees from the ISC Educational Grants Advisory Service.

ISCis Ireland

5 Sandycove Avenue East
Sandycove
County Dublin, Republic of Ireland
Tel. 353 1280 9545
email palmercarter@eircom.net

Information on member schools in Northern Ireland and the Irish Republic.

Independent Schools of the British Isles (ISBI)

Which School Ltd
Tilshead House
Tilshead
Salisbury
Wiltshire SP3 4RX
Tel. 01980 620575
www.isbi.com

The information on schools is provided by the schools themselves; includes independent and fee paying, residential, special needs, state boarding schools, summer and international schools. Contact details of principal educational psychologists and special needs placement officers in all UK education authorities also on website.

Institute of Family Therapy

24–32 Stephenson Way
London NW1 2HX
Tel. 020 7391 9150
email ift@psyc.bbk.ac.uk
www.instituteoffamilytherapy.org.uk

Clinical services for families and couples facing wide range of relationship difficulties. The new Centre for Child Focused Practice is a service for children, young people and their families facing a variety of difficulties.

Islamic Homeschooling Advisory Network

PO Box 30671
London E1 0TG
Tel. 020 8851 1866
email info@islamichomeeducation.co.uk
www.islamichomeeducation.co.uk

Membership organization providing information, advice and support to Muslim parents home educating or seeking other alternatives for their children.

Kidscape

2 Grosvenor Gardens
London SW1W 0DH
Tel. 020 7730 3300
Helpline: 08451 205 204
www.kidscape.org.uk

Registered charity helping to prevent bullying and child abuse. Helpline is for parents, guardians, concerned relatives and friends.

Montessori St Nicholas Charity

24 Prince's Gate
London SW7 1PT
Tel. 020 7584 9987
email centre@montessori.org.uk
www.montessori.org.uk

The charity fosters communication and unity within the movement. Ten regions, including Northern Ireland.

Muslim Youth Helpline

4th Floor Barkat House
116–118 Finchley Road
London NW3 5HT
Tel. 0870 774 3518
Helpline 0808 808 2008
email help@myh.org.uk
admin email info@myh.org.uk
www.myh.org.uk
Confidential helpline run by young people trained in basic Islamic counselling
skills.

NAGC YouthAgency

Suite 14 Challenge House
Sherwood Drive
Bletchley
Milton Keynes MK3 6DP
Tel. 0845 450 0221
email youthagency@rmplc.co.uk
www.youthagency.org.uk
Provides membership network for young people aged between 11 and 20 across
Britain who have exceptional gifts and talents.

National Academy for Gifted and Talented Youth

The University of Warwick
Coventry CV4 7AL
Tel. 024 7657 4213
email gifted@warwick.ac.uk
www.nagty.ac.uk
Established by government in 2002 with role to drive forward improvements in
gifted and talented education in England.

National Association for Able Children in Education (NACE)

PO Box 242
Arnolds Way
Oxford OX2 9FR
Tel. 01865 861879
email info@nace.co.uk
www.nace.co.uk

Charity established 1984 to bring together and support all those with an interest in the education of able, gifted and talented children.

National Association for Gifted Children

Suite 14 Challenge House
Sherwood Drive
Bletchley
Milton Keynes MK3 6DP
Helpline 0845 450 0221
email amazingchildren@nagcbritain.org.uk
www.nagcbritain.org.uk

Registered charity and membership organization. Provides help, support and encouragement to gifted and talented children and their families.

National Association for Gifted Children in Scotland

PO Box 2024
Glasgow G32 9YD
email nagcs@btinternet.com

Scottish charity, run by volunteers, offering support to parents and children.

National Association for Special Educational Needs (NASEN)

NASEN House
4/5 Amber Business Village
Amber Close
Amington
Tamworth
Staffordshire B77 4RP
Tel. 01827 311500
email welcome@nasen.org.uk
www.nasen.org.uk

The leading organization in the UK which aims to promote the education, training, advancement and development of all those with special educational needs.

National Autistic Society

393 City Road
London EC1V 1NG
Tel. 020 7833 2299
Helpline 0845 070 4004
email nas@nas.org.uk
www.nas.org.uk

Registered charity to champion rights and interest of all people with autism and Asperger Syndrome. Information, publications, branches run by parents.

NAS Cymru

Glamorgan House
Monastery Road
Neath Abbey
Neath SA10 7DH
Tel. 01792 815915
email wales@nas.org.uk

NAS Scotland

Central Chambers
1st Floor 109 Hope Street
Glasgow G2 6LL
Tel. 0141 221 8090
email scotland@nas.org.uk

National Children's Bureau

Young NCB
8 Wakley Street
London EC1V 7QE
Tel. 020 7843 6000
www.youngncb.org.uk

Website open to all children and young people. Through the free membership network children and young people can be actively involved in issues that affect and interest them. Two sections: under 13 and 14–18-year-olds.

Northern Ireland Dyslexia Association

17a Upper Newtonards Road
Belfast BT4 3HT
Tel. 028 9065 9212
email help@nida.org.uk
www.nida.org.uk

Northern Ireland Education Department

Rathgael House
43 Balloo Road
Bangor
County Down BT19 7PR
Tel. 028 9127 9279
email mail@deni.gov.uk
www.deni.gov.uk
Information for parents includes assessment and examinations, transfer selection,
bullying statement.

Parentline Plus

Tel. 020 7284 5600 – central office
Helpline: 0808 800 2222
email helpline service on website is secure and confidential
www.parentlineplus.org.uk
Registered charity supporting anyone parenting a child. Parents Together groups
for England and Wales available by telephone (free of charge).

ParentLine Scotland

Children 1st
83 Whitehouse Loan
Edinburgh EH9 1AT
Tel. 0131 446 2300
Helpline 0808 800 2222
email on website
www.parentlinescotland.org.uk
Supports families under stress.

Parents' Advice Centre

Franklin House
12 Brunswick Street
Belfast BT2 7GE
Tel. 01232 238800
24-hour helpline offers listening, support, guidance and counselling relating to
any family problem.

Qualifications and Curriculum Authority

83 Piccadilly
London W1J 8QA
Tel. 020 7509 5555
email gtweb@qca.org.uk
www.nc.uk.net/gt
Non-departmental body sponsored by Department for Education and Skills
provides guidance on teaching the gifted and talented.

Rethink

30 Tabernacle Street
London DC2 4DD
Tel. 0845 456 0455 (general enquiries)
Adviceline 020 8974 6814
email advice@rethink.org
www.rethink.org
Registered charity helping everyone affected by severe mental illness to recover a
better quality of life.

Rethink Northern Ireland

Wyndhurst
Knockbracken Health Care Park
Saintfield Road
Belfast BT8 8BH
Tel. 028 9040 2323
email info.nireland@rethink.org

Samaritans

Tel. 0845 790 9090
email jo@samaritans.org
www.samaritans.org
Administrative contact:
The Upper Mill
Kingston Road
Ewell
Surrey KT17 2AF
Tel. 020 8394 8300
email admin@samaritans.org
Telephone helpline available 24 hours. 203 local branches throughout the UK.

Schoolhouse Home Education Association

PO Box 28496
Edinburgh EH4 4YU
Tel. 0870 745 0968
www.schoolhouse.org.uk
Email via website.
Provides information, support and legal aspects for home educators and those considering educating at home in Scotland.

SCIS/ISIS Scotland

21 Melville Street
Edinburgh EH3 7PE
Tel. 0131 220 2106
email information@scis.org.uk
www.scis.org.uk
Independent Schools Council and Information Service for Scotland.

Scottish Executive

School Education
Victoria Quay
Edinburgh EH6 6QQ
Tel. 0845 774 1741 Scottish Executive Central Enquiry Unit
email ceu@scotland.gov.uk
www.scotland.gov.uk
Parent zone on website offers information on schools. Access via www.scotland.gov.uk, click school education, click going to school, then parent zone.

Scottish Network for Able Pupils (SNAP)

University of Glasgow
Faculty of Education
11 Eldon Street
Glasgow G3 6NH
Tel. 0141 330 3071
email snap@educ.gla.ac.uk
www.ablepupils.com

Concerned with issues related to children and young people's abilities, including exceptional individuals with remarkable abilities for age and stage.

Steiner Waldorf Schools Fellowship

Kidbrooke Park
Forest Row
East Sussex RH18 5JB
Tel. 01342 822115
email mail@swsf.org.uk
www.steinerwaldorf.org.uk

Emphasis on whole development of the child; spiritual, physical, moral well-being and academic progress.

Stepfamily Scotland

5 Coates Place
Edinburgh EH3 7AA
Tel. 0131 225 8005
Helpline 0845 122 8655
email info@stepfamilyscotland.org.uk
www.stepfamily.org.uk

Confidential helpline provides support and information for any member of the family.

Tomorrow's Achievers

email via the website
www.masterclasses.co.uk

The Gabbitas, Truman and Thring Education Trust runs masterclasses for 5–18-year-old exceptionally able children and young people. Held throughout the year in different parts of the country.

Westminster Institute of Education

Oxford Brookes University
Harcourt Hill Campus
Oxford OX2 9AT
Tel. 01865 488600
email wioe@brookes.ac.uk
www.brookes.ac.uk/schools/education/rescon/cpdgifted
This link provides a resource for education professionals and all those involved
and interested in the education of able, gifted and talented learners.

WISC

Hazelhurst
Ledbury Road
Dymock
Gloucestershire GL18 2AG
Tel. 01531 890150
email ibrwn6@aol.com
www.iscis.org.uk
Independent Schools Council Information for Wales.

Young Minds

48–50 St John Street
London EC1M 4DG
Tel. 020 7336 8445
email enquiries@youngminds.org.uk
www.youngminds.org.uk
Information and advice for anyone concerned about the mental health of children
and young people. Produces leaflets on range of topics to help young people
understand when they feel troubled and where to find help.

Young Minds Parents' Information Service

101–8 Clerkenwell Road
London EC1M 5SA
Tel. 0800 018 2138
www.youngminds.org.uk/pis
Free and confidential service to hear parents' concerns and help them find a way
forward.

Young NCB

National Children's Bureau
8 Wakley Street
London EC1V 7QE
Tel. 020 7843 6000
www.youngncb.org.uk
Website open to all young people with two sections: under 13 and 14–18 years.
Provides a network for involvement in issues that affect and interest young
people.

International

European Council for High Ability (ECHA)

Secretariat of ECHA, Johanna Raffan
NACE National Office
PO Box 242
Oxford OX2 9FR
UK
Tel. 01865 861879
email secretariat@echa.ws
www.echa.ws
International organization of researchers, teachers, school administrators and
parents who are concerned with giftedness, talent and high ability. Promotes
awareness of gifted children and provides information on their best development.

Hoagies: the all-things-gifted resource

www.hoagiesgifted.org
From across the world resources, ideas and links on this website provide an
extensive source of information for parents. Includes section for children and
teens, with suggestions for toys, books, software and links to other websites.

World Council for Gifted and Talented Children

370 S. Carmalo Avenue
Pasadena CA 91107
USA
Tel. 626 584 9751
email worldgt@earthlink.net
www.worldgifted.org
Exists to focus world attention on gifted and talented children. Hosts a biennial
conference and publishes the journal *Gifted and Talented International*.

United States
American Academy of Child and Adolescent Psychiatry
3615 Wisconsin Ave N.W.
Washington, D.C. 20016-3007
Voice 202 966 7300
http://www.aacap.org/index.htm
National professional medical association dedicated to treating and improving the
quality of life for children, adolescents and families affected by mental, behavioural or developmental disorders. Fact sheets and online information for parents.
AACAP does not provide individual consultations, or referrals to specific
child/adolescent psychiatrists.

American Association for Gifted Children
American Association for Gifted Children at Duke University
Box 90270
Durham, North Carolina 27708-0270
Tel. 919 783 6152
email megayle@aol.com
www.aagc.org
Advocacy organization for gifted children, providing information for parents and
teachers and a thrice-yearly newsletter.

Belin-Blank International Center for Gifted Education
University of Iowa College of Education
600 Blank Honors Center
Iowa City, IA 52242-0454
Tel. 800 336 6463 or 319 335 6148
email belinblank@uiowa.edu
www.uiowa.edu
Vision to inspire and serve the worldwide gifted community of students, educators
and families. Includes section for parents.

Center for Gifted Education
College of William and Mary
PO Box 8795
Williamsburg, VA 23187-8795
Tel. 757 221 2362
email cfge@wm.edu
http://cfge.wm.edu

Conducts research and provides graduate education programs and professional development for individuals in the field of gifted education. Provides programs for precollegiate learners and their families, including enrichment programs.

Center for Nonviolent Communication

2428 Foothill Boulevard, Suite E
La Crescenta, CA 91214
Tel. 818 957 9393
www.cnvc.org
Email via website.
Global organization founded by Dr Marshall B. Rosenberg in 1984. Lists certified trainers in England and Scotland.

Center for Talent Development

School of Education and Social Policy
Northwestern University
617 Dartmouth Place
Evanston, Illinois 60208-4175
Tel. 847 491 3782
email ctd@northwestern.edu
www.ctd.northwestern.edu
Conducts the Midwest Academic Talent Search, provides Summer academic programs and school year enrichment programs including the LearningLinks Distance Program. Provides conferences and seminars for parents.

Childhelp USA

15757 N. 78th Street
Scottsdale, AZ 85260
Tel. 480 922 8212
National Child Abuse Hotline 800 4 A CHILD (800 422 4453)
www.childhelpusa.org
Meeting the needs of abused and neglected children through a 24-hour helpline, research and advocacy, training and education, treatment centers, counseling and foster care.

Council for Exceptional Children (CEC)

1110 North Glebe Road
Suite 300
Arlington, VA 22201
Tel. 703 620 3660
email service@cec.sped.org
www.cec.sped.org

The largest international professional organization dedicated to improving educational outcomes for individuals with exceptionalities, students with disabilities, and/or the gifted. CEC advocates for appropriate governmental policies, sets professional standards, provides continual professional development, and more.

Davidson Institute for Talent Development

9665 Gateway Drive, Suite B
Reno, NV 89521
Tel. 775 852 3483
email info@ditd.org
www.ditd.org

Website provides details of a new public gifted school, the Davidson Academy of Nevada; the THINK Summer Institute; GT–Cyberspace; the Educators Guild; programs and scholarships; and more.

Duke University Talent Identification Program

Box 90780, Duke University
Durham, NC 27708-0780
Tel. 919 668 9100, 8a.m. to 5p.m. EST, Monday to Friday
Texas Office:
406 E. 11th Street, Suite 301
Austin, TX 78701
Tel. 512 473 8400
email via online forms on website
www.tip.duke.edu

Identifies gifted children and supports them by providing programs and activities accessible to their parents and teachers.

Education Program for Gifted Youth

Ventura Hall
Stanford University
Stanford, CA 94305-4115
Tel. 800 372 EPGY or 650 329 9920
email epgy-info@epgy.stanford.edu
www-epgy.stanford.edu/epgy/
Provides e-learning courses for gifted and talented students.

ERICEC

See Information Center on Disabilities and Gifted Education.

Family Support America

205 West Randolph Street
Suite 2222
Chicago, IL 60606
Tel. 312 338 0900
email info@familysupportamerica.org
www.familysupportamerica.org
Nationally recognized movement to strengthen and support families. Publishes books, organizes conferences and provides an online national database of family support programs.

Gifted Child Today Magazine

Baylor University School of Education
PO Box 97304
Waco, TX 76798-7304
Tel. 254 710 6116
http://www.prufrock.com/client/client_pages/prufrock_jm_giftchild.cfm
National resource for teachers and parents, with online resources available at the website.

Gifted Development Center
1452 Marion Street
Denver, Colorado 80218
Tel. 303 837 8378
email gifted@gifteddevelopment.com
www.gifteddevelopment.com
Information about identification, assessment, counseling, learning styles,
programs, presentations and resources for gifted children and adults.

GT World
http://gtworld.org/links.html
Online support community for gifted children and their carers. Provides information, links and articles as well as operating five mailing lists.

www.homeschool.com
Provides online information, resources and support for homeschooling families.

http://homeschooling.about.com
Provides online information about homeschooling.

Information Center on Disabilities and Gifted Education
http://ericec.org
Provided by the Council for Exceptional Children, ERICEC is an online information center about giftedness and dual exceptionalities as well as other special
needs.

International Dyslexia Organization
Chester Building
Suite 382
8600 LaSalle Road
Baltimore, Maryland 21286-2044
Tel. 410 296 0232
email via website
www.interdys.org
Dedicated to the study and treatment of the learning disability, dyslexia. Provides
information and funds research.

Jacob. K. Javits Gifted and Talented Students Education Program
See US Department of Education.

Johns Hopkins University Center for Talented Youth
5801 Smith Ave 400 McAuley Hall
Baltimore, Maryland 21209
Tel. 410 735 4100
email ctyinfo@jhu.edu
www.jhu.edu/~gifted/
Provides information, research, talent search and summer programs as well as distance education, counseling and assessment.

John Templeton Foundation
300 Conschocken State Road
Suite 500
West Conshohocken, PA 19428
Tel. 610 941 2828
email info@templeton.org
www.templeton.org
Provides research on the neuroscience of creativity and intelligence, a bibliography of benefits of accelerated progression for highly gifted children, and communicates the nature, development and benefits of scientific genius and creativity.

www.kidsource.com/kidsource/pages/ed.gifted.html
Online list of articles and digests providing ideas, guidance and activities for both parents and educators of gifted children.

MAAP Services for Autism and Asperger Syndrome
Susan J. Moreno, Editor
MAAP Services, Inc.
PO Box 524
Crown Point, IN 46307
Tel. 219 662 1311
email: chart@netnitco.net
www.maapservices.org
Non-profit organization dedicated to providing information and advice to families of more advanced individuals with Autism, Asperger Syndrome, and Pervasive Developmental Disorder (PDD) through a quarterly newsletter, information and advice.

www.midnightbeach.com/hs/

Provides online information about homeschooling.

National Association for Gifted Children

1707 L Street, N.W., Suite 550
Washington, DC 20036
Tel. 202 785 4268
email nagc@nagc.org
www.nagc.org
Trains teachers, encourages parents and educates administrators and policymakers on how to develop and support gifted children.

National Education Association Bullying Awareness Campaign

e-mail Gbarker@nea.org.
http://www.nea.org/schoolsafety/bullying.html
Information for parents, schools and communities.

National Research Center on the Gifted and Talented

See US Department of Education.

Ohio Association for Gifted Children

501 Morrison Road
Suite 103
Columbus, OH 43230
Tel. 614 337 0386
www.oagc.com
Local support organization.

State Resources for Gifted Education

http://ericec.org/fact/stateres.html
Provides a list of State Department of Education offices responsible for gifted education and state-wide advocacy groups.

Supporting Emotional Needs of the Gifted (SENG)

PO Box 6074
Scottsdale, AZ 85261
Tel. 773 907 8092
email office@sengifted.org
www.sengifted.org
Seeks to inform gifted individuals, their families, and the professionals who work
with them about the unique social and emotional needs of gifted persons.

Summer Institute for the Gifted

River Plaza
9 West Broad Street
Stamford, CT 06902-3788
Tel. 866 303 4744
email sig.info@giftedstudy.com
www.giftedstudy.com
Provides educational and social opportunities for academically gifted children.

Dr Sylvia Rimm

Educational Assessment Service, Inc.
W6050 Apple Road
Watertown, WI 53098
Tel. 800 795 7466
email srimm@sylviarimm.com
www.sylviarimm.com
Child psychologist, broadcaster, speaker and writer specializing in gifted under-
achievers and how girls can achieve.

www.uniquelygifted.org

Collection of resources for families with gifted/special needs children and for
professionals who work with them. Includes introductory articles, personal experience and refers to other websites.

US Department of Education
www.ed.gov

Includes details of:

The Jacob. K. Javits Gifted and Talented Students Education Program
US Department of Education
Office of Elementary and Secondary Education
400 Maryland Ave, SW
Washington, DC 20202-6200
Tel. 202 260 7813
email patricia.ross@ed.gov
http://www.ed.gov/programs/javits/index.html

State Education Authorities, Local Education Authorities, or both, may apply for grants to fund demonstration projects, innovative strategies and activities to enhance schools' abilities to meet the needs of gifted and talented students. Priority is given to models serving students who are under-represented in gifted and talented programs such as economically disadvantaged, limited English proficient and disabled students. Priority is also given to state and local efforts to improve services for gifted and talented students. The Javits Program also funds:

The National Research Center on the Gifted and Talented
University of Connecticut
2131 Hillside Road
Unit 3007
Storrs, CT 06269-3007
Tel. 860 486 4676
http://www.gifted.uconn.edu/nrcgt/nrconlin.html

A nationwide cooperative of researchers, practitioners, policy makers, and others. Conducts research into aspects of giftedness and disseminates information to practitioners, parents, policy-makers and other researchers.

Canada
Association for Bright Children of Ontario
Box 156
Suite 100
2 Bloor Street West
Toronto, ON M4W 2G7
Tel. 416 925 6136
email abcinfo@abcontario.ca
www.abcontario.ca

An all-volunteer, provincially incorporated support and advocacy group, dedicated to providing information and support to parents of bright and gifted children/adolescents through newsletters, networking, an annual conference and local workshops.

Calgary Action for Bright Children (CABC)
PO Box 36093
Lakeview Postal Outlet
Calgary, AB T3E
Tel. 403 244 8801
email cabc@abccalgary.org
www.abccalgary.org
Aims to promote growth of awareness, understanding and services for gifted children and their families, through meetings with feature speakers, panel discussions, conferences and through special programs for children and families.

Gifted Canada
www3.bc.sympatico.ca/giftedcanada
Bilingual website helps Canadian parents become aware of resources for gifted children and their families.

Mensa Canada Society
Suite 310
4 Cataraqui Street
Kingston
Ontario, K7K 1Z7
Tel. 613 547 0824
email info@canada.mensa.org
www.canada.mensa.org
Bilingual website. Part of Mensa International, the international high-IQ society.

Ontario Gifted
PO Box 2003
Richmond Hill
Ontario, L4E 1A3
email ontario.gifted@sympatico.ca
www.ontariogifted.org
Resources and information for parents of gifted children.

Australia

www.austega.com/gifted

Information on gifted and talented children, including links to other websites, articles, home-schooling and resources.

Australian Association for the Education of Gifted and Talented

email info@aaegt.net.au

www.aaegt.net.au

Offers general information, links to websites, resources for parents and teachers, online learning and fun for children. Includes Education Department websites for gifted and talented children with special needs.

Australian Mensa Inc.

PO Box 213

Toorak, Vic 3142

Tel. 1902 260 594

email gifted_children@au.mensa.org

www.au.mensa.org

The gifted children's coordinator responds to requests for help and advice.

GERRIC

Gifted Education Research Resource and Information Centre

Faculty of Arts, The School of Education

University of New South Wales

Tel. 02 9385 1972

email gerric@unsw.edu.au

www.arts.unsw.edu.au/gerric/

Offers vacation programmes for gifted children of all ages; courses for their parents in regional and remote areas; counselling services; conferences, seminars and workshops for teachers.

Gifted and Talented Children's Association South Australia

Office/Resource Centre: Annesley College

89 Greenhill Road, Wayville

Postal Address: PO Box 1

Highgate 5073

Tel. 08 8373 0500

email via website

www.gtcasa.asn.au

Voluntary organization concerned about excellence in all aspects of children's development.

Gifted and Talented Children's Association of Western Australia Inc. (GATCH WA)

c/o Meerilinga
PO Box 1177
West Leederville, WA 6901
Tel. (message bank) 08 9487 0122
email gatca-wa@gatcawa.org
www.gatcawa.org

Serves gifted children, their parents, their teachers and all those wishing to ensure that children of high ability are supported socially and intellectually – at home and at school.

www.gifted-children.com.au

Provides a communication channel for those involved with gifted children, supporting parents, disseminating information and promoting the needs of their families.

NSW Association for Gifted and Talented Children Inc.

c/o Hilltop Road Public School
Hilltop Road
Merryland, NSW 2160
Tel. 02 9633 5399
email via website
www.nswagtc.org.au

Information and support for teachers and parents of gifted children.

Queensland Association for Gifted and Talented Children Inc.

282 Stafford Road
Stafford, Q 4053
Tel. 07 3352 4288
email office@gagtc.org.au
www.gagtc.oreg.au

Provides an information and support service staffed by trained volunteers.

Tasmanian Association for the Gifted Inc. (TAG)

GPO Box 1942
Hobart, Tas 7001
email office@tasgifted.org.au
www.tasgifted.org.au
Non-profit based organization offering meetings, seminars, workshops and telephone counselling.

Victorian Association for Gifted and Talented Children Inc. (VAGTC)

PO Box 132
Caufield South, Vic 3162
Tel. 04 0205 6140
email via website
www.vagtc.asn.au
Supportive network of parents and educators with telephone support and advice.

New Zealand

Te Kete Ipurangi – The Online Learning Centre

PO Box 19098
Wellington
Tel. 04 801 0462
email gifted@tki.org.nz
www.tki.org.nz/e/community/gifted
New Zealand Ministry of Education initiative providing support for parents.

The New Zealand Association for Gifted Children

PO Box 46
Waitomo Caves
Tel. 09 521 5964
email president@giftedchildren.org.nz or membership@giftedchildren.org.nz
www.giftedchildren.org.nz

Index

Page numbers in *italic* refer to
end-of-chapter notes.

academic potential *see* potential
acceleration 124–5
  case study, Kai 124
acceptance 58, 61, 166, 182, 212, 213
adolescence 80, 103, 170, 178–88,
  188–9
  case study, Asperger Syndrome 166–7
  economic aspects 179, 184–5
  friends 182
  gifted adolescents 181–4
    case studies
      Helen 181
      Will 182–3
  impact on the family 185–8
    case studies
      Francesca 186–7
      Rick, Jodi and Ben 186
      Vijay, Sara and Shantha 186
  intellectual and emotional aspects
    178, 179–84
    case studies
      Bella 36
      Jean 179
      Ravi 179
      Tasha 179
      Thomas 180
  musically gifted adolescents 206–8
  physical and sexual aspects 178–9,
    185
Amis, Martin 187
Asperger Syndrome 163–75, *176–7*
  brainstorm diagram 168
  case study 166–9
  characteristics 165–6, 167–9
  diagnosis 51–2, 163–4, *175*

friends 174–5
helpful responses to AS behaviour
  169–72
helping children to live with AS
  173–5

baby, new 58, 65
  case study, Neil 44–7
bad dreams 78
boredom 23, 113–14
boundaries 73–6, 103
  case study, Latasha 75–6
Brahms, Johannes 201
brainstorm *168*
Branch, Margaret 125
bullying 47–8, 84, 94, 98
  case studies
    Natasha 150
    Prisca 116

Cambridge Latin Project 192
challenging behaviour 27, 28–9, 79–81
change 44–5
Common Entrance Examination 27, *54*,
  143
communication 129–37, 211–18, *219*,
  226–32
  acknowledging emotions 213
    case study, John 213–14
  asking for what you need 216
    case study, Sam 216–17
  asking what others need 217
    case study, Isaiah and Maya 218
  case studies
    Martin 226–7
    Naomi and James 131–4
    Siân and Rhiannon 134–5
  expressing appreciation 217–18
    case study, Isaiah and Maya 218
  expressing understanding 214–15
    case study, Mark 215
  identifying needs 213
    case study, John 213–14
  listening 214
    case study, Mark 215

communication *cont.*
    non-verbal expression 214
        case study, Mark 215
    using clear language 216
        case study, Sam 216–17
    win/win outcomes 217
        case study, Isaiah and Maya 218
creativity 27, 197–9
    case studies
        Aaron 198
        Henry 198
        Lim 197–8
    see also musically gifted children
current affairs 43

day-dreaming 61, 99, 197
Department for Education and Skills
    (DfES UK) 14–5, 127, *145*
doubly exceptional *see* special needs
dyslexia 33, 159, *161–2*
dyspraxia *161–2*

eating disorders 160, 184
ego 62, 63
emotional skills 43–7
    lagging behind intellectual skills 34,
        43, 95
    language 32, 101–3
        case study, Sally 102–3
        example, Mahmud 102
Essen, J. 100
exams 34–5
    A level 41, *54*, 139, 193
        case studies
            Alex 36–7
            Jacek 50
            Liana and Alan 40
    case study, Hoda 35
    Common Entrance 27, *54*, 143
    GCSE *54*, 167
        case study, Charlene 41
    NVQ 167, *175*
    O level *54*
        case study, Reuben 37

failure
    emotional impact of 39–41, 68–9
        case studies
            Alan 40
            Charlene 41
    of one sibling 68–70
        case studies
            Eric and Dan 68
            Tracey and Craig 68–9
    value of 29–30
        case study, Dominic 29
    see also perfectionism
family dynamics 57–64
family rules 60–3
    case study, Aiko and Mai 60–1
Freeman, J. 42
friends *see* gifted children; parents of
    gifted children

genius 14–5
gifted children *56, 89, 147*
    a minority 13, 50, 96
    cautious 35–6
        case study, Paul and Khalid 35
    challenging 27, 28–9, 79–81
        case studies
            Amir 27
            Earl and Mrs Senior 29
            Morag 119
            Prem 79
    energetic 24
        case study, Georgie 24
    feeling different 47–9, 49–52, 91–3,
        96–7, 100, 211–13
        case studies
            Angharad and Huw 48
            Jacek 50
    friends 22, 32, 48–9, 50, 63, 91–2,
        101, 143
    grown-up 83–6
    hiding their gifts 50, 96, 97, 123
    intellectual characteristics 22–6
    intellectual inconsistencies 33–42
    intellectual quirks 27–30
    making connexions 24–5

needing each other 100
  case study, Lui 100
parents *see* parents of gifted children
quick-learning 23, 29, 102, 113–14
  case study, Dominic 29
self-esteem 25, 32, 33–7, 47–8, 62,
  63, *89*, 98, 115, 117, 182, *219*
sense of humour 27–8
sensitive 43–4, 76–8
unheard 96–7
urge to learn 23–4
  case study, Joshua and Mrs Thomlin
    24
see also boundaries; creativity;
  emotional skills; failure; language;
  multi-talented children; musically
  gifted children; social skills
giftedness
  acceptance and communication 17,
    211–13
  characteristics 22–54, 115
  definitions 13–5
  inconsistent 33–4
  milestones 48, 71, 223, 224, 225
  some more acceptable than others
    224–6
  and special needs 159–60
  what to tell the child 52–3
  see also creativity, multi-talented
    children; musically gifted children;
    sporting
grandparents 57, 84, 95, 187
  case study, Didier 63
guiding gifted children *56, 89, 147, 219*
  anxieties 76–8
    case studies
      Selina 45
      Winston 78
  balanced approach 25–6, 30
  challenging authority 79–80
  comparisons with siblings 67–69
  emotional skills 46–7, 101–3
    case studies
      Richard, Amy and Suzy 77
      Sally 102–3

example, Mahmud 102
friends 108
giving choices 80
musically gifted children 202–9
providing a safe place to be heard
  97–101
  case study, Lui 100
self-doubt and perfectionism 37–42,
  55–6
separating the child from his
  behaviour 30, 42
sibling rivalry 68–70
  case studies
    David and Wyn 69–70
    Tracey and Craig 68–9
social skills 107–8
starting school 122
see also boundaries

Hambourg, Michal 200, 233
health visitors 81, *88*, 105–6,
  case studies
    Fatima and Yasmin 58
    Joan 110
home as a haven 51, 90, 98–101, 102–3
  case study, Sally 102–3
home education 148–56
  academic issues 149–50, 153
    case study, Sameen 149
  impact on parents 152–5
  parent–child independence 151–3,
    153–4
    case study, Paige 151
  return to school 154–5
    case study, Sunita and Sheetal
      154–5
  social issues 150–2
    case studies
      Mavis and Frank 150
      Natasha 150
      Sunita and Sheetal 150
  friends 152

identification 15
Illingworth, R.S. 178
Independent Schools Council (ISC UK)
    141
intelligence 22–6
    bell curve 13–14
internal maps 212–13

jealousy 222–6
    case studies
        Julie and Seb, Clare and Jonty
            230–2
        Tessa 224, 225
jokes see sense of humour

language 30–33
    comparative and descriptive 228–9
        case studies
            Jack and Jill 229
            Julie and Seb, Clare and Jonty
                230–2
    effects on relationships 30–3, 48, 71,
        79
        case studies
            Nicola 30
            William 31
    emotional vocabulary 101–3
    enjoyment 28
        case study, Milly 28
    gifted linguists 190–2
        case studies
            Freddie 191
            Molly 191
            Wesley 190–1
    perfectionism 35, 55–6
    power and limitations 31–2
        case studies
            Anthony and James 31
            Darren 32
            Helen 32
            Helga 31
            Mary 32
    translation 191–2
        case study, Wesley 190–1

see also reactions to parents of gifted
    children
law
    case study, Asperger Syndrome
        166–7, 170
    legal requirements on schools 127–8
linguists see language
Lucado, M. 115–16

Mason, P. 100
Meckstroth, E. 52, 66, 97
Moore, J. 100
multi-talented children 193–6
    case studies
        Joe and Gwen 193, 195
        Joseph Needham 193–4
        Keri 193, 195
        Sasha 194–5
musically gifted children 200–9
    adolescents 206–8
    case study, Aaron 198
    courses (UK) 209–10
    Hambourg, Michal, personal
        experience 200–2
    Hambourg, Michal, research 202–4
    music competitions 208
    music schools (UK) 210
    supporting musically gifted children
        203–9

National Association for Gifted Children
    (NAGC UK) 16, 19, 110, 125
Needham, Joseph 193–4
nursery teachers see teachers

parents of gifted children 56, 89, 147,
    189, 219
    a minority 13, 108–9
    challenges to authority 79–81
        case study, Prem 79
    emotional demands 76–8, 104
        case studies
            Richard, Amy and Suzy 77
            Winston 78

feeling helpless 81–3
  case study, Sean 81
feeling inadequate 84
  case study, Sean 81
friends 71, 75, 86, 106–7, 109–10
impact of own experiences 59–60,
  66–7, 83–6, 125–7
  case studies
    Alison, Megan and Lucy 66
    Fran and Steve 59
intellectual demands 71–6
  case studies
    Bernhard 74
    Brigitte 72
    Latasha 75–6
    Peter 75
isolation 13, 59, 104, 106–7, 109
joys 69–70, 72
need to be heard 109–10, 125–7
  case study, Joan 110
providing a haven for their children
  51
'pushy' see 'Pushy Parent'
relationship with schools see schools
talking about giftedness 222
tensions between parents 59–60
wanting child to fit in 48, 81–2
see also boundaries; guiding gifted
  children; reactions to gifted
  children; reactions to parents of
  gifted children; schools
perfectionism 34–42, 55–6
  case studies
    Alex 36–7
    Bella 36, 38–9
    Hoda 35
    Oliver 34
    Reuben 37
  in parents 81–3
physical development 224
  case studies
    Fatima and Yasmin 58
    Mercedes 61
    Patrick and Connor 105, 223
    Samantha 58

see also special needs
Popper, K. 202
potential 14, 36, 41, 99, 101, 149, 152,
  160, 197
pregnancy see baby, new
private schools see schools
'Pushy Parent' 23–4, 83, 117, 123–40
Puttick, G. 203–4, 209

reaching potential see potential
reactions to gifted children 25–6, 27,
  81, 104–8
  case studies
    Fatima and Yasmin 58
    Sunil 59
  hostility 222–6
  jealousy 222–6
  mixed messages 91
  pressure to conform 91–3
    case studies
      Claire 92
      Tom and Fabio 92
  pressure to socialize 93–5
    case studies
      Emma 95
      Frances 95
  see also reactions to parents of gifted
    children
reactions to parents of gifted children
  104–8, 222–32
  case studies
    Kelly 223
    Patrick and Connor 105, 223
    Wayne 222
  power of language 228–32
    case studies
      Jack and Jill 229
      Julie and Seb, Clare and Jonty
        230–2
  responsibility and choices 226–8
    case studies
      Julie and Seb, Clare and Jonty
        230–2
      Martin 226–7
  see also reactions to gifted children

Reynolds, Dorothy 48, 126

Samaritans, The 131
schools *147*
    and parents 84–6, 121–4, 125–39
        case study, Siân and Rhiannon
            134–5
        example, Hari 136–7
        planning and lists 134–5
        record keeping 128
    comprehensive 95, *111*, 140
    failing to provide for the gifted
            113–14, 122–4
        case studies
            Michael 116
            Prisca 114–15, 116
    hierarchy 128
    independent *see* private
    infant, junior and senior *54*
    legal requirements 127–8
    middle 77, *88*, 116, 124
    prep 48, *54*, 143
    primary 49, *54*, 124, 127, 142,
            198–9
    private *88*, 139–44
        case study, Jonathan 142
    providing well for the gifted 112–13,
            122
    secondary *54*, 124, 127, 198
    year group (UK) *54*
    see also acceleration; home education;
            starting school; teachers
self-confidence 34–7, 42, *89*, *219*
    case studies
        Hoda 35
        Oliver 34
sense of humour 27–8
siblings 57–8, 64–70, *89*
    case studies
        Alison, Megan and Lucy 66
        Asher, Ruth and Cathie 67
        David and Wyn 69–70
        Eric and Dan 68
        Geoff and Angela, Edward and
            Nicholas 65

Jenny and Rob 65
Murray and Jamie 65
Pippa and Nick 62–3
Ranjit and Jaswinder 66–7
Tracey and Craig 68–9
see also baby, new
social skills 47–49, 63, 91–5
    case studies
        Claire 92
        Emma 95
        Frances 95
        Tom and Fabio 92
    see also Asperger Syndrome
special needs 14, 159–60, *161–2*, *176–7*
    case study, Tony 160
    see also Asperger Syndrome; dyslexia
sporting gifts 224–5
    case study, Tessa 224, 225
starting school 94–5, 112–14, 121–2,
        122–3, 148–9
    case study, Seetal 25
Statement of Special Educational Needs
        (SEN) 160, 166, *175*
statistics 13–4, 139
Stopper, M. *160*
stretching 99–100, 197
suicide 160, 180

tantrums 79, 101, 187
    case studies
        Aiko and Mai 60
        Mercedes 61
teachers 112–13, *147*
    bullying, case study, Prisca 116
    challenges of providing for gifted
        children 119–21
    case studies
        Harriet Proctor 118
        Morag 119
        Tyron 120
    doubting children's abilities 123–4
    case studies
        Barnaby and Miss Lee 25
        Prisca 114–15
        Seetal 25

stress 118–21, 129, 130, 137
training 117, 118–19
  case studies
    Kiri 117
    Uma 117
  see also schools
teenagers *see* adolescence
toddlers 48–9, 72, 79–80, 93–5, 101,
  103
  case studies
    Aiko and Mai 60–1
    Brigitte 72
    Didier 63
    Jack and Jill 229
    Pippa and Nick 62–3
    Sunil 59
    William 31
  see also tantrums
Tolan, S. 52, 66, 97
Transactional Analysis 187
Treffinger, D. 136
Turner, M. 202–3

university 40, 65, 150, 152, 182, 193
  case studies
    Dominic 29
    Frances 95
    Hoda 35
    Mary 32
    Tracey and Craig 68–9
  class of degree *88*

Webb, J. 52, 66, 97

year group (UK) *54*
Ysaye 201